The Political Economy of Corporatism

edited by
WYN GRANT

MACMILLAN

First published 1985

Published by
Higher and Further Education Division
MACMILLAN PUBLISHERS LTD
Houndmills, Basingstoke, Hampshire RG21 2XS
and London
Companies and representatives
throughout the world

Filmsetting by Vantage Photosetting Co. Ltd
Eastleigh and London

Printed in Hong Kong

British Library Cataloguing in Publication Data
The Political economy of corporatism. —
(Sociology, politics and cities)
1. Corporate state
I. Grant, Wyn   II. Series
321.9   HD3611
ISBN 0-333-36898-3
ISBN 0-333-36899-1 Pbk

*To the participants in the International
Institute of Management project on
business interest associations*

Contents

General Editor's Preface

SOCIOLOGY, POLITICS AND CITIES

Cities are the focal points of economic, political and cultural life in most countries. They are the places where the results of past and present economic and political conflicts leave their most obvious marks. To understand the changing characteristics of cities, it is therefore necessary to comprehend the relationships between economic and political forces and the influence they have on the lives of different citizens.

The series 'Sociology, Politics and Cities' provides a vehicle for the exploration of these relationships. As they cannot be understood within the confines of traditional single disciplinary boundaries, the series aims to be transdisciplinary and includes works which combine, in different ways, such subjects as sociology, economics, politics and history in so far as they contribute to the understanding of cities.

The series also aims to contribute to cross-national understanding of cities. This is because, although Britain was the first country to experience a revolution in manufacturing industry, and the consequent industrial urbanisation, it has now reached a stage of de-industrialisation combined with de-urbanisation which needs to be set in an international context. The British economy is no longer in the world's first division. Events in its cities are increasingly determined by world rather than purely national economics. The understanding of this global context and how it is affecting cities in other countries is now an important part of urban analysis.

The series is also concerned with what private and public action should be recommended in cities. It is therefore interested in public and private policies with respect to cities and their regions.

The general aim of the series 'Sociology, Politics and Cities' is therefore to encourage and stimulate a continuing analysis of cities in capitalist, socialist and underdeveloped economies. It is concerned to develop theoretical understanding of these phenomena based upon empirical analyses. On the bases of such understanding the series is also concerned with the formulation and evaluation of relevant urban policies.

London 1985   James Simmie

Foreword

I have been involved for a number of years in research stimulated and informed by neo-corporatist writing, but, despite a number of volumes on the subject, it became apparent that the most recent theoretical work and empirical research findings were not available in a convenient form. Moreover, in teaching students about neo-corporatism, I became aware that they found the subject a confusing one, not least because of the limits of the available literature for teaching purposes. This volume attempts to bring together the latest theoretical work and empirical research in the area in a form that will be useful both to academics interested in neo-corporatism, and to students approaching the subject for the first time. The introduction is particularly intended to provide students unfamiliar with the literature with an overview of the subject as a whole.

I have incurred many intellectual debts in the preparation of this volume. Philippe Schmitter provided me with hospitality in Chicago, Berlin and Florence during the gestation of this book, listened patiently to my attempts to formulate my ideas more coherently, and helped me to straighten out my thinking: an extended conversation on the subject whilst walking round Stratford upon Avon on a cold winter day was particularly helpful. Wolfgang Streeck provided me with hospitality in Berlin and Florence, and was of considerable assistance to me in arriving at a better understanding of corporatism in theory and practice. Philippe and Wolfgang co-ordinated the International Institute of Management project on business interest associations and brought together an exceptional group of scholars from eleven countries to whom this book is dedicated. Among them, special thanks must go to William Coleman of McMaster

University for his advice and assistance. Hanspeter Kriesi of the Sociological Institute of the University of Zürich provided me with many insights into corporatist arrangements in Switzerland, and also retrieved my luggage from the Swiss customs. Frans van Waarden of the University of Leiden was a constructive and formidable adversary in many disputations.

I also benefited considerably in intellectual terms from my membership of the Corporatism and Accountability Sub-Committee of the Economic and Social Research Council under the chairmanship of Professor R. Dore. Professor G. Botz invited me to a conference on neo-corporatism at the University of Salzburg at an important point in the development of this book and, by allowing me to test my ideas at an early stage of development, prevented me from arriving at conclusions that would have been too unorthodox. Jane Sargent and Helen Rainbird were hard-working research assistants and intellectually invigorating colleagues on two projects related to neo-corporatist themes.

A number of individuals read through the introduction and I am grateful to the following for their comments: Malcolm Anderson, University of Edinburgh; Graham Cox, University of Bath; Ron Dore, Technical Change Centre; Grant Jordan, University of Aberdeen; Shiv Nath, University of Warwick; and William Paterson, University of Warwick. The responsibility for any errors, omissions or poor judgements remains mine.

I am most grateful to the contributors to this volume for their comments on the introduction and their forbearance and energy in responding to requests for revised drafts of their chapters. James Simmie was a helpful and understanding series editor, and Steve Kennedy at Macmillan was patient, tolerant and supportive through a number of delays and difficulties.

Last but not least, I must thank my wife, Maggie, and our children, Sophia, Rosalind and Amelia, for once again putting up with the strains of having a writer in the house. As Amelia commented, 'You take so long to produce your books and when they come out they are so boring.' I hope, nevertheless, that some readers will find that this book has something to offer them.

Leamington Spa, October 1984   Wyn Grant

Notes on the Contributors

Alan Cawson is Lecturer in Politics at the University of Sussex, and was a Jean Monnet Fellow at the European University Institute, Florence, in 1984–5. He is the author of *Corporatism and Welfare* and a number of articles on corporatism, democracy and state theory.

Colin Crouch is Reader in Sociology at the London School of Economics and Political Science. He is the author of *Class Conflict and the Industrial Relations Crisis*, *The Politics of Industrial Relations* and *Trade Unions: The Logic of Collective Action*.

Wyn Grant is Senior Lecturer in Politics, and a member of the Institute for Employment Research, at the University of Warwick. He is Associate Editor of *Political Studies*, author of *The Political Economy of Industrial Policy* and *Independent Local Politics in England and Wales*, and co-author of *The CBI* and *The Politics of Economic Policymaking*.

Roger King is Head of the Department of Behavioural Sciences at Huddersfield Polytechnic. He is the editor of *Capital and Politics*, and co-author of *The Middle Class*, *Respectable Rebels* and *The British Right*.

Bernd Marin is Professor of Comparative Political and Social Research at the European University Institute in Florence, and was formerly Deputy Director of the Institute for Conflict Research in Vienna and Universitätsdozent at the University of Vienna. He directs the International Bureau of Political and Social Research, Florence-Vienna. Among his books are *Politische Organisation sozialwissenschaftlicher Forschungsarbeit*, *Wachstumskrisen in Österreich?* Vol. 1, *Grundlagen* (with M. Wagner), Vol. 2, *Szenarios*, and *Die Paritätische Kommission*.

Jane Sargent is currently completing a PhD thesis for the London School of Economics on British interest group representation in the European Communities. She has published articles on this topic in a number of journals including the *Journal of Common Market Studies* and *West European Politics*. In 1984 she was appointed PR/Research Officer for the Retail Consortium.

Peter Saunders is Reader in Sociology in the School of Cultural and Community Studies at the University of Sussex. He is author of *Urban Politics: A Sociological Interpretation, Social Theory and the Urban Question*, and (with John Dearlove) *An Introduction to British Politics*.

Philippe C. Schmitter is Professor of Political and Social Sciences at the European University Institute, and was formerly at the University of Chicago. Recent publications include 'Democratic Theory and Neo-Corporatist Practice' in *Social Research* 1983. An edited collection of essays (with Wolfgang Streeck) on *Private Interest Government* will soon be appearing, as will three volumes on *Political Life After Authoritarian Rule in Latin America and Southern Europe* (with Guillermo O'Donnell and Laurence Whitehead).

James Simmie is Lecturer in Urban Sociology at University College, London. He is the author of *The Sociology of Internal Migration, Citizens in Conflict* and *Power, Property and Corporatism*.

Chapter 1

Introduction

Wyn Grant

What is neo-corporatism?

Since the middle of the 1970s a large and diverse literature, written from a variety of theoretical perspectives and drawing on a range of empirical studies, has appeared on the significance for modern Western societies of what is variously called neo-, quasi-, liberal or societal corporatism, sometimes tripartism, and increasingly just 'corporatism'. The debate on corporatism represents an attempt to understand the reciprocal relationships that have developed between the state and major organised interests in Western countries in the post-war period. The revival and recasting of corporatist explanations of these historical changes was a response to a widespread feeling among academics that conventional pluralist theories did not provide an adequate apparatus to handle the changes that were taking place in the relationship between the state and interest groups based on the division of labour in society: the process by which such groups were transformed from representative lobbies into what Middlemas (1979, p. 372) terms 'governing institutions'. The limitations of pluralist explanations, the distinction between pluralism and corporatism, and the recent attempts of some writers to defend pluralist characterisations are discussed more fully below. However, the fundamental criticism that was made of pluralist explanations was that they assumed too passive a role for the state, and in particular emphasised the variety of ways in which 'lobbies' sought to exert influence on different parts of government, to the neglect of the influence that government exerted on supposedly autonomous interests. Pluralist explanations could not capture the process whereby 'what had been merely interest groups crossed the political threshold and became part of the extended state' (Middlemas, 1979, p. 373).

The student approaching the topic of neo-corporatism for the first time will quickly become aware that he or she is encountering one of the most important and lively contemporary debates in the social sciences. He or she will not have read very far into the literature before becoming confused by the substance of what is being talked about. As Panitch comments, 'the first thing that strikes one as one reads through the recent literature on modern corporatism is the profound lack of agreement on what the concept actually refers to' (Panitch, 1980, p. 159). Similarly, Wilson (1983, p. 109) observes, 'Ten years of discussion of neo-corporatism seems not to have clarified the definition of the term but to have muddied it up'. This introduction attempts to provide a number of signposts through the literature that has accumulated over the last decade, as a prelude to the individual contributions which bring together the latest work of some of the leading theoreticians working in the field, together with results from some of the major empirical research projects that have been stimulated by the neo-corporatist debate. A concluding section points to some directions which future research might usefully take.

It will be evident that there are some differences of approach and interpretation between the authors. That is unavoidable when one is trying to encompass a debate that has attracted 'scholars of many disciplines, backgrounds and convictions' (Schmitter, 1982, p. 278). No attempt has been made to impose a particular orthodoxy on the contributors, but they have been encouraged, as far as possible, not to confine their discussions to Britain but to introduce as wide a range as possible of comparative material. The ultimate test of the utility of neo-corporatism as a set of explanations that help us to understand apparently similar developments in a number of societies will lie in the area of comparative politics and sociology. The fact that – particularly at the macro level – corporatist arrangements in Britain have exhibited limited development is, when viewed in a comparative perspective, interesting, but not a devastating blow to corporatist explanations. Indeed, it is salutary to compare Crouch's account of a decentralised, pluralist, collective bargaining system in Britain with Marin's chapter which explains the working of neo-corporatist arrangements in Austria. The former system has been associated with a failure on the part of the trade unions to achieve their broader objectives and a loss of support for the unions themselves, combined with the failure of successive administrations to achieve their economic objectives; the latter system has seen continued union participation in a widely supported system of bargaining with a broad framework of concern, which has facilitated the achievement of such economic objectives as relatively low unemployment, low inflation and a good record of economic growth.

One of the difficulties that arises in handling the concept of corporatism is that some writers confuse it with a variety of pluralism which involves intensive consultation with interest groups, but does not involve the sharing of state authority with them. The incentive for the state to share its authority in this way is that it can 'build support for the enactment and implementation of its policies by granting privileged participation to a sectoral interest group sufficiently powerful to deliver the support of its benefiting constituency' (Chubb, 1983, p. 26). However, although the state has powerful incentives to engage in corporatist bargaining, the emergence of such arrangements must not be characterised simply as a state-led process; rather, one is observing an 'osmotic process whereby the modern state and modern interest associations seek each other out' (Schmitter, 1979, p. 27).

There are boundary problems that arise in making a distinction between pluralism and corporatism, but the difficulty of distinguishing between an intensive consultative relationship and one that involves designated organisations in the implementation of policy can be overcome by making use of Crouch's distinction between contestation, pluralist bargaining and bargained corporatism (see Crouch's chapter and Crouch, 1983a); or Atkinson and Coleman's development of Lowi's concept of 'sponsored pluralism' which they distinguish from 'pressure pluralism' (Atkinson and Coleman, 1983).

I use the term 'corporatism' (as a shorthand for liberal or neo-corporatism) to refer to a process of interest intermediation which involves the negotiation of policy between state agencies and interest organisations arising from the division of labour in society, where the policy agreements are implemented through

the collaboration of the interest organisations and their willingness and ability to secure the compliance of their members. The
elements of negotiation and implementation are both essential
to my understanding of corporatism. The arbitrary imposition
of state policies through interest organisations, without any
prior negotiations, does not constitute liberal corporatism as I
understand it; equally, the negotiation of understandings, with
no obligation on the part of interest organisations to secure the
compliance of their members, does not constitute a corporatist
arrangement as I interpret the term.

Most of the discussion of corporatism so far has been focused
on the macro level, on tripartite bargaining between government, labour and capital on a national basis (supranational
discussions have also been neglected, and such discussions
within the European Community are analysed in Jane Sargent's
chapter). However, there has been an increasing recognition
among scholars in the field of the need to disaggregate
corporatism, and to study the phenomenon at the meso (or
industry sector) and even micro (firm) level (see, for example,
Wassenberg, 1982; Schmitter, 1982). A distinctive contribution
of this volume to the continuing debate on corporatism is that it
reports on the results of a number of research projects investigat-
ing corporatist phenomena below the macro level, thereby
enhancing our understanding of corporatism as a phenomenon
that can flourish in particular sectors or locations even when it is
absent in a country at the national level. The cumulative impact
of such arrangements on the organisation of a society could be as
important as highly publicised but weakly enforced tripartite
bargaining at the macro level.

The historical development of corporatism

A central problem that arises in any attempt to handle the
historical development of corporatist ideas and practices is that
corporatism has been advocated by 'an extraordinary variety of
theorists, ideologues and activists . . . for widely divergent
motives, interests and reasons' (Schmitter, 1979, p. 9). This
introduction is not intended to provide a conspectus of the
intellectual development of corporatist thought: such reviews
are available elsewhere (Harris, 1972; Newman, 1981). There
will be a brief discussion of the development of corporatist

arrangements in the post-war period, but only after some of the more important earlier influences on corporatist thought have first been indicated.

The association of a fundamentally undemocratic form of corporatism with fascism, and in particular with Mussolini's Italy, is too well known to require documentation here, but the severing of the historical association with fascism was a key prerequisite of the revival of corporatism as a doctrine that was compatible with, and indeed could contribute to, the development of modern liberal democracies. In making this transformation, it was possible to rely to some extent on pre-fascist discussions of corporatism in Catholic social thought: such influences were important in winning acceptance for doctrines that were neo-corporatist in all but name in a number of smaller European democracies in the immediate post-war period, particularly the Netherlands.

In their original form, Catholic conceptions of corporatism could be said to have had a number of reactionary ideas inherent in them. Leo XIII's famous encyclical of 1891, *Rerum Novarum*, was an attempt to formulate a Roman Catholic response to the development of trade unionism among the working classes. Leo XIII regretted the fact that there had been no replacement for the mediaeval guilds, thus, as he saw it, exposing workers 'to the hard-heartedness of employers and the greed of unchecked competition' (Freemantle, 1956, p.167). Leo XIII rejected the attainability of equality, or any idea that class conflict was inevitable. Turning to solutions, Leo XIII advocated what was in effect a form of bargained corporatism: 'employers and workmen may of themselves effect much in the matter of which we are treating, by means of such associations and organizations . . . which draw the two classes more closely together' (Freemantle, 1956, p.188). The encyclical goes on to discuss in some detail the formation of Catholic trade unions. In his 1931 encyclical, *Quadragesimo Anno*, which celebrated the fortieth anniversary of the publication of *Rerum Novarum*, Pius XI praised the earlier encyclical because it had 'boldly attacked and overturned the idols of Liberalism' (Freemantle, 1956, p.230). Pius XI described self-governing organisations for industries and professions as 'if not essential, at least natural to civil society' (Freemantle, 1956, p.232).

Neo-corporatism has generally been seen as a doctrinal companion of social democracy, and there is no doubt that social democrats have given a considerable impetus to the spread of corporatist arrangements, both in theory and practice. However, neo-corporatism also received a considerable impetus in Europe from Christian democracy, an impetus that was largely missing in Britain. Social democrats found neo-corporatist ideas generally compatible with their way of thinking, particularly when it became understood that neo-corporatist arrangements could enhance the role of the trade unions in society. Catholic social thought, which combined a reactionary nostalgia for the passing of the mediaeval guild system with a forward-looking attempt to seek harmony within the framework of a modern industrial society, was important because it contributed to an acceptance of neo-corporatist ideas where they were most likely to be rejected, on the right of the political spectrum. In the late 1970s and 1980s, the influence of Catholic social thought on parties of the Right in Europe seems to have waned, while neo-liberal ideas have gained ground, and it is this erosion of support towards the Right of the political spectrum that provides one of the most important contemporary challenges to the survival of corporatist arrangements.

However, perhaps more important than these particular traditions of thought were the circumstances experienced in the aftermath of the Second World War by many war-ravaged countries in Europe, particularly the smaller ones that had had their entire territories occupied. There was a new willingness to attempt to bridge differences between capital and labour in the task of reconstruction. A classic case was Austria, which is often regarded as offering the prototype of effective corporatist arrangements. Under the First Republic, Austria had suffered civil war, annexation and, then, occupation by the Allied Powers. As Marin points out in his chapter, the organisational infrastructure of corporatist co-operation dates back to the nineteenth century, but political coexistence between the opposing class 'camps' was not possible in the circumstances of the First Republic. Co-operation within corporatist arrangements only became possible after the Second World War, when extensive nationalisation weakened the power of business interests, thus bringing about a more even balance of power between capital and labour (see also Marin and Traxler, 1984).

This brief consideration of the Austrian case confirms the observation that there is no one historical pattern of corporatist development, no inexorable unfolding of a grand corporatist design. As Schmitter explains in his chapter, with the possible exceptions of Belgium and the Netherlands, neo-corporatist arrangements have been the largely unintended outcome of disparate interest conflicts and policy crises in which none of the class or state actors involved was capable of imposing its preferred solution upon the others. Corporatist arrangements typically emerged as second-best compromises which no one really wanted or defended openly, thus leading to their general invisibility, their uneven distribution and their precarious legitimacy. One might add that this unintended and unacknowledged character of corporatist arrangements is one of the features of the phenomenon that makes the debate about it often difficult to follow.

Corporatist arrangements seem to have been most successful at the macro level in small countries, and it could be that the historical verdict on corporatism will be that it is a phenomenon of small countries in prosperous times. Apart from the fact that they have more centralised labour movements which favour corporatist arrangements (see Crouch, 1983a) small countries have a particular incentive to facilitate co-operation between state, labour and capital, since if they are to retain their highly specialised niches in export markets, on which they depend for their prosperity, active co-operation between the social partners is necessary to facilitate a continuous process of industrial adjustment (see Zysman, 1983, pp. 317–18).

What corporatism is not

One of the prevalent sources of confusion in the corporatist literature is that the term is often used in ways which I would regard as invalid. Of course, no one has the right to issue licences that prescribe the ways in which the word should be used, or to proscribe its use in particular circumstances. However, it is important that each particular writer should make clear what limits he or she would set on the use of the term. For example, I would not use the term in the sweeping way in which it is deployed by Gamble, who states that 'The corporatist thesis suggested that institutional bases of power outside Parliament were now much more important than anything which occurred within Parliament itself for the formulation and implementation of policy' (Gamble, 1984, p.170).

Corporatism is not étatisme. Corporatism is interventionist, but it is indirectly rather than directly interventionist; its character is, of course, action by the state in conjunction with the organisations that are based on the division of labour in society. In order for this to be possible, the state does, of course, have to modify its objectives, and the means of attaining them, in a way that would not be necessary if the state was taking direct action. However, in the long run, more may be achieved by co-operation than through direct state action which may, ultimately, start to undermine the state's most important possession – its ability to exercise legitimate power. Moreover, indirect intervention may preclude the necessity for direct intervention. Drawing attention to the way in which the German state has been more willing than the British state to intervene in the organisation of private interests, Streeck comments:

> Ironically, but hardly unintended, the interventionist policy of the German State on the organisational forms of social interests enables it in many cases to abstain from direct economic intervention since it provides interest groups with a capacity to find viable solutions between and for themselves. (Streeck, 1984, p.145)

One account of corporatism that treats it as a form of direct intervention is that by Winkler, who defines corporatism as an alternative economic system to capitalism and socialism, one based on a combination of private ownership and state control. Winkler's vision of the corporate state involves an attempt 'to exercise direct control over the internal decision-making of companies and over the bargaining strategies of unions' (Winkler, 1977, p.82). Winkler treats his model as a probabilistic prediction, not to be fulfilled, despite its Orwellian undertones, by 1984, but 'before the end of the 1980s' (p.87). One cannot yet say, of course, whether the Thatcher government will simply turn out to be an aberrant interregnum in the path of corporatist economic development, so that Winkler's vision of a future society characterised by 'fascism with a human face' may eventually be fulfilled, albeit perhaps a few years behind schedule. However, whether or not the model is eventually shown to have predictive value, and despite the fact that it has been an important element in the debate on corporatism (particularly when one also takes account of Winkler's work on the subject with Pahl), the phenomenon discussed does not represent corporatism as I understand the term.

Even more confusion is caused in the minds of students by the term 'tripartism', which many of them incorrectly equate with 'corporatism'. I regard tripartism as a weak form of liberal corporatism in which the state, capital and labour engage in macro-level discussions on economic policy which, however, only result in general guidelines for the conduct of policy; impose no firm responsibilities on the partners to implement any policies to which they have agreed; and are not linked, except in the most tenuous way, to discussions at the meso or micro levels. While tripartism is an attempt to develop policy through a partnership of the state and the major producer interests, the organisation of the arrangement is a complete inversion of the successful Austrian variety of corporatism, which is highly regulated at the base, but characterised by complete informality at the top, with discussion in the Parity Commission ending up as an 'intimate face-to-face talk exclusively between two people – the president of the chamber of commerce representing capital and the president of the trade union confederation representing organised labour' (Marin, 1983a, p. 209). Marin's work stresses the importance of a pyramid of institutionalisation in successful corporatist arrangements. Tripartism all too often represents an attempt to impose corporatist arrangements by the state from the top down, rather than building on arrangements that have evolved between capital and labour.

Tripartism, in the sense defined, approximates to much of what has happened at the macro level in Britain, but does not amount to an effective corporatist arrangement. The 1974–9 Labour government in Britain, and the preceding Heath government in its last two years of office, made a considerable effort to work in co-operation with the representatives of capital and labour. The Queen's Speech and other major policy statements contained declarations such as 'My Ministers will co-operate closely with the Trades Union Congress and the Confederation of British Industry' (Queen's Speech, 1 November 1978, column 5). However, as Crouch points out in his chapter, national co-operation was only able to exert influence over shop-floor autonomy for a short period.

Corporatist arrangements can, of course, be made between the state and groups arising from the division of labour other than organisations represented capital and labour, e.g. professional organisations of various kinds ranging from the field of medicine to that of sport. Moreover, as Simmie points out in his chapter, capital and labour must be joined by land as the three major categories of factors of production. Indeed, virtually all forms of production require land on which to combine capital and labour. Disputes over land use involve political bargains which diverge increasingly from the pluralist democratic and accountable paradigm.

Two further points of clarification relate not to the nature of corporatism *per se*, but to the orientation of this book. This book is concerned with societal corporatism rather than state corporatism, a distinction that is fully explained in Schmitter (1979). In summary, this distinction is concerned both with power and influence relations and with the developmental pattern by which corporatism emerges. State corporatism involves the creation of 'corporations' which 'were created by and kept as auxillary and dependent organs of the state' (Schmitter, 1979, p. 20). Historical examples are to be found in fascist Italy, Petanist France and Salazar's Portugal. However, Coleman's (1984) study of the Quebec construction industry shows that it is possible to find examples of state corporatism at the meso level in Western democracies. Lehmbruch (1983) discusses the application of the concept of state corporatism to socialist countries.

Societal corporatism is characterised by the existence of singular, non-competitive, hierarchically ordered representative organisations which are autonomous in their origins. Through an osmotic process, they develop a symbiotic relationship with the state, so that the legitimacy of the state becomes in part reliant on the active consent of recognised interest organisations. Societal corporatism has been characteristic of Western countries such as Norway and the Netherlands, but trends in some East European societies could lead to arrangements at the meso level which would have sufficient autonomy from the state to be labelled as examples of societal corporatism.

A second point of clarification is that no particular position is taken in this book on the desirability or otherwise of corporatist arrangements; the emphasis is on analysis rather than prescription. Readers will quickly become aware that contributors differ in their views about the desirability of corporatist arrangements; what they share is a willingness to explore systematically the issues raised by the neo-corporatist debate. I have been described as a 'pro-corporatist' (Jordan, 1983, p. 3), but I would maintain that I am only a pro-corporatist in the sense that I believe that the corporatist paradigm has triggered off an important and stimulating debate on the way in which political structures attempt to cope with economic and social change.

As far as Britain is concerned, I have always been sceptical about the possibility of bringing about effective corporatist arrangements at the macro level, because of the structure of industrial relations, the limited authority exercised over their members by the representative organisations of *both* labour and capital, the absence of a co-operative relationship between them, and the persistence of individualistic values in the society. As Streeck comments, 'It is conceivable that there are societies that, for whatever reason, have not and cannot acquire the capacity to develop corporatist structures, and Britain with its long liberal traditions could indeed be such a society' (Streeck, 1984, p. 148).

However, there has been an excessive preoccupation with macro-level solutions in Britain. Corporatist arrangements do flourish in favourable circumstances at the meso level, and such arrangements may be able to make a greater contribution in the longer run to the task of evolving industrial adjustment policies which undertake the difficult but necessary task of promoting change and winning the support, or at least the acquiescence, of those affected. A working example of such an arrangement in Britain is that of the Milk Marketing Boards and the Joint Committee in the dairy industry, which permit the balancing and reconciliation of the potentially divergent interests of government, farmers, dairy manufacturers and individual consumers (see Grant, 1983a, 1983b).

The political economy of corporatism

Books on a wide range of topics now contain the words 'political economy' in their title, but the use of the term in the title of this book is not a marketing device, but reflects a genuine effort by the editor to bring the insights of political science and sociology to bear on the analysis of economic problems. (see, for example, Grant, 1981; Grant and Nath, 1984.) I share Zysman's belief in the central importance of 'the political capacity of government to promote the process of adjustment' (Zysman, 1983, p. 15). This task is often pursued in co-operation with the organisational representatives of labour and capital. Hence the corporatist debate relates to some of the central issues of economic policy, and those issues are a core concern of corporatist analysts. There is, therefore, a real sense in which the corporatist debate is a central part of the effort to develop a genuine political economy, i.e. one that does not use economic theories to explain political outcomes, but combines the insights of a number of social science disciplines in the exploration of common concerns.

The relationship between incomes policies and neo-corporatist arrangements, for instance, has been a central concern of corporatist analysis. Helander (1982) has discussed how the adoption of incomes policies led to the emergence of a liberal corporatist sub-system in the Finnish polity. More generally, it could be argued that one of the mainsprings of the development of neo-corporatism was the adoption of a full employment commitment by most western states in the immediate post-war period. This tended to produce wage-push inflation, leading governments to turn to a variety of incomes policies in an attempt to maintain full employment and low rates of inflation. The word 'variety' is important here, because some of the most effective arrangements seem to have been largely confined to bilateral deals between capital and labour, with the state hovering benevolently (or with an air of quiet menace) in the background. However, whatever the precise arrangements adopted, the pursuit of an incomes policy does make the state more reliant on the representatives of capital and labour for their consent and collaboration.

However, one must be careful not to overstate the importance of incomes policy and to imply that it was the only motor behind the adoption of neo-corporatist arrangements. If it had been, then the developments that have taken place might have been largely confined to the macro level, and would have appeared and disappeared with the presence or absence of incomes policies. In fact, some corporatist arrangements have predated the emergence of incomes policies, and others have endured their disappearance (see Marin, 1982a, p. 63ff). One reason is that corporatist arrangements are sometimes rooted in law, and cannot therefore be easily dismantled, even if there is some desire to do so. Moreover, whatever their precise legal status, 'Corporatist institutions, once established, make it difficult for the constituent parts to regain their previous autonomy' (Streeck, 1984, p. 154).

Corporatist arrangements have been important in the conduct of industrial relations and the general regulation of the labour market, although I would not go so far as Strinati, (1982, p. 23) and define corporatism as 'a particular form of state control of industrial relations'. Crouch's chapter in fact provides a general model for the analysis of corporatism in industrial relations, which stresses the importance of the direct relationship between capital and labour, with the state's role in the process being crucial but limited. Crouch emphasises that we should not use corporatism as a synonym for state intervention or state-led incomes policy.

In terms of a more specific aspect of industrial relations, one might point to the existence of corporatist arrangements in a number of countries, even Britain, in the area of training policy. The underlying cause of this resort to corporatist solutions is not hard to find: left to the market, firms are likely to support training in a form and at a level which does not meet the long-term needs of the economy, yet straightforward state intervention may be based on highly imperfect information and comprehension of the problems, and may meet resistance from employers and unions to an extent that policy objectives cannot be attained. A simple state subsidy would not resolve the problem because, apart from the difficulty of ensuring that it was used in a way compatible with policy objectives, it would not allow employers and unions to make a direct input to the formulation and implementation of training policy. Corporatist arrangements in training policy are particularly likely to be needed in industries such as construction, which is skill-intensive but has a highly mobile work-force. In such circumstances, a market solution would fall short even of the short-term needs of employers, and effective state-backed co-operation between employers and unions is likely to develop, a hypothesis supported by empirical evidence from Britain and West Germany (Streeck, 1983; Rainbird and Grant, 1984).

Problems of structural adjustment in Western societies, which have become more severe since the first oil shock, have led the majority of Western states to adopt industrial policies of various kinds which seek to facilitate the process of adjustment. These industrial policies characteristically involve intervention in particular industrial sectors. However, in order to execute such intervention successfully, it is necessary to have access to expertise about the sectors which is not normally in the possession of the state, but of the trade associations and trade unions in the sector concerned.

If all that was required was access to expertise, then all that might develop would be a close consultative relationship. However, industrial policies usually rely on a mixture of exhortation and financial inducements, rather than direct state intervention, i.e. indirect intervention of the kind which relies on corporatist arrangements. In order for the policies to be effectively implemented, it is necessary to have the active co-operation of those concerned. The most effective way of reaching individual workers is usually through their union, and, given the number of firms in many sectors suffering structural problems, the only feasible way of reaching them is through trade associations. Thus, the pursuit of an industrial policy can lead to the development of corporatist arrangements at a meso level. As Atkinson and Coleman comment:

> Corporatism will be closely associated with industrial policy because the success of the latter is dependent on how readily producer groups will agree to accept the inevitable dislocations associated with economic adjustment. As a distinctive policy network corporatism promises to deliver consensus on the goals and instruments of policy and to be a vehicle through which the state can share responsibility for implementation as well as policy direction. (Atkinson and Coleman, 1983, p. 8).

Corporatist arrangements may not only be fostered at the sectoral level or at the nation state level. Economic policy increasingly involves international arrangements, and these may help (or hinder) the emergence and survival of corporatist arrangements. For example, the Organisation for Economic Cooperation and Development's advocacy of 'positive adjust-ment' polcies may indirectly foster corporatist arrangements at the meso level. It has also been argued that the interventions of the European Community, when combined with the impor-tance it attaches to dealings with interest organisations, par-ticularly the so-called 'social partners', may lead to the development of corporatist arrangements at the Community level, or at the member state level.

As Jane Sargent's chapter shows, the reality is a little more complex. The Commission does develop relationships with corporate interest groups, partly to give it more legitimacy in its dealings with the Council of Ministers, and partly to reduce its workload by delegating particular policy implementation res-ponsibilities to designated groups. However, organised interests could not really be described as partners in policy formation, and much of the emphasis in recent years has been on the development of the European Parliament rather than corporat-ist arrangements, although the ESPRIT programme is an interesting example of the development of a corporatist partner-ship at the micro level with individual firms. Against this, some aspects of Community policy, particularly competition policy, have led to the dismantling, or at least have undermined, existing corporatist arrangements in Britain.

Sargent concludes that the Community exhibits a combina-tion of weak corporatist arrangements which, in any case, tend to favour capital rather than labour, and weak pluralist and parliamentary arrangements. Both are prevented from further development by a number of underlying tensions within the Community, and these are discussed in the chapter. The European Community is, therefore, unlikely to boost the spread of corporatist arrangements in the way that some commentators have assumed was likely to happen. Sargent's chapter fills a major gap in the existing literature on corporatism, as discussion of corporatism at the Community level has been strangely neglected by academics.

The dual politics thesis

Although it is possible to identify various policy arenas in which corporatist arrangements are likely to develop, such an exercise does not of itself provide a systematic explanation of the dispersal of corporatist arrangements across different parts of the economy and polity. The importance of the dual politics thesis, which is extensively discussed in the chapters by Cawson and Saunders, is that it does offer such an explanation.

As Saunders explains in Chapter 6, what the dual politics thesis attempts to do is to relate work on corporatism to work on other aspects of political processes in order to develop a framework through which to link a diversity of contemporary empirical concerns with the broader theoretical issues of political science and political economy. The thesis suggests that there is a tendency for political activity concerning issues of production to become focused on central state agencies, to foster relatively exclusive corporatist forms of interest mediation, and to be informed principally by values which emphasise the rights of private property and the importance of sustaining private sector profitability. Conversely, there is also a tendency for consumption questions to be relegated to peripheral or localised state agencies where a plurality of interests become involved in political competition to realise their objectives, and where the actions of participants are often informed by values stressing the rights of citizenship and the importance of meeting different social needs.

In Chapter 6, Saunders compares political processes at different levels of state organisation (the local and the regional) and across different types of policy areas (production and consumption interventions). In sympathy with the comparative objective of this book, he compares research conducted in two different countries (Australia and England). In all three case studies, the development of corporatist forms reflected pressure from private sector interests for relatively exclusive access to state agencies, a theme which is also taken up in Simmie's chapter. Saunders concludes (p. 172) that 'the most fertile ground for the emergence of corporatist forms of urban service provision relates (as suggested by the dual politics thesis) to those interventions where producer interests are most directly affected and where the resulting tendency towards corporatism is reinforced by the existence of non-local and non-elected agencies which are staffed by individuals who are sympathetic to the concerns expressed by propertied interests'.

Corporatism at the local level

There has been very little discussion so far about corporatism at the level of local governments, and one of the objectives of Cawson's chapter is an attempt to remedy this neglect. Cawson does not simply trawl the corporatist net on a new fishing ground, so to speak, in the hope of catching new corporatist species, but seeks to establish the local within a more general theory of interest politics and state intervention. He argues that corporatism is unlikely to become as significant at the local level as elsewhere, but shifts in the mode of state intervention, partly in response to the economic crisis of recent years, have led to more locally based attempts to influence the behaviour of local economies which involve a search for interest organisations which might become corporatist partners in policy-making.

In Chapter 7, which focuses on land-use planning mechanisms at the local level, Simmie argues that participation in the procedures of local physical planning authorities is characterised more by corporatist than by pluralist forms of interest mediation. Although both forms may still be observed, there is a tendency for the former to develop at the expense of the latter. Both Cawson and Simmie therefore see tendencies towards more corporatist arrangements at the local level, although, arising from the different emphases in their interpretations of corporatism, Simmie sees such developments as more extensive and wide-ranging than Cawson. Cawson concludes that the most striking examples of the corporatist policy mode at the local level turn out to be where the local defines the object of policy rather than characterises the nature of the interests involved. Simmie emphasises the ownership and control of land by the production and capital sectors of the political economy and draws attention to the exclusive tendencies inherent in land use planning arrangements. This emphasis on exclusivity fits in with Cawson's conclusion that the kinds of corporatist interventions that may reshape the local political economy will be determined outside the reach of local political organisation.

It is therefore important to be aware of the limitations of local level corporatism, both in terms of its spread and the degree of influence that is exerted over organised interests by public policy-makers. As the chapters by Saunders and Simmie show, what often results is additional privileges for already privileged groups in society. This emphasis on the reinforcement of existing privileges adds to the importance of King's chapter, which shows that increased involvement by local authorities in economic policy-making and the encouragement of central government have been instrumental in the development of corporatist arrangements at the local level that have involved chambers of commerce as representatives of business. However, despite the increased involvement of chambers of commerce in public policy implementation, King points out that there is little sign of increased control exerted downwards on members by chamber officers. King concludes that the corporatist tendencies that can be observed in government–chamber relationships are less an instance of state-induced restraint on the chambers than a recognition by the state of its relative powerlessness to influence the accumulation of capital.

Although it is procedurally helpful to separate out local corporatism as an object of analysis, it is important, as has been pointed out, to locate such phenomena within a broader theoretical understanding of the relationship between state and society. Effective meso- and micro-level corporatist arrangements can be found in countries which have no corporatist arrangements at the macro level, but this does not mean that there is no relationship between the arrangements at the different levels. Work by Marin stresses the importance of the dialectic between the different levels of interest intermediation (see Marin, 1982a, p. 74ff and Marin, 1983a, pp. 215–6). If structures below the macro level are to be stable and permanent, they must to some extent rely on support from the macro level, while macro-level structures are sustained and strengthened by effective corporatist arrangements at the meso and micro levels.

The pluralist counter-attack

Pluralist theorists have not been slow to respond to criticisms of their approach by corporatist writers. There are a number of

points in the pluralist response which merit serious consideration. Four main arguments will be considered here: that
corporatist writers have misrepresented the diversity and
richness of pluralist writing; that despite their emphasis on the
state, corporatists have had little to say about it; that, in any
case, corporatism is nothing more than a particular form of
pluralism; and that there is uncertainty in corporatist writing
about the relationship between structure and function.

Almond (1983) sets out a defence of the richness and variety
of pluralist literature which makes the more general point that
political science tends to suffer from an imperfect professional
memory and thereby fails to cumulate its literature in a way that
would yield valuable comparative perspectives and theoretical
insights. Thus, as the limitations of a 'new wave' of literature are
exposed, political scientists rediscover the wave before the last
one. In a sense (although Almond does not use this phrase),
political scientists are always having to rediscover the wheel. For
example, classic pluralist writers such as Truman devoted
considerable attention to the relationship between interest
groups and government, with government acting not as a
neutral force, but one that established and maintained a
measure of order in the relationships between groups (see
Truman, 1951, pp. 45 and 106).

Almond's article is a salutary reminder of the importance of a
familiarity with earlier literature. As far as the pluralist
literature is concerned, its diversity is a source of strength – it
provides a range of explanations with which one could fill the
intellectual equivalent of a supermarket trolley – but it is also a
source of weakness. It is difficult to arrive at a clear statement of
the pluralist position that could be used to inform empirical
research. In a sense, this makes the task of the defenders of
pluralism much easier, because they can present a constantly
moving target to their critics. It could be said, of course, that
corporatism suffers from similar weaknesses, and it may have
been afflicted by the transmission of the virus of intellectual
confusion which is present in some pluralist writing.

Wilson argues that, 'A very basic question left unanswered in
most discussions of neo-corporatism is, what is the state?'
(Wilson, 1983, pp. 111–12). Part of the problem is, of course,
that one of the concomitants of corporatism is a dissolution of

the boundary between the public and the private (see Schmitter, 1982). As Schmitter points out in this volume, the modern state has been forced to share its formerly exclusive powers with other institutions in (and outside) its own society so that he claims that, 'What is left is an amorphous complex of agencies with very ill-defined boundaries, performing a great variety of not very distinctive functions' (p. 33).

It should also be pointed out that there are important empirical variations in the role of the state in corporatist arrangements in different countries at different times. As Crouch has observed, the state may play a range of roles 'while remaining within the compass of liberal interest organisation', although 'certain possibilities are excluded at each end of the range. At one extreme, a state committed to working with organised interests will limit the extent of its own *direct* interventions . . . At the other extreme, such a state can never be *laissez faire*, leaving matters to regulation by interest groups without taking any interest in the outcomes (Crouch, 1983b, p. 456).

One of the most potentially damaging charges made against theorists who use the term corporatism is that it is simply a variety or sub-type of pluralism (see, for example, Almond, 1983). If it is no more than a sub-type, then the intellectual distinctiveness of corporatism, and its potential contribution to the debate about relationships between the state and organised producer interests, would be considerably diminished. Corporatist writers have never denied that 'Pluralism and corporatism share a number of basic assumptions' (Schmitter, 1979, p. 15). One may also accept Martin's point (1983a, p. 102) that societal corporatism is closer to pluralism than it is to state corporatism without undermining Schmitter's argument (1979, p. 15) that pluralism differs markedly from corporatism as an ideal type.

However, the attempt to assimilate corporatism as a variety of pluralism cannot be left unchallenged. There are a number of crucial differences between corporatist and pluralist approaches. As Crouch (1983b) has emphasised, the essence of neo-corporatism is to be found in the notion of intermediation which takes us beyond the pluralist analysis of bargaining between groups and government. In particular, Crouch emphasises the importance of groups engaged in corporatist bargaining being able to discipline and control their members to comply with agreements negotiated with the state or other parties.

It may be doubted whether pluralism can properly be described as a theory of interest intermediation. It is rather a theory of bargaining between autonomous, often competing, groups and a fragmented state in which the emphasis is on the flow of influence from the groups to the state with an inbuilt set of checks and balances which supposedly prevent any one group from becoming too powerful, e.g., the development of so-called countervailing groups. Intermediation means that group leaderships have to ensure that their memberships comply with the agreements they have arrived at with the state or other organised interests. As Cox and Hayward point out, for a system of corporatism to work, 'the representatives of capital and labour must have the *capacity* to discipline their own members to accept the compromises to which the leadership of these bodies agree in the common interest' (Cox and Hayward, 1983, p. 219). What corporatism offers is the possiblity of arriving at *effective* bargains, in the sense that they can be secured and implemented, rather than being simply talked about in the hope that changes in the behaviour of the discussants will follow. One consequence of the imposition of discipline on group members that accompanies corporatist arrangements is that a tension is set up within the interest organisations between representation and self-regulation. It is the exploration of this tension within organised interests that is one of the central concerns of corporatist research.

As has been pointed out, corporatist analysis focuses on the groups that arise out of the division of labour in society, whereas pluralism is concerned with the analysis of any organised (or latent) interest. Cawson (1982, p. 38) notes that 'Corporate groups are defined by their location in the social and economic division of labour; their identity is given by the *function* that their members perform in society and the economy'. In particular, as Berger (1981a, p. 13) emphasises, 'In industrial capitalist countries with liberal democratic governments, organisations representing labour and capital are not simply groups like any others. They are both less variable in their indentification of interests and more powerful in relation to other groups'.

'Productive confusion': structural and policy approaches

Corporatist writers could be accused by their critics of failing to resolve the choice of approach between starting from policy arenas and working back to the structures found within them, and working from structures in defined sectors towards policy issues. In fact, as Schmitter argues, 'the most productive confusion in the dialogue on neo-corporatism has been that which has "opposed" those who define it as a distinctive mode for organising the conflicting functional interests . . . and those who identify it as a distinctive mode for making and implementing public policy' (Schmitter, 1982, p. 262). Attempts to resolve this productive confusion have led to some interesting research findings which are discussed later in this section.

The approach to corporatism as a mode of policy-making and implementation (which Schmitter labels 'corporatism$_2$') is particularly identified with the work of Lehmbruch, who has 'laid the emphasis on "patterns of policy formation"' (Lehmbruch, 1982, p. 8), although he also emphasises the importance of 'a close relationship between the large interest organisations and political parties' (Lehmbruch, 1983, p. 158) and the significance of a high degree of co-operation between large organised social groups themselves as a 'distinguishing trait' of liberal corporatism (Lehmbruch, 1979, p. 54). The advantage of this approach is that it allows the investigator to tackle pressing questions of public policy in the light of neo-corporatist theory. The risk is that structural explanations may be brought in as residual variables when other explanations have failed without a proper understanding of the structures concerned.

An alternative approach, as developed in the International Institute of Management's international comparative project on business interest associations, co-ordinated by Schmitter and Streeck, is to proceed from a structural analysis of the interest organisations in defined economic sectors, in this particular case business interest associations. Thus the International Institute of Management project starts from the base of a thorough study of economic conditions in each sector and incorporates an analysis of the relevant state structures and other interlocutors such as trade unions. One positive consequence of this strategy is that it is possible to make comparisons across countries at the meso level. Material is also collected on the 'rules of the game' that shape associative activity and on the historical development of the system of associations. Only when the data on these structures have been collected, including an analysis of the interaction with the state of the interests being studied, are policy issues in the form of *Schwerpunkte* (points of emphasis) analysed. Thus although it takes longer to arrive at the study of particular policy issues, when they *are* studied, the analysis proceeds on the basis of a full understanding of the capabilities and orientations of the relevant actors.

In as yet unpublished research for a comparative study of food processing industry associations and agricultural policy, Coleman has noted that in two of the countries being studied, the supposedly unstable situation occurs of a pluralist structure of representation and a concertation structure of control. In both of the countries studied (Canada and Switzerland), fragmented and unco-ordinated associational systems are involved in the task of economic regulation as private interest governments, and there is no reason to suppose that this policy system is unstable.

Who benefits?

Any account of neo-corporatism must be as much concerned with outcomes as with processes: in other words, it must attempt to answer the question, 'Who benefits?' There has been no lack of speculation on this issue in the literature, mainly in relation to two themes: do workers lose out as a result of being ensnared in corporatist arrangements; and are policies with extensive corporatist arrangements better able to meet their economic objectives than thosee which lack such arrangements?

Panitch argues that, 'Above all else, [corporatism] is a political structure designed to integrate the organised working class in the capitalist state' (Panitch, 1980, p. 175). There is no doubt that particular governments at particular times have seen corporatist bargains with trade unions as a way of damping down labour discontent and, in particular, of keeping wage settlements down to 'acceptable' levels (acceptable to the government, that is). There is also no doubt that labour has come away from particular corporatist experiments, especially the more temporary ones, with little to show for its co-operation with government policies. Work by Cameron, drawing on data from a wide range of OECD countries, suggests that there is a relationship between corporatism and labour quiescence. Nevertheless,

> Cameron finds no evidence that under corporatism labour loses out in factor shares and, if anything, the 'social wage' is higher. But from the standpoint of the working class as a whole, the major advantage must be reckoned as the preservation of high levels of employment, even if some groups within the working class are denied gains that militancy could have brought. (Goldthorpe, 1984, p. 8)

Although capitalists and other privileged groups such as the professions are supposed to give less and receive more from corporatist arrangements than the workers, they tend to be less enthusiastic about them. In countries such as Britain, this may have something to do with a continuing attachment on the part of such groups to an ideology of the minimalist state. However, it does seem possible that the price that capitalists have to pay for participation in corporatist arrangements, at whatever level, tends to rise over the long run. The entry price may be low, but the costs of membership rise over time, and exit becomes increasingly difficult, as Sargent's (1983) study of the Pharmaceutical Price Regulation Scheme shows. Neo-corporatist arrangements tend to expand from discussions of such questions as wage restraint into areas which start to threaten the property rights of capitalists, thus raising the price paid for social peace (see Schmitter, 1982). Sweden has generally been regarded as an example of, at least, bipartite (capital–labour) corporatism (even if the Swedes do not like the term being applied to their country) and when employers decide to take to the streets in Sweden to protest about wage-earner funds, it suggests that the angelic chorus in the corporatist heaven does not always sing with an upper-class accent.

Offe, (1981, pp. 153–4) has argued that the political status that unions gain through involvement in policy-making arrangements with the state could enhance working-class power, while Crouch (1982a) has advanced the view that bargained corporatism offers the possiblity of the extension of democracy in the management of industrial affairs. Corporatism at least has the potential of changing the balance of political power in favour of the weaker side in a capitalist market society (organised labour). Whether it does so will depend on the balance of forces, and the bargains arrived at, in particular cases. (For evidence that corporatist arrangements have strengthened organised labour in the Austrian case, see Marin 1982a, pp. 321ff).

The general attraction of corporatism, leaving aside sectional gains, is that it offers the possibility of transforming the process of economic management into a non-zero-sum game, so that everyone is better off than they would be in the absence of corporatist arrangements (although some may gain more than others). There is, however, a risk that organised interests will benefit at the expense of the unorganised, or that interests included in the process of policy negotiation will benefit at the expense of those excluded. (One example is small firms: see Crouch, 1982a, p. 175.) A more general issue that arises is how the interests of individual consumers can be taken into account in bargains between the state and producer groups. In Britain, the publicly financed National Consumer Council could be seen as an attempt to incorporate consumer interests into bargaining arrangements between the state and producer groups, particularly given that it has been allocated a seat on the National Economic Development Council. However, giving a public status to consumer 'representatives' can pose as many problems as it solves.

Even if it could be established that there were some losers from corporatist bargaining, corporatist arrangements might attract support it if could be demonstrated that they facilitated the achievement of key economic objective such as low inflation and fuller employment. Deciding whether corporatist arrangements have any impact on macroeconomic outcomes involves a number of difficult methodological problems, not least specifying which countries have accepted corporatist arrangements at which times. Nevertheless, there is a growing body of evidence that suggests that corporatist arrangements may have beneficial macroeconomic consequences: for example, Schmidt (1982) suggests that corporatist arrangements may have facilitated the management of domestic labour markets and softened the impact of the business cycle. The review of the available evidence commissioned by the Corporatism and Accountability Sub-Committee of the Government and Law Committee of the Economic and Social Research Council should, when it becomes available, help to focus and carry forward the debate on this crucial issue.

Corporatism as a middle-range theory

Writers on neo-corporatism are not searching for a 'philosopher's stone' (Martin, 1983b), whatever their critics may claim. The claim made by mainstream writers on neo-corporatism is more modest. They would argue that, stripped of its pejorative associations with fascism, neo-corporatism can help us to understand certain important tendencies that have occurred in a number of Western societies. It is not presumed that these tendencies will persist for ever, or that corporatism is 'something a polity has or does not have' (Schmitter, 1982, p. 265). Neo-corporatism offers us a middle range theory of interest intermediation. As explained by Merton, middle range theory lies between all-inclusive general theories of social systems that are too remote from social reality to account for what is observed, and detailed descriptions of particular phenomena that are not generalised at all. Middle range theory does involve abstractions, but they are close enough to what is observed to facilitate empirical testing (see Merton, 1957, pp. 39ff, and Saunders, Chapter 6 of this volume).

The way in which organised interests based on the division of labour relate to the state and each other raises some of the central questions facing modern Western societies, not least the distribution of power within them, and how the divergent claims of different social groups can be reconciled, if at all. The relative lack of neo-corporatist practices in some societies can tell us as much about those societies as neo-corporatism can help us to understand societies in which such arrangements are highly developed. Neo-corporatism should not be seen, in any sense, either prescriptively or analytically, as a 'final solution' to some of the most important and pressing problems facing Western societies. It is, however, a phenomenon and a paradigm that will have to be worked through and fully understood before we can comprehend what lies beyond it. In the final section, attention will be drawn to two paradigms which might take the debate further.

Issues for future research

One central problem that has received attention, but which would benefit from further debate, is the relationship between corporatism and democratic theory. As Schmitter (1983a, p. 15) points out, at the very least neo-corporatism should be compatible with the prevailing 'procedural minimum' of democracy – civic freedom, universal suffrage, etc. The fundamental question that has to be tackled is whether a society with extensive corporatist arrangements can better, or at least as well, serve the ideals embodied in theories of respective democracy than traditional forms of government based on territorially elected parties. Part of the problem is that although there is a variety of ways in which corporatist arrangements and parliamentary institutions can be related to one another (see Coombes, 1982), the adoption of corporatist arrangements does imply a willingness on the part of government to share power with designated interest organisations rather than with Parliament. From a more positive point of view, corporatism does offer new opportunities for citizen participation in a strengthened tier of intermediary organisations. The acceptability of corporatism in the long run may depend as much on its capacity to create such new opportunities for participation and its ability to develop a balanced relationship with parliamentary forms of representation, as on its contribution to economic performance. So far, as Schmitter points out in this volume, neo-corporatism has been a consumer, not a producer, of legitimacy, with the state as its supplier.

One solution to this dilemma might appear to be to give more explicit recognition to corporatist arrangements, and to underpin them with a corporatist ideology. However, as far as the first suggestion is concerned, it should be recognised that the term 'corporate state' still has negative associations in the eyes of many political influentials and the public at large, even if academics have come to treat corporatism as a phenomenon which requires systematic exploration rather than outright condemnation. Moreover, many corporatist arrangements have grown up on an *ad hoc* basis, and the participants would either deny that they were corporatist, or if convinced that they were, might withdraw their support from them. As Marin explains in Chapter 4, corporatism is a 'self-denying' concept which is characterised by moral ambivalence, a lack of political legitimacy and an absence of normative foundation.

If corporatist arrangements are successful (e.g. in attaining stated economic policy goals), then they may not require any explicit ideological legitimation. However, the problem of excluded interests remains and would benefit from further empirical research. This is often conceived in terms of weak, poorly organised or underprivileged groups being kept away from the warmth of the corporatist hearth. However, there is another kind of exclusion that is particularly important in the British case: the isolation of privileged interests from corporatist arrangements. As Crouch points out in Chapter 3, the financial sector in Britain has been an 'excluded zone' from corporatist influence, a phenomenon which, although highly developed in the British case, is not confined to that country. The financial sector in Britain has been allowed to maintain many privileged self-regulatory arrangements of its own, and these are likely to continue in the future, even if under greater state surveillance than in the past. The research programme approved by the Corporatism and Accountability Sub-Committee of the Government and Law Committee of the ESRC includes awards to a number of projects concerned with the financial sector, and the results of this research will build on existing knowledge to leave us much better informed about how privileged the corporatist arrangements in the financial sector are.

The general relationship between interest organisations and political parties has been a surprisingly neglected topic in political science, and this is no less true of the corporatist literature. Lehmbruch has devoted some attention to this question, but there is scope for considerable further research. As Marin's examination of the Austrian case in this volume shows, under well-developed corporatist arrangements, the boundaries between interest organisations and political parties dissolve. Political parties are incorporated into interest associations,

associations into political parties. This apparent consequence of a high level of corporatist development does pose further questions about democratic theory, as most Western democracies accord central importance to the way in which political parties with voluntary memberships draw up policy programmes, submit them to the electorate, and then implement them if they gain office. The reality is, of course, somewhat different, but constitutional myths have their own importance, and the structured choice offered by political parties is such a key feature of modern Western democracies that any transformation of their role would have important implications for democratic theory and practice.

New paradigms?

The corporatist debate has not yet reached a stage of development where one can say with any confidence which paradigms are likely to contribute to the new synthesis that will eventually emerge from it. However, there are two promising possibilities. One is the model of *associative order* developed by Streeck and Schmitter (1984) and discussed by Schmitter in his contribution to this book. One of the merits of the Streeck–Schmitter approach is that it sets out the properties of an associative model of social order in a way that facilitates further work in the area, including empirical research. Schmitter explains the essential features of the associative order approach in his contribution to this volume:

> Our point is not that this 'new' order is somehow destined to prevail over the others, or even to assume an equivalent significance in all advanced industrial/capitalist societies, but that modern social order is composed of a mix of institutions with different actors, motives, media of exchange, resources, decision rules, cleavage patterns and normative foundations – and that the traditional trio of community, market and state fails to explore all the possible bases and combinations. (p. 51)

The concept of *organisational development* was presented in the research design for the International Institute of Management project on business interest associations (Schmitter and Streeck, 1981). Although developed for the study of business interest associations, it could be applied to other organisations engaged in corporatist bargaining. There are two basic notions involved in the concept of organisational development: coping with organised complexity, and achieving and maintaining organisational autonomy. Organised complexity is concerned with how representative associations cope with the considerable diversity of underlying interests they attempt to organise. This diversity can be overcome through intra-organisational differentiation and through external co-ordination between independent associations. Organisational autonomy refers to the supply of resources needed for an organisation's development, but also to its capacity to determine its objectives and select the means and strategies to pursue them independently. Developed, stable organisations with long-term objectives are more likely to appeal to the state as prospective partners in governance.

Collaborative work by the writer with Coleman on the international comparison of business interest associations serving particular industries deliberately eschewed the use of the term 'corporatism' and concentrated instead on the notion of organisational development (Coleman and Grant, 1984). It was found that the concept of organisational development did provide a framework within which to explore such issues as the capacity of associations to undertake public policy functions and to engage in long-term strategic thinking about the problems of their industries. In the particular cases examined, British associations were found to display a higher level of organisational development than their Canadian counterparts, and the British associations were better able to assume responsibility for public policy implementation as private governments.

Wilson concludes from his review of the corporatist literature that neo-corporatism 'may turn out to be an intellectual blind alley leading nowhere if [it] turns out to be limited to a few groups, certain issues, and particular or passing circumstances in some countries' (Wilson, 1983, p. 121). There has been a drift away from corporatist arrangements in Britain, although that may consist of a replacement of tripartite arrangements by more exclusive, bipartite arrangements with privileged interests, rather than the complete disappearance of the sharing of policy responsibilities with producer interests (see Harrison, 1984).

In any case, whatever happens in particular countries (and it should be remembered that empirical research has shown that there are far more corporatist arrangements at the meso level than would have been thought likely a decade ago), the debate on neo-corporatism will have been worthwhile. It has infuriated some academics, stimulated others, and probably induced frustration and despair in most of its participants at one time or another. However, the fact that such a lively and wide-ranging debate has been possible suggests that Western social science, if less well funded than it once was, is still healthy in the sense that it is able to engage complex and difficult issues that are relevant to current policy problems. If nothing else, the debate has given a much needed stimulus to the cross-national study of interest organisations, which, after a brief flurry of interest in the late 1950s, had languished in the doldrums for too long. Long after the dust of the theoretical and terminological disputes has settled, these comparative studies will stand as a monument to a debate which brought together scholars from different countries, disciplines, forms of training and political perspectives to work together in an effort to understand changes in the relationship between the state and organised interests in their societies.

Chapter 2

Neo-corporatism and the State

Philippe C. Schmitter

The 'state' has become a bit like the weather. Social scientists in recent years have been talking a great deal about it, but have not been able to do much with it. Articles and books now display the concept prominently in their titles, but no one seems quite sure what it is. We have been exhorted somehow to 'bring it back' into our analyses (Skocpol, 1982), but we have not been told where it fits.[1]

The burgeoning literature on neo-corporatism has contributed significantly to this revival of interest in the state (Cawson, 1978; Maraffi, 1983), but it has not resolved the problem of what or why the invocation of such a portentous concept adds to our understanding of politics in advanced industrial/capitalist societies. On the one hand, it has been (correctly) credited with calling our attention to the many ways in which the structure and action of public authorities affect the identification and organisation of interests; on the other hand, it has been (rightly) criticised for not telling us enough about the circumstances and motives under which these authorities intervene to change the ways in which individuals and groups perceive their interests and act collectively to defend them. In short, it is one thing to put the state into a theory and quite another thing to have a theory of the state.

'State theory'?

But is it really possible any longer to speak of *a* state theory or a theory of *the* state in the advanced industrial/capitalist societies of Western Europe and North America (Jessop, 1982)? Most of the conditions which previously allowed theorists to treat the state as a distinctive social institution are no longer present to the same degree. For example, its imputed capacity for *unity of action* seems dubious in the face of abundant evidence of competitiveness and incoherence among its multiple agencies and levels. *Sovereignty* used to be considered the hallmark of stateness, but few would argue that, today, even the largest and most powerful of state units have the ultimate capacity to determine autonomously and authoritatively the allocation of all private goods and public status within their respective territories. 'Internal' capitalist relations have long restricted the state's effective exercise of sovereignty, but the more recent development of transnational processes and supranational regimes have added so many new external constraints that the claim is no longer credible. Indeed, the very concept of sovereignty now seems quaint and has become virtually extinct in normal or academic usage.

Other allegedly distinctive properties of the state – its association with a particular nation and the spirit of nationalism; its capacity for the defence of a specific territory; its pretence to embody the common and universal interests of the citizenry; its claim to centrality in all political calculations; its staffing by a special stratum of the population; its organisation according to unique (bureaucratic) principles – have not so much disappeared as weakened, or lost their exclusiveness. The modern state has either diminished in its command of these properties, or has been forced to share them with other institutions in (and outside) its own society. What is left is an amorphous complex of agencies with ill-defined boundaries, performing a great variety of not very distinctive functions. As a symbolic and systemic totality, the state may still command a relative superiority of coercive power within a given territory and a legitimate authority to use that power to enforce certain norms, but even these capacities are subject to unprecedented contestation and restriction. In short, we are being asked to bring the state back into our analyses precisely when it least resembles what it was historically and theoretically. If we are to do this effectively, we cannot merely revive or retrieve out-dated assumptions about this institution. We must revise and reconstruct them.

Paradoxically, what seems to have motivated this new fashion is the claim, advanced by social scientists from a wide range of political perspectives, that the contemporary state has been 'taking weighty, autonomous initiatives' (Skocpol, 1982, p. 1) which go beyond or against the demands and interests of existing social groups. Precisely when its distinctiveness, its unity and its sovereignty have diminished, the state in Western Europe and North America appears to have increased its capacity to penetrate society with its policies – to affect citizen behaviour, to extract resources, to collect information, to regulate economic exchanges, to distribute goods and services – and to do this with a degree of 'relative autonomy' which seems both puzzling and unprecedented. Indeed, this emergent property has provided the central focus, the principal *explanandum* and *explanans*, of contemporary efforts at theorising about the state.

The mere fact that so many schools of thought have uncovered this analytical lodestone does not, however, imply that there is agreement on what this autonomy means, why it is significant, or how it is to be measured. Conservatives interpret what has happened in recent decades as a decline in the state's 'real-historical' mission to pursue distinctively public or civic goals, and attribute its cause largely to a change in the pattern of recruitment whereby ambitious, self-serving, middle-class professionals have displaced disinterested and public-minded aristocrats in the control of state agencies. Traditional liberals point to the unprecedented growth in the volume and variety of state activities and argue that relative autonomy emerges as an unanticipated consequence from the sheer complexity and fragmentation of these efforts at regulation and subsidisation, with each agency and agent competing for power, status and budget shares. For many Marxists, the phenomenon lies not in behavioural or institutional factors, but in functional ones. Capitalism, at this stage in its development, requires a functional apparatus that is capable of ensuring the general conditions for capital accumulation and social cohesion. To do this, the state must acquire an independent strategic capacity to forge unity within the dominant class, overriding its particularistic interests, and to extract consensus from subordinate classes, co-opting and/or manipulating their partial interests.

So, there is agreement among 'state-centred' theorists that relative autonomy is something important, but disagreement among them concerning what it is and why it exists. The state may (some would say, must) formulate and implement policies that are not merely reflective of established preferences and articulated demands of groups, strata and classes within society, but it is not clear whether this capacity is a permanent attribute or an episodic occurrence, a functional necessity or a contingent choice, a consistent property or an issue-specific response. Underlying these theoretical (and, at times, scholastic) divergences is the central issue of whether the state has 'interests' of its own – and the distinctive resources to make them prevail in the face of resistance by those with conflicting interests. This, in turn, is linked to the question of whether the state can design its own 'policy instruments', i.e. whether it can choose the terrain and format for its interaction with social groups and can impose upon these groups the conception of interests and mode of collective action that it prefers. This is where neo-corporatism might enter the picture as one possible mode of restructuring state–society relations.

Political design?

Regardless of the school of neo-corporatism – and there are many – its students would agree that it is unlikely to emerge or persist without the active connivance or complicity of state agencies. Interest associations will not attain the status of monopoly representatives or form comprehensive hierarchies of sectoral and class co-ordination without some degree of official recognition, if not encouragement. Nor will they become regular, integral participants in policy-making or acquire direct responsibilities for policy implementation without the tacit agreement, if not the active promotion, of public officials. State actions are therefore necessary but not sufficient causes of neo-corporatist arrangements. In democratic polities, stage agents can try to bring about such patterns, but their efforts can fail (see McBride, 1983, for a case study of this). Affected groups may refuse to organise themselves appropriately; targeted organisations can turn down the invitation to participate; incorporated associations can defect if they find the costs of collaborating too high. To use an Italian expression, neo-corporatism depends on a *scambio politico*, a political exchange in which organised interests and state agencies calculatedly, if not always willingly and enthusiastically, agree to a particular pattern of formal representation and substantive negotiation (Pizzorno, 1978; Ceri, 1980–1; Rusconi, 1981 and 1983; Mutti, 1983; Regini, 1983).

From this perspective, such arrangements cannot be seen as a deliberate act of state control over the expression of class or group interests (see Panitch, 1979 and 1981; Jessop, 1978; Strinati, 1979 and 1982) – whether the state is interpreted as acting out of its institutional self-interest or as enforcing the general class interest of the bourgeoisie. Rather, this sort of compromise is possible only where some degree of balance exists in the organised expression of class forces, and where the organised expression of other interest cleavages in the society ethnic, religious, generational, positional, gender-related, etc. – can be disregarded or set momentarily aside. This is not to say that the classes involved must have achieved a parity of power – that capital and labour must have the same capacity to influence state policy or to extract benefits from public authorities – for neo-corporatist arrangements to come about. If this were the case, they would be exceedingly rare and of very limited duration. Rather, the relevant interlocutors must be in a situation of mutual deterrence, each sufficiently capable of organised collective action to prevent the other from realising its interests directly through social control and/or economic exploitation, and each sufficiently incapable of unilateral manipulation of public authority to impose its interests indirectly through the state. In such a context of imposed bargaining (Crouch, 1977), both the room and the necessity for intervention increase. State agents acquire the capacity to make an independent and significant contribution towards the negotiation of a more stable and institutionalised interest compromise and, at the same time, are empowered to extract some 'public-regarding' concessions from the bargaining associations. Such a relative autonomy is neither *behavioural* in the sense that it depends on the preferences of civil servants (Nordlinger, 1981), nor is it *functional* in the sense that it stems from the imperatives of ensuring the long-run imperatives of capitalist reproduction (Poulantzas, 1972 and 1975), nor is it *tactical* in the sense of just disguising the interests of a non-ruling dominant class behind the facade of state neutrality (Block, 1977). It is *structural* and grounded in the institutional interests of the state.

The more comprehensive neo-corporatist arrangements, at least as they have emerged in the political democraticies of Western Europe since the Second World War, have not been the result of the wilful calculation of some autonomous state actor or the hegemonic project of some progressive class fraction. They have not come about through deliberate, grandiose efforts at 'political design' (Anderson, 1977). With the possible exception of the immediate post-war settlements in Belgium and the Netherlands, they have been the largely unintended outcome of a series of disparate interest conflicts and policy crises in which none of the class or state actors involved was capable of imposing its preferred solution upon the others. Typically, they began as second-best compromises which no one really wanted or defended openly: hence their general invisibility, their uneven distribution and their precarious legitimacy. State actors would usually have preferred authoritative regulation; business re-presentatives an allocation through market forces; and labour leaders a redistribution of wealth and/or a redefinition of property rights. Neo-corporatism satisfies none of these projects, but incorporates elements of all of them. It is, therefore, both conservative in that it reflects existing property and power relations, and potentially transformative in that it subjects them to explicit and repeated negotiation. Class compromise is thereby moved from the plane of individualistic adaptation and parliamentary manoeuvre to that of inter-organisational bar-gaining and contract formation.

All this would be unnecessary if the state really was as autonomous as some have argued in its recruitment patterns, informational resources, agenda-setting and implementation capacities. Pierre Birnbaum, for example, has argued that France – the only country in the world with a real state in his opinion – is incapable of developing neo-corporatist arran-gements (Birnbaum, 1982a, p. 111; for a rather different version of state–interest association relationships in France, see Hall, 1982 and Pontusson, 1983; and of corporatism in that country, see Schain, 1980 and Goetschy, 1983). Conversely, where the state lacks autonomy due to the overwhelming hegemony of capitalist interests, neo-corporatist bargaining will be rejected as a heretical and wasteful impediment to the efficient operation of market forces. The United States has frequently been cited as a case in point (Wilson, 1982), although even there some traces of corporatism have been discerned (Wolfe, 1977; Lustig, 1982; Milward and Francisco, 1983). Great Britain, which was (erroneously in my view) earlier placed in the avant-garde of neo-corporatism (Harris, 1972; Pahl and Winkler, 1975; Winkler, 1976; Newman, 1981), has more recently been identified as a place where the balance of organised class forces and state capacities is no longer (not yet?) appropriate for the task (Crouch, 1979; Jessop, 1980; Regini, 1983).

Policy instrument?

If the emergence of such arrangements cannot be attributed to some grand political design of the state or some hegemonic class fraction, can they be assigned the more modest status of a policy instrument, a format chosen to resolve particular problems; and if so, why that and not some other means of coping with interest conflicts? The mere existence of mutual deterrence and organisational stalemate may make stable and comprehensive neo-corporatism possible, but they do not make it inevitable or desirable. It is not the only instrument available in the policy repertoire of advanced capitalism. Indicative planning, public ownership of productive assets, selective subsidisation, state regulation, control of the money supply and centralised executive authority all offer alternative means for dealing with its conflicts and contradictions. Not only have these been tried (with varying degrees of success), but many constitute 'first preferences' of powerful constituencies and are often more compatible with cultural norms and democratic values than the second-best and dubiously legitimate institutions of neo-corporatism.

One answer that has been proposed is that such arrangements are preferred and promoted, not by the relatively autonomous state, but by relatively autonomous groups within it, i.e. by specific bureaux and agencies. In response to their discrete needs for information, compliance, legitimacy and support *vis-à-vis* competing units, civil servants seek to co-opt their clients and find systems of functional representation useful for these purposes. No doubt one could find many instances where public officials have taken the lead in establishing such relationships, rewarded interests which formed or merged into monopolistic associations, encouraged representatives to take a longer-term and more 'responsible' view of their member interests and sought to insulate policy deliberation from partisan, territorial and/or popular pressures.

Civil servants are likely to be much less enthusiastic about effectively sharing decision-making power with interest associations and especially about devolving to them the authority and material resources necessary for the implementation of policies. Nor are they likely, in a liberal-democratic polity, to be able to control as much as they would like the processes of leadership selection and demand formation within formally co-opted associations – unless it is in the calculated interest of these groups to consent to such adjustments. Efforts by zealous and autonomous authorities to go beyond these implicit limits would be thwarted by defections, either by association leaders or their disillusioned followers. Also, if the dominant motive in the formation of neo-corporatist arrangements were the co-optive preference of civil servants, this could only explain the proliferation of bipartite or tripartite forums of functional representation attached to particular bureaux or agencies, not the emergence of comprehensive trans-sectoral institutions for negotiating and implementing macroeconomic and social policy throughout the polity. These require much more extensive *political*, i.e. party and parliamentary, support (Armingeon, 1982; Armingeon *et al.*, 1983); Lehmbruch, 1983; Lehmbruch and Halle, 1983). Admittedly, social pacts of this scope are not that common and have had a precarious existence in many countries; nevertheless, they do constitute the most salient and powerful utilisation of this policy instrument, its best claim to being a means for significant restructuring of the relations between civil society and the state apparatus.

This suggests (to me) that, while neo-corporatism may not be 'architectural', it is not purely 'artisanal'. The macro-functional imperatives of capitalist reproduction may be too vague and indeterminant to explain its emergence – especially its very uneven distribution across sectors and countries in Western Europe and North America – and the micro-behavioural preferences of civil servants may be too circumscribed and ineffectual to explain its significance, especially its differential contribution to political and economic outcomes in these countries (Schmitter, 1981a; Schmidt, 1982, 1983; Cameron, 1978, 1983). The answer, I propose, lies at the meso level, i.e. in the relationship between the interests of class/sectoral organisa-tions and the interests of the state as an institution. The former are defined less (and less) by the elevated goal of attaining hegemony and imposing a distinctive 'class project' upon the whole of society, and more (and more) by the prosaic objective of influencing public policy to ensure a stable or expanding share of rewards within the existing order. To do this under contemporary circumstances, classes must get organised, and that requires overcoming the 'free-riding' limitations imposed by voluntary membership and the 'free-booting' temptations inherent in individualistic or particularistic access to political power (see Schmitter, 1981b, for a more complete exposition of this argument). This in turn implies a possible organisational interest in exploiting state authority to resolve the paradox inherent in liberal associability, i.e. by making (*de jure* or *de facto*) member contributions and compliances compulsory. In such cases, group consent to neo-corporatist arrangements may not just be contingent upon the satisfaction of immediate member preferences. Where meso calculations of this sort have asserted themselves, classes may eventually come to learn that it is in their interest to have their preferences and behaviours governed by intermediary organisations and subjected to state interests.

State interests, however, have proved as difficult to define and intractable to measure as has 'relative autonomy'. Tracking down what is distinctive to this particular historical mode of organising political space requires, first, that its institutional interests be distinguished analytically from those of two sets of actors, governments and civil servants, who occupy positions within the state and who frequently claim to be acting in defence of its interests. Unfortunately, the literature fails to make this distinction consistently, and this has added greatly to the confusion about the role of the state in establishing and maintaining neo-corporatist arrangements.

Government interests can be defined structurally in terms of ensuring the reproduction of an existing distribution of public offices and established means of gaining access to them, and conjuncturally in terms of seeking to remain in control of those offices. In stable liberal democracies, this means that there is a likelihood that politicians will act to preserve government based on electoral accountability and territorial representation, and will take whatever steps are feasible and tolerable to promote their (or their party's) re-election. Neither of these generic interests is intrinsically favourable to neo-corporatism. Indeed, the contrary is more likely to be the case. Only where party competition has been temporarily suspended, as during a grand coalition government, or where such arrangements can be shown not to threaten regime norms or incumbency resources, are they likely to be promoted or tolerated by government interests in the strict sense in which they have been defined here.

Civil servant interests also have their structural and conjunctural aspects. On the one hand, the employees of the state have an interest in perpetuating an ensemble of institutional identities, recruitment patterns, cultural norms and professional standards which define their particular status in society. On the other hand, they have a set of status-related preferences with regard to salaries, perquisites, job security, career opportunities, budget shares, and so forth for which they periodically struggle and which bring them into conflict with other social groups. As noted above, a given agency or subset of civil servants may develop an interest in promoting neo-corporatism as a means for coping with a specific policy problem, but it is by no means clear whether they, as a *Stand*, have some inherent propensity for this sort of arrangement. Its tendencies to blur the line between public and private institutions, to require extensive consultation with affected groups, to acquire devolved resources from the state and, in the extreme case, to take over substantial responsibility for the implementation of policies could all be interpreted as antithetic to the long-term interests of civil servants.

State interests are obviously difficult to distinguish empirically from those of its principal agents – governments and civil servants – even if it is possible to point to numerous situations in which the efforts of these groups to get re-elected or rewarded have clearly undermined the objective or subjective capacity of a given state. Nevertheless, any politician coming to power or any functionary taking office is likely to learn fairly quickly what these are and what limits they impose upon his or her actions. First and foremost, the interests of a state are defined by the inter-state system of which it is a part. The 'compellingness' of this interdependence with units claiming similar capacities and status is not a constant. Relative size, geographical location, material and human resources may seem relatively fixed, but their significance as constraints and opportunities varies with such factors as military technology, strategic doctrine, balances of power, alliance patterns, and so forth. Western Europe since the end of the Second World War has witnessed some enormous changes in the threat potential within its regional sub-system, as well as the gradual erosion of illusions of national aggrandisement and imperial domination. Barring a dramatic shift in the global balance of power and attendant adjustments in military security, the international interests of its states have focused and will continue to focus to an unprecedented degree on gaining advantage within a highly competitive world economic system. Neo-corporatism has reflected this development in paradoxical fashion. It has been promoted at the sectoral level as a device for protecting domestic (and, more recently, regional) interests from external competitors, and it has been exploited at the level of the entire economy as a means for improving a country's external competitiveness. This has periodically brought about a convergence of state interests and the interests of specific class segments (of labour as well as capital, not to mention agriculture as a whole), but it is questionable whether such arrangements would have emerged had the former's interests not been at stake. States with less internationally penetrated or vulnerable economies have made much less use of them.

The other realm in which a distinctive state interest is discernible concerns the exercise of its most important attribute: legitimate authority. This is backed ultimately by the resource which, at least in theory, it is supposed to monopolise – physical coercion – but if this were to be relied upon too frequently the 'economy' of the state form of political organisation would diminish greatly. So, in addition to defending its territorial integrity and international status, the state must safeguard its vital interest in the efficacy of the decisions (laws and decrees) which it alone has the capacity to promulgate (*Eigengesetzlichkeit* in the incomparable German jargon). In part it does so by developing and perfecting the capacity to punish those who transgress these norms. But its special ability to extract voluntary compliance depends also on the credibility of its symbolic status as that unique social institution which embodies and protects the public interest, i.e. those interests which all its citizens/subjects have in common yet cannot realise because they are divided into competing and conflicting groups. However false this universality may seem to critics at a given moment, and however fraudulently a given government or administrative apparatus may manipulate it to serve its own interests, the state must uphold such a claim, at the expense of all other social institutions. Historically, as Max Weber has pointed out, this has involved reliance upon a variety of formulae or belief systems. In modern states, the legal-rational one is predominant, and neo-corporatist arrangements have a complex relation with it.

As we have hinted above, such arrangements depend crucially on authority in order to extract members' compliance, and normally the only available legitimate source for this is the state in which they are embedded. One can imagine that in restricted contexts and at certain moments, associations could secure compliant behaviour from some combination of intellectual persuasion, social coercion, historic vulnerability and/or leader charisma, but for larger groups and longer periods these sources are not likely to remain reliable, especially if they are seeking to enforce a conception of group interests that diverges from individual perceptions of immediate benefits. For this they need what the Austrians call 'a whip in the window', i.e. a credible and legitimate capacity to call upon state authority to back their bargains and contracts. State actors may be willing, indeed eager, to devolve such a *compétence* to non-state organisations by granting them an exclusive public status and by backing their agreements with the status of public law – provided this does not undermine the state's claim to universalistic defence of the public interest or generate demands on the state's command over scarce resources. By such a process of devolution (*Staatsentlastung*), authorities are relieved of direct responsibility for intervening in matters of considerable complexity and controversy while retaining their symbolic status as sovereigns and enhancing their real ability as guardians of public order.

In practice, however, neo-corporatist arrangements are not always so compatible with state interests. They may result in a substantial increase in claims on scarce public resources in the form of subsidies, fiscal exemptions, subsidiary programmes, etc. which are extracted as compensations in order to ensure agreement among the contracting social parties. They may produce negative externalities for excluded interests in the form of higher prices, restricted access, unemployment, pollution, etc. which cause affected groups to respond in unconventional ways by questioning the state's commitment to protecting the general interest. Most subversively, the establishment of so many quasi-independent sites where generally binding regulations can be elaborated through arcane processes among restricted private participants and implemented without accountability to a wider public (and occasionally without reference to con-stitutional norms) may undermine confidence in the very institution of public law itself. Especially where neo-corporatism has become entrenched on a segmental basis, the rights and duties attached to property, production relations, job security, remuneration, fringe benefits, pricing, credit, entry into the market, and so forth become highly differentiated by class, sector of production and profession. The modern liberal state is thereby deprived of one of its most important symbolic resour-ces: the universality of its legal order.

If the perspective developed above has any merit, the emergence of neo-corporatism (and its persistence) cannot be predicted from the micro-motives of interested private in-dividuals or public employees. Nor can it be analysed exclusive-ly in terms of the macro-functional imperatives of either the capitalist economy or the democratic polity. These demands and constraints no doubt should play a role in understanding the contingent conditions that might favour the choice of this policy instrument rather than another, but the structural point of departure lies at the meso level in an arrangement of mutual convenience between representatives of interest associations and representatives of state authority. Both have something to offer each other which neither may be able to obtain on their own. Both also have something to fear from each other. The interest organisations may have the aggregated information and, most of all, the capacity to deliver the compliance of their members with respect to specific aspects of public policy. What they have to fear is co-option, their transformation into dependent recipients of public favours and passive agents of state policy. State authorities have the capacity to provide attractive and selective rewards, and to accord public status to consenting organisations which could protect them from those who would offer rival representation or undermine established positions. Their fear is that, by so doing, they will become colonised by the groups they have empowered and will lose their distinctive and exclusive status as protectors of the public interest, and thereby their legitimacy before the public at large.

Whether this delicate *quid pro quo* will be tried and, if so, whether it will prosper, is not to be predicted from behavioural surveys of individual preferences or from functionalist analyses of system properties. What is relevant are power configurations and organisational opportunities. Hence neo-corporatist arrangements are more likely to emerge where class hegemony is no longer a plausible option (e.g. where socialist or social-democratic voting strength and presence in government is high) and where rival projects do not divide class actors (e.g. where interest associations are not internally divided by ideology, ethnicity or religion). They are also more likely to be found in nations which never had or have given up pretensions to great power status (e.g. small, neutral countries or larger ones that have suffered international defeat) and in economies that are specially subject to external competition (e.g. those with a high proportion of GNP in imports and exports). Looking at specific sectors or policy areas within countries, one would expect that the neo-corporatist temptation would be greatest in the case of interest organisations whose potential members are so large in number and dispersed in location that voluntary associability is severely impaired (e.g. farmers and the petty bourgeois), whose member interactions are particularly competitive and potentially ruinous (e.g. the construction industry and retail trade), and/or whose categoric goods can only be produced reliably when backed by coercive authority (e.g. restrictions on entry, access to scarce materials, price-fixing, limitations on technological innovation). On the side of the state, authorities will be more tempted to enter into neo-corporatist commitments where they cannot obtain the necessary information on their own and/or where they cannot implement policy without the active consent of targeted groups (e.g. where they seek to intervene in matters related to production, investment and employment rather than the more traditional areas of infrastructure provision, income distribution, consumer protection or social welfare).

As for the level of the state at which such political exchanges are structured, that obviously depends a great deal on formal, constitutional structure. National arrangements among peak associations attempting to set comprehensive parameters on wages, working conditions, employment practices, fiscal systems, welfare benefits, prices, etc. were what initially attracted the attention of scholars. More recently, they have been particularly inventive in discovering 'local corporatisms', although these often seem little more than mechanisms for the direct consultation of functional interests without the wider implications for intermediation or devolution implied in the national agreements (Hernes and Selvik, 1981; Dickens and Goodwin, 1981; Flynn, 1983; King, 1983; Milward and Francisco, 1983; Cawson, this volume). Ironically, the privileged site has long been that of professional categories and economic sectors where the associational desiderata, agency needs and policy characteristics have converged to form quite stable and well-insulated arrangements of mutual convenience, often at high cost to the economy at large. (For a particularly striking example of such a convergence across countries which otherwise have very different interest configurations, see the monographs on the dairy industry by Grant, 1983a; 1983b van Waarden, 1983; Traxler, 1983; or on the food-processing industry more generally by Coleman and Jacek, 1982, and Farago, Ruf and Wieder, 1984). The net result of such 'sectoral' or 'selective' corporatisms is a pattern of entrenched policy segmentation which renders more difficult and less effective efforts at either comprehensive concertation or monetary control. Moreover, the forging of 'crisis cartels' to deal with the problems of declining industries seems to be extending this ad-hocracy with serious implications for the governability and competitiveness of national economies (Esser and Fach, 1981; Esser, 1982).

Regardless of the opportunity structure from which they

emerge, the nature of the interests incorporated in them, the level of the state at which they operate, or the scope of public policy they are capable of affecting, neo-corporatist arrangements ultimately depend on their success or failure at establishing what an increasing number of analysts have come to call 'private governments'. It is to this theme that we now turn.

Private interest governments?

The concept of 'private government' has been given such diverse meanings (McConnell, 1966; Gilb, 1966; Lakoff and Rich, 1973; Lowi, 1979; Buxbaum, 1981; Thompson, 1983) that it seems necessary first, to define it clearly and, second, to explain its relationship to neo-corporatism. A private interest government (PIG is the unfortunate acronym) exists where a non-state association allocates goods, services or status that are monopolistic in nature and indispensable for members; it is therefore capable of affecting and potentially controlling their behaviour, and does so with the specific encouragement, licence or subsidisation of the state, thus imposing certain public standards and responsibilities on the behaviour of the association. In short, a PIG is based on group self-regulation through formally private organisations, empowered by a devolution of public interest. The insertion of the word 'interest' in the middle of the concept is intended to convey the meaning that a generic social category is involved – classes, sectors or professions are the usual ones – and that this group is expected to act from calculatedly self-regarding motives.

This definition excludes many groups that have been called 'private governments' in the past: secret societies, organised crime, guerrilla movements, business corporations, cartels, para-state agencies, 'quangos', etc. All these may distribute monopolistic and indispensable goods and hence be capable *de facto* of controlling the behaviour of their clients, followers, beneficiaries or victims, but they either do not have members in the same sense as an interest association, or they do not represent a generic social category, and/or they have not received a mandate for exercising public functions.

What may be more difficult is to distinguish PIGs from other configurations or organised interest–state interaction which can also fit the neo-corporatist profile. One that has received a great deal of attention, especially in the North American literature, is that of 'privatised government' in which an association – in all likelihood a monopolistic one – captures or colonises a particular agency of the state and is able to make private use of its public powers of regulation, taxation, subsidisation, etc. (McConnell, 1966; Lowi, 1979). A second configuration, which has especially preoccupied scholars working on Latin America and Southern Europe, emerges where a state – usually under authoritarian rule – creates, co-opts or controls an interest association and is thus able to use it to coerce its leaders or members (Malloy, 1977). In both these cases, one finds elements of neo-corporatism whether conceived as interest intermediation or as policy-making. But neither colonisation of the state nor subordination to it constitute private interest governance in the sense I am proposing here.

Leaving aside those PIGs that have been inherited from the medieval/early modern past, and which somehow survived the Napoleonic and Liberal assaults of the nineteenth century on guild privileges, their contemporary emergence depends on a particular, and often highly contingent, distribution of resources across the public and private organisations which agree to form them. Especially crucial is the role of the state. It must be, on the one hand, autonomous enough in the policy arena at issue not to be 'colonisable' by the interest or interests involved, and credible enough to threaten these interests with a worse possible outcome – usually direct regulation – if they do not agree to respect the 'public-regarding' provisions it imposes. On the other hand, the state must be weak enough to recognise that the costs of implementing a given policy authoritatively will exceed its likely benefits, and willing enough to devolve some of its most distinctive resource – legitimate coercion – to organisations which it does not administratively control. In this political exchange, public authorities are neither brokers nor mediators. They are not just fashioning a policy instrument that will modify relationships between civil society and themselves, but consenting (and in some cases, conniving) in the creation of new measures of social control that will affect relationships within civil society itself.

From this perspective, the emergence of private interest governance is not synonymous with the emergence of representational monopolies or institutionalised participation in policy-making; it is just a possible and contingent outcome of such developments. An increase in the variety and scope of state activities does *not* make it a functional requisite. An increase in the frequency with which public agents take weighty, autonomous initiatives does *not* make it a political imperative. An increase in the spread of bureaucratic organisation in society does *not* make it a rationalistic necessity. However, these might contribute to its likelihood. The emergence of PIGs depends on a distinctively political calculus involving a specific distribution of existing power capabilities and an anticipated reaction with regard to future impact upon affected interests.

Moreover, the success of such arrangements is by no means assured, even where they have been well-established. On the state side, so to speak, their viability and desirability depends on their public-regarding content and state-respecting form. This, in turn, is contingent in democratic regimes upon such factors as maintaining a rough electoral balance of class and sectoral forces, ensuring the application of professional standards of civil service conduct, respecting the material interests and career goals of state employees, and sustaining some degree of community consciousness and public attention to the policies involved. Perhaps even more crucial to guaranteeing that PIGs will not degenerate over time into 'privatised governance' is the need to sustain an independent and adversarial relationship between the privileged interests incorporated within them. This may be very difficult to ensure where the beneficiaries of such arrangements are relatively concentrated (and well-organised) and their victims are relatively dispersed (and usually poorly organised).

Seen from the associational perspective, the obvious danger is that PIGs will develop over time into mechanisms of state control or exploitation, either because co-option undermines the capacity of leaders to take autonomous action, or because complicity undermines their legitimacy in the eyes of their members. In the neo-corporatist discussion so far, the evaluative accent has been placed upon 'asymmetry' in the distribution of benefits and organisational capacity among participating class actors – mostly, capital and labour. However important this question may be (and evaluations of it have changed rather dramatically in recent years), the emphasis on private interest governance shifts the axis somewhat and asks what are the longer-term distributional consequences for the state and non-state interests involved. Just as it was previously assumed that capitalist interests always prevailed over worker interests, so it is often presumed that the state (and the public at large) will always be exploited by PIGs. Why this *must* be the case brings us back to that contested concept of the relative autonomy of the modern state. If this is simply fraudulent or tactical, i.e. the state is really at the instrumental service of the bourgeoisie – appearances to the contrary notwithstanding – then private interest governance is just an ideological illusion. If its relative autonomy has a functionalist basis, PIGs have a useful role to play in policing the long-term interests of the dominant class and suborning those of the dominated class, but in the event of any significant conflict the capitalist state will reveal its true colours (Offe, 1983). If, however, the basis of its relative autonomy is structural, then the emergence of PIGs to cover specific policy sectors or to set trans-sectoral, macroeconomic parameters is a development of much greater significance. It remains vulnerable to cyclical fluctuations in the influence of class groups and to structural trends which undermine their capacity to deliver the compliance of their members – both of which are problems that may affect trade unions more severely than business and professional associations (Baglioni and Santi, 1982; Carrieri and Donolo, 1983) – but this by no means ensures that state authorities will always be incapable of asserting and defending the interests of less organised and underprivileged publics. Nor is it necessarily the case that government interests, as expressed through traditional liberal/pluralist forms, e.g. territorial representation and partisan competition, would do a better job of this.

Associative-corporative order?

In a recent (1984) essay, Wolfgang Streeck and I have speculated that, to the extent that neo-corporatist trends have resulted in private interest governments of varying scope, composition and viability, it may be possible to speak of a new 'model' of social order with its own distinctive logic of action and reproduction (for other efforts at placing neo-corporatism within prevailing models of social order, see Crouch, 1981; Cawson, 1982). Philosophical thought and social science has thus far been dominated by three such models, each identified by a different central institution, namely the *community*, the *market* and the *state* which embodies and enforces a distinctive axial principle. The models are: *spontaneous solidarity, dispersed competition* and *hierarchic control*. Table 2.1 outlines the properties that are assumed by these much-discussed models; the market model is subdivided into economic and political 'sections'. In Table 2.2 we have suggested how those of a possible *associative-corporative* order with its guiding principle of *organisational concertation* might differ from these. Our point is not that this 'new' order is somehow destined to prevail over the others, or even to assume an equivalent significance in all advanced industrial/capitalist societies, but that modern social order is composed of a mix of institutions with different actors, motives, media of exchange, resources, decision rules, cleavage patterns and normative foundations – and that the traditional trio of community, market and state fails to explore all the possible bases and combinations. The *idea* of a distinctive associative order is, of course, not new. Hegel was perhaps the first to advance a conception of *Korporationen* as the highest expression of civil society, and he was followed by a long list of nineteenth-century theorists, religious and secular, who advocated some form of organic-corporative order as an alternative to the anomic decline in community, the anarchic competition of the market, and the possible tyranny of the nation state. The *fact* of a distinctive associative order has always been on historical display, so to speak, in the experiences of the late mediaeval cities of Italy, France, Catalonia, the Rhineland and the Hanseatic North, whose social and political systems were based for a brief period on a guild structure. (For an excellent recent case-study of ancient 'municipal corporatism', see Najemy, 1982). Interestingly, when John Maynard Keynes reflected in 1926 on the consequences of 'the end of *laissez-faire* in the disorder following the First World War and searched for the bases of a possible new order 'somewhere between the individual

TABLE 2.1   *The properties of 'community', 'market' and 'state' social order*

	Community
1. Guiding *Principle* of coordination and allocation	Spontaneous solidarity
2. Predominant, modal, collective *Actor* Other *Actors*	Families Clans, lineages, communes, localities, sodalities
3. Enabling *Conditions* for actor entry and inclusion	Ascriptive member status
4. Principal *Medium of exchange*	Esteem
5. Principal *Product of exchange*	Compacts
6. Predominant *Resource(s)*	Respect, trust, inherited status
7. Principal *Motive(s)* of superordinate actors Principal *Motive(s)* of subordinate actors Common *Motive/calculus*	Esteem of followers Belonging to group, desire to share in common values 'Satisfying identity'
8. Principal *Decision rule(s)*	Common consent, unanimous agreement
9. Modal *Type of goods* produced and distributed	Solidaristic goods
10. Principal *Line of cleavage* Other *Cleavages*	Natives vs foreigners Clan rivalries, generation gaps, conflicts over turf, inheritance claims, personal disputes
11. Predominant *Normative-legal foundation*	Customary practices
12. Principal *Pay-off(s)*	Mutual affection, collective identity

and the modern state', he looked backward to those previous experiences and proposed 'a return . . . towards mediaeval conceptions of separate autonomies' as a way out of the impasse (Keynes, 1963). At the risk of being accused of reactionary nostalgia, Streeck and I have followed Keynes's advice and asked what such an order might look like if it were to emerge in

Market	State
Dispersed competition	Hierarchical control
Firms / parties	Bureaucratic agencies
Entrepreneurs/politicians, consumers & workers / voters	Subjects (taxpayers, law abiders, conscripts, etc.) civil servants, clients, claimants
Ability to pay / eligibility to vote	Legal authorisation, 'jurisdiction'
Money / votes	Coercion
Contracts / incumbencies	Authoritative regulation
Economic / political entrepreneurship, calculative rationality	Legitimate control over the means of coercion, authoritative distribution of positions, administrative & legal expertise, procedural correctness
Profit / electoral victory	Career advancement, bureaucratic stability
Material benefit / exercise of 'voice'	Fear of punishment
'Maximising advantage' / 'minimum winning coalition'	'Minimising risk', 'Maximising predictability'
Consumer / majority preference	Authoritative formal adjudication imperative certification
Private goods	Collective goods
Sellers vs buyers / Parties vs voters Capital vs labour / producers vs consumers / importers vs exporters / incumbents vs opposition territorial, ethnic, religious, linguistic, ideological divisions, etc.	Rulers vs ruled Supervisors vs subordinates overlaps of jurisdiction conflicts between levels of government, interstate rivalries, etc.
Property rights/constitutional guarantees	Formal administrative procedures
Material prosperity / citizen accountability	External security, equitable and predictable treatment, efficient mobilisation of resources

the contemporary world.

At its core is a distinctive principle of interaction and allocation of resources among a privileged set of actors. These are organisations defined by their common purpose of defending and promoting interests – mostly class, sectoral and professional associations. Their central principle is that of inter-organ-

TABLE 2.2   *The properties of an associative model of social order*

1. Guiding *Principle* of interaction and allocation	Inter- and Intra-organisational concertation
2. Predominant, modal, *Collective actor* Other *Actors*	Functionally defined interest groups, members (firms, consortia, individuals, social groupings), interlocutors (state agencies, parties, movements)
3. Enabling *Conditions* for actor entry and inclusion	Capacity for mutual disruption, attainment of monopoly status, willingness and capacity to compromise, symmetry of organisational capacity
4. Principal *Medium of exchange*	Mutual recognition of status and entitlements Compliance of members
5. Principal *Product of exchange*	Pacts
6. Predominant *Resource(s)*	Guaranteed access, compulsory contributions and membership, institutionalised forums of representation, centralisation, comprehensive scope, jurisdiction and control over member behaviour, delegated tasks, inter-organisational trust
7. Principal *Motive(s)* of superordinate actors Principal *Motive(s)* of subordinate actors Common *Motive/calculus*	Expansion of organisational role, organisational development, career advancement Lessened uncertainty, proportional shares, 'Satisficing (mini-maxing) interests'
8. Principal *decision rule(s)*	Parity representation, proportional adjustment, concurrent consent
9. Modal *Type of goods* produced and distributed	Categoric goods
10. Principal *Lines of cleavage* Other *Cleavages*	Members vs group leaders vs (state) interlocutors Included vs excluded (social movements) Well organised vs less well organised Established vs rival groups Over- vs under-represented Majority vs minority segments National vs regional vs local interests (parties, maverick enterprises, community representatives, local notables)
11. Predominant *Normative-legal foundation*	*Pacta sunt servanda*, Freedom of association
12. Principal *Pay-off(s)*	Less class exploitation, more symmetric distribution of benefits, greater predictability and stability of socio-economic outcomes (social peace)

isational concertation, i.e. negotiation among a limited and exclusive set of actors who mutually recognise each other's status and entitlements and are capable of reaching and implementing relatively stable compromises (*pacts* or *social contracts*). An associative-corporative order is, therefore, based primarily upon interaction between complex organisations and, secondly, upon their interactions with their members and the state, whose resources or support are necessary for the concerted compromise to take effect and to remain binding upon all those affected.

It is when we turn to the 'enabling conditions' in Table 2.2 that the distinctiveness of an associative-corporative order becomes most manifest, especially in contrast to that postulated by pluralist theories based on pressure politics. For some time, the dominant way of analysing collective action in defence of interests relied on an uneasy amalgam of community and market assumptions. According to that, interest associations sprung into existence spontaneously and acted autonomously on the basis of a unity of shared norms and perceptions – both community properties. They attracted members on a voluntary basis, formed into multiple, overlapping and competing units, entered into shifting 'parallelograms of group forces' according to the issue at hand, used whatever means tended to produce the best immediate results, and gained influence roughly proportional to the intensity of their preferences and the magnitude of their resources – all characteristics of market-like relations. The emergent neo-corporatist paradigm of the 1970s challenged each of these assumptions and suggested that a different logic of collective action might be more apposite.

In a first approximation, this logic can be characterised as follows. In a community, member preferences are *interdependent*, based on shared norms and jointly produced satisfactions. In a market order, the actions of competitors are *independent* as no single actor is supposed to have a determinant and predictable impact upon the eventual allocation of satisfactions. In a state-dominated model, actors are *dependent* upon hierarchical co-ordination, which makes their choices heteronomously determined and asymmetrically predictable according to the structure of legitimate authority and coercive capacity. In an associative-corporative order, actors are *strategically interdependent* in the sense that actions of select organisations do have a determinant and predictable effect (positive or negative) on the satisfaction of each other's interests, and this is what induces them to search for relatively stable pacts. For this to occur, contracting associations have to have attained, if not a symmetry in resources, then at least reciprocal capacities for affecting each other and for representing and controlling the behaviour of their members (and, where necessary, the reactions of possible mavericks). This usually implies that they have an effective monopoly in their status as intermediaries for a given class, sector or profession. As long as interest associations are fragmented into rival communities, organised into competing markets for members and/or resources, or manipulated from above by state authority, then the enabling conditions for a distinctive associative-corporative order do not exist. Since this is the case for many policy arenas and even for many whole societies, it is obviously not appropriate to speak in these cases of a fourth order alongside the community, market and state. It would be even less appropriate to speak of its emergence as an ineluctable necessity if general social order is to survive. Some capitalist economies seem to do quite well with little or no help from PIGs, even if their ruling institutions may be less governable (Schmitter, 1981a).

The medium or 'currency' in which the associative model deals is *influence*, conditioned by mutual recognition of status and entitlements. Of course, concerting groups may occasionally bring to bear on a given issue their customary solidarity, their monetary resources, their bloc votes and even their credible threats to use coercion should the negotiative process break down, but in the course of their normal interaction they make 'reasonable' demands on each other and pay 'prudent' respect to state and public concerns. Fundamentally, they are informing each other about the magnitude and intensity of their preferences and the strategies they would adopt if agreement is not reached. They offer, in return for the satisfaction of some uncertain part of these preferences, to deliver the compliance of their members. As many have pointed out (Nedelmann and Meier, 1979, were perhaps the first to do so), such exchanges depend on political factors and can be quite unstable solutions. Their viability and efficacy can, however, be considerably enhanced if, as a result of iterative efforts at concertation, the participating associations manage to acquire new resources. Inter-organisational trust is perhaps the most important (and difficult to measure) of those mentioned under rubric 6 in Table 2.2. Others are guaranteed access, compulsory contributions and/or membership, institutionalised (if often informal) forums for intermediation, centralised administrative structure, comprehensive scope of representation, legal jurisdiction and enhanced control over member behaviour, and delegated policy tasks. As we have noted above, many of these emergent properties require the complicity – if not the active collaboration – of state authorities.

The motivational structure of an associative-corporative order is perhaps less distinctive from community, market and state arrangements than its other attributes, at least with regard to superordinate actors. Like their 'brethren' in state agencies, the motives of association leaders and administrators should be largely determined by the needs of the organisational context within which they operate and from which they draw most of their resources. At the centre of these are desires for organisational development, administrative stability and strategic autonomy (Schmitter and Streeck, 1981). Eventually, this should lead to a professionalisation of management within all of the interacting associations and a consequent decline in their dependence upon voluntary support and elected leadership.

The motives of subordinate actors, i.e. of group members, are more difficult to discern and to sustain since they are being forced to give up what may often be attractive opportunities for acting individually or collectively through other channels. In exchange for this, they are compelled to accept compromised, longer-term and more public-regarding obligations negotiated on their behalf by their respective class, sectoral or professional representatives. This may be less of a problem for those categories of interest where individual actors are very weak and dispersed, e.g. farmers, unskilled workers, the petty bourgeois, but it could pose a serious challenge in those categories where 'going it alone' through market power or state influence is a real alternative, e.g. capitalists and privileged professions. Presumably what motivates subordinates to conform to group-negotiated pacts is a decrease in uncertainty about aggregate outcomes and an increase in their assurance of receiving a proportionately more equitable share of whatever is disputed and distributed than would otherwise be the case. If one adds to these motives the probability that certain conditions of macro-societal performance, e.g. lower inflation, less unemployment and lower strike rates, will be superior in societies whose markets have been 'tamed' by associative-corporative action, then we have an even more compelling reason for understanding member conformity (Schmidt, 1982, 1983; Cameron, 1983; Shonfield, 1984).

One could argue that what happens is a shift in the rationality of social choice. In communities, the calculus rests on 'satisfying identity'; in markets – economic or political – on 'maximising preferences or forging minimum winning coalitions'; and in states on 'minimising risk/maximising predictability'. What associations in a prospective corporative order strive for is something more prosaic, but quite rational given the structural complexity and informational overload of modern societies, namely 'satisficing interests'. By deliberate mutual adjustments in their expectations and successive iterations of their exchanges, these privileged actors may avoid the temptation to exploit momentary positional advantages to the maximum and the fate of landing in the worst possible outcome in which all lose. In short, they manage to solve the prisoners' dilemma inherent in unconstrained interest politics through the development of inter-organisational trust, backed by devolved public authority. The price paid for this is a lengthy and cumbersome deliberation process and a series of 'second-best' compromises which are often difficult to justify on aesthetic or normative grounds.

Communities presumably decide by unanimous consent, markets by consumer preference or majority rule, and states by authoritative adjudication. An associative-corporative arrangement or private interest government makes its choices by a highly complicated formula which begins with parity representation, works through a sequence of proportional adjustments such as 'splitting the difference' or 'package-dealing', and then ratifies the final pact by concurrent consent. All this takes time and is vulnerable to substantive and normative assaults from community, market and state sources. Usually, the deliberations are kept informal and secretive in an effort to insulate them as much as possible from outside pressure or from dissidents from within associational ranks (Marin, 1982a, 1982b, 1983a,

1983b). The arcane 'weighting' of influences and the complex calculation of proportionality and equity may seem, especially to outsiders, to involve arbitrary standards and mysterious forces – nothing like the neat and obvious decision rules of solidaristic unanimity, consumer sovereignty, majority vote or authoritative interpretation characteristic of the other three models of social order. These elements of lack of accountability to individual citizens and inequality in group access – combined with the unavoidably compromised nature of the decisions eventually made – can create a rather serious legitimacy problem for associative-corporative arrangements and expose them to strenuous normative attack by the proponents of community, market and state.

Public legitimation?

Neo-corporatist arrangements in general, and private interest governments in particular, require legitimation if they are to function effectively and durably. Their actions must stand a high probability of being obeyed voluntarily (but not necessarily enthusiastically) by those affected by them, as well as by those participating in them. Whatever the underlying role played by devolutions of state authority, if enough citizens reject them on either substantive or procedural grounds, then the costs of arriving at such agreements and especially of implementing them would quickly exceed their utility.

As many have observed, neo-corporatism faces a serious legitimation problem. At first this was seen largely in terms of its unfortunate etymological association with certain inter-war experiences in authoritarian *corporativismo, corporatisme, Korporativismus*, etc. Indeed, in some countries such as France, the discussion has been virtually paralysed until quite recently by this linguistic difficulty. The more inventive Italians and Germans rather quickly resolved the issue by dropping out the 'iv' and referring to *corporatismo* and *Korporatismus* as Anglo-Saxon-imposed neologisms conveniently purged of their discredited past associations. But hiding behind this rather superficial matter is the much more substantial issue of how such transformations in the mode of interest intermediation and/or policy-making can be justified.

The matter is made more difficult by the partial and

surreptitious way in which these arrangements have crept into the interstices of community, market and state mechanisms. They have rarely been defended, even by their proponents, and their activities have often been carefully shielded from their potential opponents. Not only are their allocative mechanisms kept secret, but the very existence of private interest governments is often not known to the larger public. How many consumers of milk or clients of lawyers are aware of how the prices/fees they pay are determined? Indeed, much of the power of PIGs, especially of the segmental or selective sort, depends on such invisibility and ignorance. If their processes and consequences were better known and rendered accountable to the wider public, their legitimacy would, no doubt, suffer.

But the problem is not just one of cognition and conceptualisation. Neo-corporatist arrangements face the task of legitimating themselves in relation to two very well-entrenched 'normative complexes' of modern society. On the one hand, they must justify their existence with respect to existing community, market and state institutions; on the other hand, at least in the contemporary period, they must explain how they are compatible with the norms and procedures of political democracy.

Each of the traditional 'orders' presumptively has its own distinctive normative basis, principles of legitimacy which can be relied upon – all else failing – to generate support in the event of any particular conflict. Communities are founded on a sedimentation of customary practices; economic markets depend on a general acceptance of the principle of private appropriation of assets and its specific expression in an agreed set of property rights; political markets rest on a basic tolerance of social diversity and its embodiment in a framework of constitutional guarantees and electoral laws. The state owes its legitimacy, we have argued above, to its supposed indispensability as the guarantor of external security and protector of the internal public interest. Neo-corporatism enjoys no such supportive symbolic status – just the vague allegation that it somehow works to produce quantitatively more desirable market outcomes, further justified in some cultures by notions of 'self-administration', 'subsidiarity', 'social peace' and/or 'social partnership' inherited from the past. It would be no exaggeration to suggest that it has been so far a consumer, not a producer, of legitimacy, and that its supplier has largely been the state. For reasons discussed above, this transaction is a precarious one for both sides, especially where such bargains have taken the form of sectoral and selective arrangements. Continued reliance upon it may well weaken the normative basis of state authority by undermining its pretence to the universalistic, legal-rational treatment of citizens and diminish the concrete effectiveness of interest associations in delivering the voluntary compliance of their members. This is not meant to imply that a legitimacy crisis is impending which will ineluctably sweep away 'segmented corporatism' and its 'fragmented state', just that the long-run problems of this mode of intermediation and policy-making are not confined to equity in the generation of material benefits or symmetry in the development of organisational capacities – the two issues which have heretofore attracted the most critical attention.

No doubt legal scholars and legalistic ideologues are already busy explaining why it is both necessary and desirable that such a segmentation of the norm-generation process should occur and why, for them to be effective in building consensus, such disparate efforts should be left to informal arrangements with obscure *compétences* and arcane procedures and definitely not be exposed to excessive parliamentary scrutiny or centralised judicial review – much less to contentious public discussion. After all, the law has long been divided into civil/criminal, public/private, national/international domains and specialised fields covering maritime, commercial, administrative and other matters have been recognised without diminishing the state's claim to embodying legal consistency. Why not add 'dairy law', 'artisans' law', 'steel-making law' and 'health service law' and admit that each might adopt distinctive standards and obligations and be formulated by different bargaining processes? The end result could come to resemble the feudal *Ständestaat*, except that, instead of the old lumpy blocs of nobles, clergy and bourgeois (supplemented here and there by peasants), the emerging post-liberal *Ständestaat* would have to have considerably more categories of differentiated privilege and obligation. Legitimising formulae can presumably be found – the von Gierke/guild socialist/early pluralist tradition might be of some help – which would make these trends consistent with the state's institutional interest in retaining its status as the sole source of legitimate coercion and its image as the ultimate guardian of public interest. Indeed, if citizens were to have to choose between a neo-liberal *dismantlement* of state functions and a neo-socialist *development* of them, many might prefer and be prepared to justify a neo-corporatist *dispersion* of them.

Whether or not these choices will be put to them and which they will be free to select may well depend upon the second 'normative complex' of modern society that was mentioned above, namely that of political democracy. For the countries of Western Europe in the contemporary period, it is not enough that policy instruments are somehow compatible with community standards, economic principles and state interests. They must also not violate too egregiously the norms and procedures of democratic politics. Whether neo-corporatist arrangements are sufficiently compatible with existing citizen expectations to ensure their legitimacy, or whether they are potentially capable of altering those expectations to their favour is a subject that is beyond the allotted scope (and length) of this essay. Fortunately, the attention of scholars of varying persuasion (Offe, 1983; Olsen, 1983; Schmitter, 1983a) has recently begun to focus on this issue.

Chapter 3

Corporatism in Industrial Relations: a Formal Model

Colin Crouch

Introduction

When classifying industrial relations systems in terms of corporatist theory, it is useful to think of a continuum, starting at one extreme with contestative relations, moving through pluralist bargaining and bargained corporatism, and ending at authoritarian corporatism. Elsewhere (Crouch, 1983b) I have defined the poles of this continuum in terms of the role of representatives being, respectively, purely representative and purely disciplinary. But this tells us very little of the inner dynamics of different ideal typical systems. How do these different kinds of industrial relations 'work'? In particular, how, in detail, do pluralist and corporatist forms of bargaining differ? This can be done most clearly if the argument is set out formally. There is nothing that can be called mathematics in this, but readers who have a horror of formal analysis can skip the symbols, as everything is contained within the verbal account.

Our starting point is a relationship between two actors in a capitalist economy: organised labour (L) and (organised) capital (C). The relationship between L and C is a sub-set of a wider relationship between labour and capital. Only some aspects of that wider relationship become issues between the organisational representatives. For them to do so means that they have become politicised and must be resolved through some political exchange, deal or bargain. The remainder of the wider relationship is arranged by labour receiving orders from capital in exchange for payment of a wage (the wage–effort relationship), although usually orders are modified by personal give and take. The parentheses around 'organised' in the case of capital indicates that capital may appear as an individual firm in an exchange, not necessarily as a group or association of firms, while labour is always collectively organised, at least informally, if it is taking part in an exchange going beyond the simple wage–effort bargain that binds individual employees to their jobs. This reflects part of the fundamental imbalance between capital and labour, in that capital automatically possesses power by virtue of its role in the employment relationship, while labour does so only if it organises. (For a fuller account of this inequality, see Offe and Wiesenthal, 1980; and Crouch, 1982b, ch. 2.)

The question of the level at which C and L operate (e.g. shop floor, company, economic branch, nation state) will be left indeterminate until a later section (p. 79). This has considerable advantages, as it enables us to build up the relationship from its simplest components. A disadvantage is that it means postponing the entry of the state until a late stage. Given that corporatism is often presented as a theory of the state, this may seem puzzling. However, the state is active in this area only because problems exist in relations between the labour-market actors. Historically, the state has sometimes intervened after these problems have revealed themselves; sometimes it has acted anticipatorily. But analytically it makes sense to analyse the relationship that throws up the problems before examining the intervention that becomes involved in the search for a solution.

Forms of industrial relations systems

Contestation

The wider capital/labour relationship contains elements of both conflict and those matters in which the two sides prosper together. But the starting point for the relationship between L and C is normally conflict: issues enter the relationship because one side (usually labour) is dissatisfied. The simplest form of relation between L and C is therefore a zero-sum game,[1] i.e. a change to the benefit of one party can be achieved only through a concomitant change to the disadvantage of the other:

$$\Delta c + \Delta l = 0 \tag{1}$$

where c, l = shares of C and L respectively. When industrial relations take this form we can speak of contestation. Neither party can be expected voluntarily to concede such gains to the other. C may be able to achieve improvements to its share under such a system because of its position of authority in the general capital/labour relationship, but L will be able to pursue its interests against C only by waging conflict that imposes cost on C greater than the costs C would incur by making concession to L. That is, L will secure an improvement in its share only when:

$$b_c > \Delta l \qquad (2)$$

where b_c = the cost imposed on C by conflict, and where it is assumed that Δl represents an improvement in L's position that L regards as worth having. Most conflicts will impose costs on both parties, such that $b = b_c + b_l$, where b = total conflict costs, but so long as L has some expectation that $b_l < \Delta l$, it will find the conflict worth while.

The implication of this is that cases of contestation are in fact *worse* than zero-sum games: the costs of conflict impose a net loss on the aggregate share of the two parties, whatever happens to any individual party:

$$\Delta c + \Delta l = 0 - (b_c + b_l) \qquad (3)$$

The more frequently the two interact, the greater the range of issues covered in their interactions, and the more important those issues, then the greater become these losses from conflict:

$$\Delta c + \Delta l = 0 - (b_c + b_l)n \qquad (4)$$

where n = the density of interactions between the parties, 'density of interactions' being a compound expression denoting frequency, extent and importance of interaction.

This might imply that, despite the zero-sum nature of the substantive distributive relationship, the two parties share an interest in reducing conflict costs. However, there are several reasons why such an interest may not be realised. First, either C or L might believe that in the long run it will succeed in getting more concessions and a lower share of conflict costs than the opponent. Second, even if this is not the case, either (though in practice probably only C) may believe that in the long run such heavy costs will be imposed on the other by conflict that the other will lose the capacity to struggle, and that therefore it is worth tolerating heavy conflict costs on its own side while awaiting that outcome. Third, by the same token one side might believe that an overall reduction in conflict costs will only help the other side maintain a capacity for conflict that it could not otherwise afford. Where at least one side acts on at least one of these three assumptions, there will be no co-operation in a mutual reduction of conflict costs, although of course each side will try constantly to reduce its own share of these costs. Every conflict will have to be fought right through until one side acknowledges defeat; this is pure contestation. Records of industrial relations in France from the nineteenth century until recently are replete with examples of such practices (see Shorter and Tilly, 1974; Lange, Ross and Vannicelli, 1982).

However, even in these cases conflict will not be entirely unrestrained. (In reality few conflicts are truly 'unrestrained', even wars, as Simmel long ago noted – see Coser, 1956. 'Unrestrained' industrial conflict *usually* stops more or less short of acts of physical violence against persons or the destruction of physical property.) If, say, L is using pressure to secure a wage rise, then it must be willing to accept temporary truces and resumptions of normal working. Within an individual dispute, L will expect C to concede at the point where C's losses through continuing conflict become greater than the cost of making a concession to L adequate to stop the conflict, that is $b_c > \Delta l$. It does not make sense for L to continue the struggle beyond the point where C has made its maximum concession, because on those terms C will never concede; C might as well save the cost of the concessions if it must bear a conflict cost irrespective of whether it makes them: $b_c < b_c + \Delta l$. This is obvious, but in real life it is far from obvious whether maximum concession points have been reached. Workers' representatives have to make a judgement about this as best they can, and there will often be disagreement among them and between them and their members. The negotiators will be able to make deals with employers only if they can undertake to call off conflicts at points where they judge maximum concessions to have been reached. This implies a modicum of *discipline* within the workforce. Even under contestation there will therefore be occasions when workers' representatives act in the manner normally associated with corporatism, urging their members to go back to work or cease some kind of disruption. However, this is of the most minimal kind.

In general, the amount of discipline that representatives need over their members to end a conflict depends on the relationship between the different estimates made by the workers and by their representatives respectively of the likely outcome of prolonging the conflict. If these estimates are identical, they will agree when to end the struggle and the matter is simple:

$$\Delta l_e - b_{le} = \Delta l_r - b_{lr} \qquad (5)$$

where sub-scripts e and r indicate the expectations of outcomes held by workers and their representatives respectively. But several factors may lead to these expectations differing. We shall deal here with just one of them: the more that the role of representatives differs from that of ordinary workers, the more likely it is that their expectations will differ. For example, if the representatives are simply fellow workers who from time to time are called in to act as spokesmen, we might expect the gap to be smaller than if they are specialised, full-time union officers. Therefore, *ceteris paribus*, the difference between the expectations of workers and their representatives is given by:

$$\Delta l_e - b_{le} = (\Delta l_r - b_{lr})x \qquad (6)$$

where $x = $ some function of the difference in experience of representatives.

If the workers are more optimistic than their representatives concerning the outcome, the representatives will be able to secure an end to conflict only by the imposition of a degree of discipline (which may include appeals based on trust as much as the threat of negative sanctions) sufficient to bridge the gap between their respective explanations:

where $\qquad (\Delta l_e - b_{le}) > (\Delta l_r - b_{lr}),$

$$\Delta l_e - b_{le} = (\Delta l_r - b_{lr}) + d \qquad (7)$$

where $d = $ discipline

Since, under contestation, there is little specialised role for representatives (i.e. x is low), then *ceteris paribus* there is little difference between their and the workers' expectations, and there is therefore only a very small role for discipline. (If members are more pessimistic about chances of success in conflict than their representatives, statement 7 reads:

where
$$(\Delta l_e - b_{le}) < (\Delta l_r - b_{lr}),$$
$$\Delta l_e - b_{le} = (\Delta l_r - b_{lr}) - d$$

That is, conflict will be ended by workers *breaking* union discipline – which will be trying to maintain the conflict – and ending the dispute.)

Pluralist bargaining

Let us now turn to those situations in which both capital and labour decide that, in the long run, they would stand to gain from a reduction in conflict. They then develop procedures for conducting their conflicts in such a way that they avoid mutually damaging action: for example, they develop rules for deciding how disputed matters should be resolved, and have recourse to conciliation and arbitration services.[2]

For each side, these procedures constitute restraints on their own freedom of action, but they accept them because of the mutuality of the arrangement. The function of the procedural restraints is to reduce conflict costs, such that the conflict relation summarised in statement (4) above can now be expressed as:

$$\Delta c + \Delta l = 0 - ((b_c + b_l) - (p_c + p_l))n \tag{8}$$

where p_c and p_l are the procedural restraints adopted by C and L respectively. It will be seen that this arrangement does not diminish the zero-sum conflict at the heart of the relationship, but merely reduces the negative sum imposed on the parties by the need to resort to open conflict to resolve their disputes.

As C and L develop devices of this kind we begin speaking of pluralistic bargaining rather than of contestation. This does not necessarily mean there is less conflict; that will depend on the size of b_c and b_l, and on the capacity of the parties to enter into conflict. C may be unwilling to develop procedures because L's capacity to engage in conflict is too low to make the exercise worth while; this will lead to an enduring contestation model, though with actual outbreaks of conflict probably being only sporadic. But, for a given level of b_c, b_l, conflict will be lower under pluralist bargaining than under contestation.

Procedures not only enable conflicts to be played out *in parvo*. Some operate by insulating conflicts from one another, by preventing an aggregation of disputes into major cleavages. Particularly important in the history of modern capitalism has been the containment of industrial conflict so that it does not spill over into the political realm. This was a dominant theme in the literature on the institutionalisation of conflict (Dahrendorf, 1959; Harbison, 1954). Similarly, theories of pluralist politics (e.g. Dahl, 1961) stressed that in such polities no one group of actors is able to become involved in a large range of issues, and that most of the time most issues are not in play (see also the general statement of the pluralist theory of industrial relations in Clegg, 1975).

There is therefore an interesting distinction among the procedures which help to make pluralism. Some, those we have called p, bind the parties together through a procedural positive-sum game; others separate the parties from each other by disaggregating their interactions over substantive matters. In other words, these latter operate by reducing the density of interactions (n) which, as we saw above, increase conflict losses. We can therefore improve statement (8) by writing it as:

$$\Delta c + \Delta l = 0 - (b - p)\frac{n}{s} \qquad (9)$$

where s = devices for insulating conflict, and simplifying the specification of b and p for ease of reading.

This now constitutes a full statement of a pluralist relationship between C and L. It is a system that requires more of representatives than does contestation. The actors in procedures are representatives alone, and procedures work only if the representatives are able to convince their members that the representatives' experience of them serves as a better guide to the balance of power than any attempt by the members to play the matter out for themselves in 'real' conflict. As this divergence in experience develops, so, in terms of statement (7) above, more discipline is required if the representatives are to be able to deliver consent.

Within such a system, relations become less sporadic, more continuous, although individual bargains are still discrete exercises. A major motive in the construction of procedures is acceptance of the long-term nature of the relationship; neither side seeks to eliminate the other as a conflict force. This means that during each bargaining round each side is aware of the probability of future rounds and may therefore convey signals that it hopes will affect the behaviour of the opponent in the future. These signals may be negative; that is, they may try to stress how little will be available for concessions in the future. But they may be positive: one side may attempt to provide small, apparently gratuitous gains to the opponent; these are designed to act as *douceurs*, creating goodwill that may moderate the behaviour of the opponent in the next bargaining round. Within pluralism, therefore, we have the nascent development of minor substantive positive-sum exchanges, often facilitated by inter-temporal bargaining.

Bargained corporatism

If there is scope for positive-sum games, why do not all participants always introduce them on a large scale, until they dwarf the negative nature of zero-sum bargaining? This is what the wider public often asks of the two sides in industrial relations. There are in fact several good reasons for reluctance.

First, there may be a limited supply of such issues. We must remember that the *CL* relationship is that sub-set of all capital/labour relations that has been subjected to negotiation between organised actors, usually because a union has raised questions as issues. Unions will rarely bother to raise non-contentious matters; and capital will rarely want of its own accord to place them within the negotiating relationship: if it can unilaterally allocate positive-sum advances between itself and its workforce, why should it allow a union to share the credit by being seen to have helped secure these gains? Also, even if both sides stand to gain from a development, there may still be conflict about the division of the spoils. Again, management may prefer to forgo the chance to negotiate the positive-sum issue in order to protect its ability to determine the relative shares of any mutual gains which it is unilaterally able to secure.

Second, and especially for the workers' side, there is condiderable difficulty in determining whether an issue *is* a joint one. If a false identification is made, and a zero-sum issue is treated as positive-sum, they run the risk of failing to defend their members' particular interests. Given this dilemma of lack of knowledge, workers' representatives often respond by treating all issues as potentially zero-sum games, accepting any positive-sum gains as windfalls, implying nothing for long-term relations. British shop stewards may often be heard to remark that, since they never really know what management is up to, they play safe by following the rule: 'if the bosses are for it, we must be against it'. Managers less often have this dilemma, as they normally possess better knowledge; but if they feel uncertain about the likely outcomes of situations, they may also follow a policy of restricting negotiations to straightforward conflicts.

Third, it should not be assumed that the pursuit of joint interests will proceed 'innocently'. Once labour in particular has accepted a particular goal as common, capital may try to induce it to believe that its pursuit of conflict goals nullifies or at least jeopardises the chances of achieving the joint goal. (This is so obvious a tactic that employers almost routinely use it.) If the two sides start to grapple with these problems and try to play their conflicts in the context of the pursuit of certain joint interests, they begin to depart from a pluralist system towards that which we call neo-corporatism or bargained corporatism (the distinction between this and 'simple' or authoritarian corporatism will be clarified in due course; for the original use of the concept 'bargained' corporatism, see Crouch, 1977, especially pp. 262–72).

To explore this we need to consider more precisely what is involved in positive-sum bargaining. Except in the most trivial cases, the pursuit of joint interests is not painless. We must assume that, except in extreme cases, if the two sides could achieve something together from which they would both gain without cost, they would do it immediately, and the issue would not remain on the agenda long enough to become involved in complex interactions. The more normal positive-sum bargain starts with one side (say C) saying to the other: 'if you accept sacrifice k_l, you will attain gain g_l, which will be greater than k_l; and I shall gain g_c.' L will probably refuse this until it can negotiate a considerable reduction in g_c; C is asking to share the gain without making any sacrifice, and must expect its share of g to be very small. The issue is therefore likely to include many elements of a zero-sum conflict after all. It is therefore more likely that C's offer will take the form: 'If you incur sacrifice k_l and I incur sacrifice k_c, you will attain gain g_l and I shall attain g_c, both g_l and g_c being greater than k_l and k_c respectively'. Alternatively, it may be L that proposes k_c to C. The balance of g and k values on each side now being fairly incommensurable, it is more likely than an agreement will be reached, such that:

$$(g_c - k_c) > 0; \quad (g_l - k_l) > 0 \qquad (10)$$

A typical example might be: C offers to share strategic decision-making (k_c) *with* L if L will agree to a change in manning practices (k_l); from this L will gain better wages for its members because of improved efficiency (plus the chance to share in strategic decision-making) (g_l); C will gain from increased profits following the change in manning practices (g_c). It should be noted that such an exchange by no means excludes conflict. Either party may become resentful that somehow the other side seems always to achieve a better balance of g and k. However, they are both unlikely to take their dissatisfaction to the point of relinquishing the entire g, k exchange so long as they continue to gain from it more than they could reasonably expect to gain in its absence.

Often, although both sides gain more from prolonging an arrangement than from breaking it, the gains are unequally shared. This may eventually strain the tolerance of the weaker party, although it remains in its interest to try to renegotiate the arrangement rather than to wreck it. An important example was the way in which the Swedish unions' solidaristic wage policy benefited capital more than labour. From the mid-1970s the unions developed their policy of wage-earner funds as an attempt to change the terms of the relationship *within* the general framework of Swedish incomes and industrial relations policies (Martin, 1979).

Matters are made more complex by the fact that typically the parties are asked for sacrifices now in exchange for gains in the future. In estimating their g, k balance they must therefore discount the gains by a factor representing the risk that the gains will not be achieved. Looking at it from L's point of view, the deal is worth while only if:

$$(qg_l - k_l) > 0 \tag{11}$$

where $q = $ the probability that the gains will be achieved and $q < 1$.

The total gains available to L under these conditions are, at first sight, a sum of the gains from pursuing common interests plus the fruits of continuing pursuit of conflict:

$$\Delta l = ((g_l - k_l) + (z_l - (b_l - p)))\frac{n}{s} \tag{12}$$

where $z_l = L$'s gain from conflict.

But we must now recall that often the k_l being demanded is the foregoing of a zero-sum demand. In a case of that kind, L is confronted with a choice: continued pursuit of conflict demands (z_l), will reduce its co-operative gains (g_l), in the extreme case to nothing:

where $$k_l = fz_l$$

we can rewrite (12) as:

$$\Delta l = ((g_l - fz_l) + (z_l - (b_l - p)))\frac{n}{s} \tag{13}$$

where $f = $ the factor by which pursuit of conflict goals destroys the achievement of joint goals.

Therefore, L's position as it contemplates becoming involved in this kind of bargaining contains the following unattractive elements: to achieve the newly attainable goals it must give up some zero-sum goals, from which C will clearly gain; and the identity of an issue as zero-sum or joint will often be obscure and subject to manipulation by C. We must now add to these problems the relationship between L as representative and its membership.

Statement (7) above gave us the role played by organisational discipline if representatives were to persuade their members to accept their version of the point at which conflict should be ended in the minimal case of representation under contestation. In the kind of bargaining we are now considering, the representatives are usually asking their members to accept an immediate and therefore *known* sacrifice in exchange for the representatives' *estimate* of the gains that will come in exchange. The members have to make their own estimate of the quality of the representatives' estimate, without having been themselves involved in the negotiations:

$$(q_e g_l - k_l) = (q_r g_l - k_l) + d \qquad (14)$$

Given that the members are making an estimate of the credibility of the representatives' own estimate of g, it is probable that q_e will be lower than q_r, placing an increased strain on d.

One may conclude that, in the light of all these points, unions would be well advised to stay clear of all entanglements with positive-sum issues and stick to conflict, even if that means the sacrifice of some indefinable positive-sum gains. Such was, for example, the majority view of the British Trades Union Congress in 1977 when it rejected the proposals of the Bullock Committee for a system of worker-directors. Many unionists saw a great risk of the worker-directors being lured by management into discussing probably bogus mutual interests to the point where they discouraged fellow workers from pursuing conflict issues (for a discussion, see Elliott, 1978).

However, the pursuit of mutual interests does present opportunities for gain. In what ways can, say, L reduce the risks and difficulties of trying to realise them? The main basic problems are an inability to trust C, inadequacy of information available to judge the character of an issue and the contingent, future nature of gains in comparison with sacrifices. L can try to reduce these: (a) by extending its share of control over aspects of its exchange with C; (b) by similarly extending its access to relevant information; and (c) by developing a dense network of exchanges with C so that both sides become caught in a continuous flow of exchanges. This last is particularly important in reducing the imbalance of timing between sacrifices and gains. There is no need to put all weight on one big exchange, and at any one moment each side is receiving gains from past commitments as well as making and receiving further present and future commitments. Each side acquires a vested interest in demonstrating its own trustworthiness because it stands to gain from the continuation of the relationship.

All this leads in a common direction: a dense multiplication of the links binding C and L, an extension of the issues which they try jointly to regulate, or about which they at least share available knowledge. This of course threatens an important element of pluralist bargaining summarised in statement (9) above, in which conflict was limited by insulation devices (s) which limit the number, extent and importance of interactions between C and L. Bargained corporatism is therefore risky; if the zero-sum issues after all prove more important, the conflict will be intense. The inner dynamic of industrial relations under bargained corporatism can therefore be summarised as follows: in order to realise common interests, the parties are constrained to restrict their pursuit of zero-sum gains and also to expand the scope of their interactions. The equivalent of (9) for bargained corporatism is thus:

$$\Delta c + \Delta l = ((g - (fz_c, fz_l)) - (b - p)) \frac{n}{s} \qquad (15)$$

In addition, as we have seen, particular strain is placed on the relationship between representatives and members.

Such a system is not assured of success. It remains possible for the net gains expected from conflict by either party to become greater than those from pursuit of the joint aims, making it rational for them to break loose from the strain towards conflict-avoidance that the above implies. And in practice it remains impossible to resolve all problems of mistrust and of the correct identification of zero- and positive-sum issues. However, once such a system becomes established, it contains certain self-reinforcing elements. The dense nature of the web of exchanges eventually enables commitments to be traded over time in a complex way. Even zero-sum matters may acquire the appearance of positive-sum ones as concessions made at one point may be regarded as credits available to be 'cashed' at a future date. Confidence in adopting that approach is possible only when the flow of exchanges has become very dense, with a high expectation of its indefinite continuation. Eventually the system itself becomes a positive-sum game: at any one time each side has a stock of cashable credits; the practitioners on each side become experts at working the system; and they derive status from being associated with the system's achievements. There is therefore a very high premium on maintaining the system, and all involved will be very reluctant to pursue any course likely to put it in jeopardy. This itself considerably reinforces the pressure to reach agreements and to avoid conflict.

But however self-sustaining such a system may become over time, at the moment of establishment it remains very risky. Real-life instances that approximate to the model seem to have become started because there was little alternative. For example, most of the countries normally characterised as neo-corporatist (Austria, Sweden, Norway, and to a lesser extent Germany, Denmark and the Netherlands) exhibited from an early stage in their development as industrial societies strongly centralised, highly politicised interest organisations alongside a national state-led project of industrialisation (that is, n was high, s low). The establishment of classic institutionalised conflict in the Anglo-American manner was unlikely, and if these countries were to transcend heavy conflict around a model of contestation, a risk had to be taken with bargained corporatism. By the same token, the existence, at least on the employers' side, of national organisations grouped around the state made corporatism easier to achieve at a national level than in societies with fragmented or decentralised organisations confined to narrow spheres of activity.

They were further inclined in that direction by the relative prospects on g and $(z-b)$ at the time of their construction of corporatist edifices. At the end of the Second World War, Austrians and Germans, especially in the labour movement, could see little immediate prospect of either co-operative or conflictual gains, but they had recent horrifying memories of the enormous costs of all-out conflict. They were predisposed to enter corporatist structures even without much prospect of gain. Rather differently, Dutch employers and unions had seen some of the potential gains from positive-sum exchanges during their co-operation in resistance to the German occupation. Different again, in the 1920s Scandinavia had seen some of the most widespread, if not particularly violent, industrial conflict the world has known. The political ascendancy of the labour movement shortly afterwards seems to have persuaded labour that it stood to gain more from seeking its goals through national-interest forums, while capital decided that it might as well come to terms with political reality in that part of the world and at least secure in return a labour movement interested in extensive co-operation.

These societies also all have strong traditions of internal discipline within their centralised labour and business organisations – which, we have seen, is a central requirement of bargained corporatism. As Panitch (1981) has pointed out, this can impose great strain on relations between representatives and members, at least on the labour side. But this needs to be put into perspective. True, the Swedish system was showing considerable strain by the end of the 1970s, with growing unofficial strikes and, in 1980, an official general strike. But the system had existed for forty years, and has still not collapsed. The Austrian system is only now entering a period of strain as that country at last begins to suffer from the international recession; but the system had sustained Austria through its first-ever successful exercise in democracy, and by the 1970s had helped to make it one of the world's most impressive economies. Panitch's Marxist perspective prevents him from considering the possibility of the positive-sum outcomes that may have sustained support for these systems despite the discipline they imposed on workers' pursuit of short-term conflict gains. By the same token, the more obviously 'representative' system of decentralised British pluralist bargaining has witnessed in the 1980s a much more drastic loss of support from the workforce than has so far been experienced by the neo-corporatist systems mentioned above – possibly at least partly because it did not in the past provide much scope for positive-sum activity.

However, this line of argument should not be taken to mean that bargained corporatism inevitably secures better gains for capital or labour than pluralism, or even contestation. Everything depends on the particular balance of power between the parties.

Authoritarian corporatism

Why do the participants in bargained corporatism not develop their relationship to the point where zero-sum games disappear altogether? Conflict costs would then be nil, and the parties would lose the troublesome effect of the increased density of exchanges, which makes conflict more costly but which is needed for the development of corporatist stability. In other words, why not progress towards:

$$\Delta c + \Delta l = gn \qquad\qquad (16)$$

If corporatist relations become more stable and less risky the greater the proportion of total transactions that are positive as opposed to zero-sum, then surely the end point of corporatist stability must be the reduction of all transactions to positive-sum games only?

The problem with this reasoning where C and L are concerned is this: since there are real conflicts of interest at many points between labour and capital, how are zero-sum games to be suppressed? If they are simply ignored by the corporatist representatives, then other representatives will spring up to deal with them, and the corporatist system will be weakened, losing some of its central function, the reduction of conflict. Perhaps legal, police or other measures could be used to stamp out any attempt at raising conflict issues, at disturbing the corporatist peace. But if all difficulties caused for capital by labour are simply squashed, why should capital bother to go into the corporatist exchange at all? If C can be confident that L will never raise awkward and expensive conflicts, it need waste no time developing a dense network of relations with L designed to maintain good relations between them. As we saw earlier, much of the elaboration of the bargained corporatist network was needed precisely to contain the irreducible core of conflict. Once that core disappears, the network becomes irrelevant.

Although the next stage on a continuum of industrial relations systems after bargained corporatism is authoritarian corporatism, the latter can exist only if autonomous representative organisations are crushed. This helps explain two important points. First, it has been noted (Williamson, 1982) that the corporatist edifices of such countries as fascist Italy and Portugal were largely bogus, elaborate facades that did little. Corporatism entered fascism as a useful ideological device for demonstrating how the social conflicts of pre-fascist society could be ended; but once the fascists had liquidated the autonomous labour movement, there was no real need for such institutions. Second, one can understand how it is vital to actors in bargained corporatist systems that they retain their sense of identity, that they continue to rally their 'side' and develop its symbols, and that they cling tenaciously to the core of zero-sum conflict in their relationship, no matter how far they compromise it in practice. *Were the two sides to lose their sense of conflict and separateness, the whole system would become unnecessary and the representatives would lose their function.*

This is therefore another of the risks taken by bargained corporatism: the actors must in everyday practice constantly compromise the separate identities on whose strength and separateness the *raison d'être* of the system depends. Occasional major outbreaks of conflict, such as the Swedish general strike of 1980, therefore perform a function within bargained corporatism similar to that played by crime and its punishment in the Durkheimian theory of social integration.

Corporatism and 'political space'

We must now consider in more detail what is meant by the increasing density of the network of relations that characterises bargained corporatism and distinguishes it from pluralism. This discussion will also enable us to bring the state into our analysis. Relations between capital and labour can extend across two dimensions: horizontally, to embrace new issue areas (e.g. moving from central questions of labour's wage-effort bargain to include the overall level of employment in the economy, or labour's social benefits); and vertically, to embrace new levels in the scope and hierarchy of decisions (to move upwards through the capital/labour relationship is to move from shop floor, through company, economic branch, possibly region, to nation state and perhaps to supra-national bodies).

Interest groups are not at liberty to move around this space at will. They are constrained by their capacity to bring people together at a certain vertical level and around a certain set of (horizontal) issues, and by their ability to take effective action at the point in question. These two aspects are linked: the willingness of people to adhere to the interest organisation will depend on its effectiveness, and its effectiveness will depend on its ability to mobilise support. Effectiveness can for our purposes be seen as a function of a group's ability to forge relationships with other interests capable of exercising power over the issues in question. To 'forge a relationship' in this sense means to be recognised as a force to reckon with, to possess the capacity to wield sanctions in the issue area concerned.

Interests tend to have a 'base' point within political space. For trade unions this is obviously located horizontally within issues affecting pay and conditions of work for employed labour; vertically it will be at whatever point (shop, firm, industry, etc.) it has been easiest to organise workers. One can similarly identify the base points for organisations of capital. Clearly, the further an interest moves from its initial base across the space, the more difficult it finds it to forge effective relationships. In addition, irrespective of 'distance' travelled, there may be institutional barriers inhibiting the formation of certain relationships and therefore entry into certain parts of the space.

Within capitalist societies there are severe limits on the capacity of labour organisations to affect issues going beyond their exchange with given units of capital unless they can forge effective relations at the level of the nation state. It is at this level that crucial macroeconomic variables can be manipulated, and the state has unique opportunities for reaching out to all parts of the society through its capacity to make law. Sometimes unions and employers organised at the national level can determine macroeconomic variables together; they might also reach agreement on certain desirable legal changes. (The latter sometimes occurs in countries with parliaments that are deadlocked over non-economic issues, but in which national agreements are possible between organised capital and labour. Not surprisingly, Belgium has provided several instances – see Molitor, 1978, pp. 34–5.) But for this to be effective they must have, in the former case, at least the tacit approval of the state, and in the latter at least its willingness to accept their proposal. For an interest group to make an effective vertical move to the level of the state is therefore also to facilitate a range of horizontal moves. In its relations with organised interests the state therefore acts something like the hand on the cork of a bottle containing an imprisoned genie: if the hand can be persuaded to lift the cork, there is no knowing what the genie may do.

But sometimes the genie is released in the hope that he will perform some task. So far we have spoken as though the interests are striving to reach state level in order to extend their influence. Equally, the state may want to encourage groups to perceive some version of a national interest, which they will be able to do only if invited and enabled to raise their organisational capacities to the state's level. The state then faces the risk that they will seek to exercise influence in ways other than those envisaged.

Clearly, there are on this question considerable differences in the structural constraints and state policies compatible with pluralism and bargained corporatism respectively. The ability of interests to transcend their initial institutional confines is a central variable determining those devices for insulating issue areas (s) on which the two systems occupy different positions. In an ideal-typical pluralist society, the centre of gravity of the labour movement comes at a point somewhat short of the nation state. It is not highly decentralised, because an important element of the procedural rules for conflict minimisation that are crucial to pluralist bargaining is the avoidance of uncontrollable 'guerilla' conflicts. Also, access to wider political influence is not entirely prevented: pluralism is a system without rigid barriers, so organised interests will have lobbying influence, via the nation state, over areas of interest close to them. However, the insulation constraints limit the network of relations that might develop from this.

In contrast, under bargained corporatism the emphasis is on the establishment of an extensive network of relations. Not only does activity at state level enable this, but this is also the level at which interests have access to the macroeconomic variables that give them some mixture of control, predictability and information that they need if they are to commit themselves to corporatist exchange. Further still, the national level is particularly appropriate for the search for common interests. As Olson (1982) has shown, groups operating effectively at or near an 'encompassing' national level are unable to externalise any negative consequences of their actions and are therefore likely to recognise responsibility for them. Groups that are small in relation to the overall system, on the other hand, can look after their own immediate interests and ignore externalities.

There are exceptions to this. If labour lacks the power to organise at near-national level to an extent that demands attention, it may be contained at a lower level of 'company corporatism', at which it may internalise some 'general' interests at the level of the company, while being unable to do anything at higher levels. Although they are not nationally 'encompassing', such company unions are encompassing at the only level at which they are able to have an effect. This is probably the best way to account for the conduct of unions in Japan, which are in general company-level unions. Here the giant firms are able to offer reasonable assurances of predictable positive-sum gains to that minority of their employees that is established and which dominates the unions, this predictability being eased by the close corporatist relations that prevail between the corporations and the government, a corporatism in which labour plays no part. This accounts for the strange position of the literature on Japanese corporatism, in which industrial relations at company level are described as corporatist (e.g. Dore, 1973), while at national level observers speak of a 'corporatism without labour' (Pempel and Tsunekawa, 1979).

In the more typical nationally based cases, centralisation should not be taken to mean that all union activity is concentrated at national headquarters. The network of inter-dependence and predictability will be undermined if local and regional organisations are left with nothing to do but obey orders or start rebellious activities of their own. If bargained corporatism is to function effectively (and, of course, empirical cases may *not* function effectively), actors at lower levels of the movement must be given functions within the system that depend on the successful activity of the national centre. (For example, local union officials might help run a labour-market policy that has been negotiated at national level.) Meanwhile the national centre, probably with the help of state bodies, exercises influence over a wide range of external matters in order to ramify the network and render the wider context of action controllable or at least predictable.

Given adequate research knowledge of the functioning of different societies, we could map the location of capital and labour interests in political space for individual societies, and this would enable us to judge how well they fitted the requirements of pluralist or corporatist or some other systems. For example, from the account given in Chapter 4 of this volume by Bernd Marin (see also Marin, 1982a), it is clear that modern Austria resembles closely the bargained corporatism model. The labour movement is highly centralised at the national level, and through its relations with employers' organisations, with the legally established *Kammern* and with the state and the political parties, it has influence over a wide range of contextual matters, establishing the dense network of relations of the kind necessary to a bargained corporatist model.

A different picture is revealed if we attempt a preliminary sketch of the way in which the British system was developing during its brief corporatist phase of the social contract, 1974–9. During that period there were two principal decision-making centres within the unions. For many years a series of developments had strengthened the near-autonomous base of shop-floor groups in several key sectors of the economy. These were engaged in bargaining at a highly fragmented level that was less co-ordinated than that envisaged by pluralist, let alone corporatist, theory. At the same time, national government policy was pulling in exactly the opposite direction, trying to lure the national leadership, through the Trades Union Congress (TUC), into a position of centralised co-operation. It did this by offering the TUC, and some national unions, widespread influence over economic and social policy. In exchange the unions were expected to share government's national perspectives and somehow impose on the union movement as a whole a wage policy compatible with government economic policy. In other words, goverment was breaking the bounds of pluralist bargaining in a direction opposite to that being achieved by the shop-floor movement, breaking down barriers of issue-insulation that could be compatible with system stability only under conditions of neo-corporatism. But only very temporarily (1976–8) was this national structure able to exercise much influence over shop-floor autonomy.

A further problem for British corporatism was a major 'excluded zone' from corporatist influence, the financial sector (or the 'City of London'). As several accounts have suggested (Strange, 1971; Hu, 1975; Blank, 1977; Crouch, 1980; Ingham, 1982), the financial sector occupies a unique position of autonomy from the rest of the economy in Britain. For deep historical reasons stemming from the imperial role of the British polity and the way in which British industrialisation was financed, the financial sector has been far less integrated with the industrial than in many other countries, and it has stood aloof from most attempts at tripartite national policy-making. It may well be that in several other countries the financial sector would be proof against labour-movement influence, but this does not become an issue because it does not appear as such a separate sector, with interests relatively indifferent to the bulk of the employment-creating economy. In Britain this autonomy has been an issue, as its inaccessibility to national policy-making has often made a mockery of attempts to construct tripartite strategies around a national interest.

Attempts at neo-corporatism within Britain have therefore presented a strange picture. Labour has been unable to impose the co-operation on its own base that would be a precondition of the effective operation of such a system, although it has continued to lay claim to a wide political influence of a kind that would be destabilising under circumstances other than those of bargained corporatism. At the same time, the inaccessibility of the financial sector rendered labour extremely dissatisfied with the level of political influence it exercised. The incompatabilities of this arrangement, and the odd coexistence of dissatisfaction within the labour movement at its impotence over crucial policy issues alongside alarm among its opponents at the extent of its power, eventually generated the shattering of the social contract in the strikes of the 'winter of discontent' in early 1979.

Not surprisingly, the Conservative government that took office in May that year has not attempted to involve organised labour in any neo-corporatist exercises. The government has not shown the same reluctance to forge corporatist relations with business interests alone. Indeed, one consequence of its desire to withdraw from direct state intervention in the economy is greater reliance on co-operative self-government by business interests (see Grant, 1984; Harrison, 1984). It has discouraged union influence at the national political level, while the high level of unemployment has further weakened labour to the point where many sections of capital have little interest in coming to terms with it anyway. In some respects it is possible to describe the changes since 1979 as a determined return from an unsuccessful bargained corporatism to a classical pluralism, with organised labour being pressed back into its 'proper' limited confines. However, there are some indications that the government, and a few sections of capital, want to go even further. Pluralism implies strengthening (a) the middle levels of the labour movement against the shop-floor, and (b) the elaboration of procedures for dispute settlement. But it is present policy to weaken union leaderships and to break up many established procedures of dispute settlement, as the government believes that these have imparted disastrous rigidities to the labour market. The aim of weakening the role of union leaders within their organisations can be seen in legislation to increase the role of ballots in union decision-making; that of undermining procedures can be seen in the demolition of 'automatised' systems of pay determination, especially in the public services.

In the terms of the above analysis, this is a shift to contestation. The reluctance of several sections of capital to pursue the intimations of government policy (together with a certain ambiguity within government policy itself) should not be taken as a hankering after 1970s neo-corporatism: in many cases it may indicate anxiety at the implications of contestation in favour of pluralism. As we saw above, groups embark on contestation only if they envisage total victory or the consistent ability to gain victories with small conflict costs.

Conclusions

From our analysis of the detailed character of industrial relations under bargained corporatism, we can draw certain conclusions that throw an interesting light on the events of the 1970s that led to the initial upsurge of interest in the phenomenon.

First, it will be noted that we have talked in terms of relations between labour and capital. The state enters at a crucial but limited point – the means of access to the national level – and it may perform either an active or a passive role. This differs somewhat from several analyses, which have used corporatism almost as a synonym for state intervention or for state-led incomes policy. My shift of emphasis reflects the direction taken by recent research, which has turned from the dramatic events of the 1970s to consider long-standing neo-corporatist arrangements (e.g. Marin, 1982a; Korpi and Shalev, 1979; Armingeon, Lehmbruch *et al.*, 1983). One recent work (Armingeon, 1983) explicitly rejects short-term incomes policies of the kind that originally excited attention as being viable cases of neo-corporatism. The focus on the 1970s was excusable at the time. Governments, responding to inflation and other crises, turned to neo-corporatist policies and tried to initiate neo-corporatist behaviour, often through incomes policy. But the means of encouraging a phenomenon should not be mistaken for the phenomenon itself. Corporatism in industrial relations is rooted in a relation between capital and labour, normally at nation-state level. State-led incomes policy may be a means of instigating it, but it is likely to be unsuccessful if the underlying structure of organisations is unsuitable.

Second, and similarly, we have seen that bargained corporatism takes the form of a dense web of interactions, and one must take great care before labelling an individual piece of behaviour as corporatist. One example of political exchange, or a few instances of co-operative national industrial relations, bear the same relation to neo-corporatism as a single swallow does to summer. And even that analogy holds only if the summer is an English one (i.e. it may fail to arrive at all). This again helps to explain the failure of some of the limited experiments of the 1970s to take root.

Third, the above analysis of the state helps explain the paradox that the events of the 1970s are usually interpreted as demonstrating enormous power on the part of organised labour, while Marxists interpret the same events as demonstrating the capitalist nature of the state. In the first instance, the Marxists are right: the state's role was often to take the place of capital in the exchange with labour, trying to initiate corporatism in order to stabilise wage costs and reduce the disturbances being caused by labour's attempts to avoid the consequences of inflation and economic restructuring. But, at the same time, the state's interventions were often repugnant to capitalists themselves, who did not trust the state to represent their interests adequately without conceding too much in the enlarged political role implied for labour – especially if the state was being managed by labour's political allies.

Finally, we must look to the future. So far our theory has assumed that the nation state is a level of action that provides sufficient access to relevant context for organised groups. For at least two decades after the Second World War this seemed to be the case. In the new and expanding world of trading relations that developed among nations within the sphere of influence of the USA, it was possible for nation states to find profitable niches for their economies and, without recourse to protectionism, to manipulate a few policy variables that would enable them to take advantage of these niches. By the late 1970s that had ceased to be true. At least temporarily, the period of self-sustaining expansion had come to an end; in many sectors the old industrial countries were being rivalled by new, low-cost producers in the Third World (Froebel *et al.*, 1979); the wave of commodity price rises in the early 1970s distorted much economic activity; multinational agencies acquired a new level of influence over national economic policies as nations acquired large debts trying to manage the inflationary crisis (Makler *et al.*, 1982); and multinational companies not easily subordinated to national policy came to dominate increasingly large sectors of the economy.

The old industrial nations now face a major need to restructure their economies, moving capital and labour from many areas in which they used to be dominant into new ones. But they do this with less freedom of action, less scope for control or even prediction at the national level. Their map of political space begins to look very constricted, with a whole range of issues made inaccessible to actors organised at levels no higher than the nation state, even if their activity at that level is impressive. This is a strong potential challenge to bargained corporatist systems. What will the partners to corporatism do if they lack influence over the variables that determine the restructuring to which they must now commit themselves?

The corporatism of Dutch industrial relations, in an economy particularly dominated by multinationals, has already been considerably weakened by this process. The Scandinavians are beginning to experience these problems in the, for them unusual, net outflow of capital from their economies. The greater the extent that capital can find ready exit from a country, the less it will be committed to making agreements within the corporatist system, and the worse terms labour will receive. So far labour's most advanced response to this has been the very recent legislation in Sweden to give trade unions control over a proportion of the profits of industrial enterprise, through the establishment of wage-earner funds in which a proportion of company profits must be deposited (Meidner, 1976; Öhman, 1982, 1983). The objectives of this scheme have changed from time to time since the idea was first mooted in the early 1970s. There is now preoccupation with ensuring that an increasing proportion of earnings from Swedish economic activity is available for re-investment in Sweden in a manner responsive to the control of workers' organisations.

It is too early yet to decide whether the attempt will be successful; one problem is that capital is so opposed to the policy that it may prefer to withdraw from bargained corporatism to a more open conflict in industrial relations than has been normal in Sweden for the past half-century (Myrdal, 1980). In terms of the earlier analysis of this chapter, Swedish industrialists see wage-earner funds as the opening of a new zero-sum conflict arena, shifting the balance of industrial relations such that the dense web of relations threatens rather than promotes stability. For their part, the unions expect that there are still sufficient advantages for capital in the Swedish system to inhibit any drastic moves to wreck it. It is not easy to build up the dense network of relationships essential to the success of bargained corporatism, but once achieved, such a system is not likely to be dispensed with lightly, given that the costs of co-operation are often exceeded by those of conflict.

Chapter 4

Austria – The Paradigm Case of Liberal Corporatism?

Bernd Marin

A labelling paradox

Whereas outside observers and analysts unanimously consider Austria to be the prototype of the new corporatism (Lehmbruch, 1982; Schmitter, 1981a), Austrians themselves strongly resent it if their co-operative system of labour relations and interest intermediation is called 'corporatist'. Why is this so and what does it mean? While resistance to 'corporatist' claims is rooted in recent Austrian history, political objections and semantic ambiguities surrounding the paradigm case draw our attention to typical normative problems which arise in connection with the idea of corporatism as a self-denying concept. Thus, being of general theoretical significance, labelling paradoxes cannot be ignored.

'Corporatism' as a self-denying concept

In the Austrian case, the traumatic historical experience of half a decade of Austro-fascist dictatorship as a form of authoritarian state corporatism (1933–8) and the spectacular failure of this *christliche Ständestaat* (not to speak of 'corporatist' experiences under Nazi occupation), ruled out corporatist ideology and terminology from political discourse. Like Nazism, 'corporatism' remains a four-letter word in public debate.

Although this may be all too understandable, is it more than a collective idiosyncrasy? Moral indignation cannot, of course, diminish the analytical value of the corporatist perspective and prevent its scientific use: incongruence with everyday meaning even increases explanatory power in comparative research. But the outright divergence of social science concepts from the self-interpretation of political actors may also disclose something about the phenomenon itself: with 'corporatism' it points not only at an embarrassing historical legacy, but at a continual moral ambivalence, a lack of political legitimacy, an obscure absence of normative foundation.

For corporatism is still not an authentic political formula, a self-denying organising principle of institution-building. While many stabilising 'corporatist' arrangements and even undisputed practices may be found in countries like Austria, Sweden, Norway, the Netherlands, Denmark and Israel – or Switzerland and Japan – they lack the coherence and dignity of a common democratic political vision. 'Corporatist' institutions, in Austria as everywhere in 'pluralist' democratic societies of a 'liberal' character, fail to generate a genuine and widely accepted ideological legitimation. New corporatism thus remains an abstract theoretical designation, whereas the designated reality, ironically enough, hides behind a plurality of competing labels – including 'organised pluralism'. In Austria, the preferred name is *Wirtschafts- und Sozialpartnerschaft (WSP)*.

Theoretical significance of the Austrian case

Sometimes even small remnants of great empires that have fallen apart do matter, as witnesses of something more important than their size or history. As far as Austria is concerned, its post-war development contributed at least twice to challenges to liberal pluralist orthodoxy in political and social theory: first, it contributed to the 'consociationalist' approach; now it figures as the ideal type of the 'neo-corporatist' paradigm (Lijphart, 1968/ 69, 1969, 1977; Lehmbruch, 1967, 1984).

Within the new corporatist discourse, a close look at the Austrian system of co-operative labour relations and encompassing conflict regulation allows for at least three types of lesson to be drawn (partly leading to conclusions opposed to widespread assumptions):

1. *Concept generation/modification/falsification through critical case studies.* If, and to the extent that, the Austrian case is assumed to be an extreme or ideal type of strong corporatism, its constituent components can be taken to represent defining elements of the new corporatism. Empirical research and inductive generalisations, therefore, permit us to go well beyond the blueprint schemes which stimulated the research programme in the first

place (Schmitter, 1974; Winkler, 1976; Lehmbruch, 1977). But new insights should not lead us to reduce Austrian arrangements to 'unique' historical contingencies, instead of explaining them in terms of general hypotheses.

2. *Testing of practical neo-corporatist claims through internationally comparative studies.* The political promises of increased economic growth, improved performance, greater stability, reduced conflict and enhanced 'governability' and integration as a consequence of neo-corporatist intermediary interest intermediation can be tested and differentiated by carefully designed comparative studies.

3. *Disproving purely political, culturalist, historical or institutionalist approaches to new corporatism instead of a comprehensive political economic perspective, as suggested by comparative historical studies.* The extreme contrast between the Austrian First Republic (ending in civil war, Fascism and Nazi occupation) and the Second Republic, combining rapid economic and social change *and* political stability in a process of 'orderly change' needs explanation, given that historical comparison has direct theoretical implications. To the extent that the discrepancy between class struggles and co-operative conflict regulation, or overall breakdown and regime stability, cannot be accounted for by variations in institutionalised interest intermediation, a strictly institutionalist perspective ceases to be a viable approach to the new corporatism. If almost the same basic 'corporatist' institutions can lead to civil war as to peaceful co-operation, institutional arrangements may matter less than postulated – while their interdependence with different levels of economic reproduction, the balance of class forces and other dimensions of power structure matters more than conventional institutionalist corporatism would have it (Marin and Traxler, 1984). Without taking into account the non-institutional prerequisites such as the political economy and class base of corporatist institutions, nothing can be said about their more than temporary viability, as any diachronic analysis of the Austrian paradigm case demonstrates convincingly.

Common misconceptions, or what 'Wirtschafts- und Sozialpartnerschaft (WSP) /new corporatism is **not**

If, and to the extent that, the Austrian case is considered to be an ideal type of new corporatism, then some widespread misconceptions can be ruled out on the basis of empirical evidence. Thus, neo-corporatism is *not*:

1. A new socio-economic ('third') order beyond capitalism and state 'socialism', combining private ownership with state control of production (Winkler, 1976). Rather, it is a system of well-organised mixed capitalism and is fundamentally non-etatist.

2. Consequently, it is not a modern, technocratic version of authoritarian state corporatism ('wahrer Staat') (Spann, 1931), nor an institutional design of some social engineering mastermind to extend state authority by extending etatist control through 'functionalised' political organisations and private interest governments (Streeck and Schmitter, 1984). Rather, antagonistic co-operation between functional interests is free of state regulation, and any supervision by a 'big brother' is not only unnecessary but detrimental to intermediary collective self-management and autonomous co-operation.

3. Corporatist co-operation does not imply a common ideology of class harmony; it is no 'counter principle' and 'final overcoming' of the class struggle, as conservatives claim (Klose, 1970, p. 15). Rather, it transforms class conflicts into a permanent war of manoeuvre between interest associations over organisational advantages within the institutional system; it does not simply 'institutionalise' class struggle, as Dahrendorf suggests (1959, pp. 64ff), but converts it into conflicts over the rules of the game of co-operative conflict resolution (Marin, 1982b, pp. 332ff).

4. Consequently, it is also not a political structure designed (above all) to integrate the organised working class in the capitalist state; it is not a 'subordination' of labour organisations (Panitch, 1979). Although it does not challenge a reformist bourgeois hegemony, it is politically underdetermined: it may benefit labour or capital (or both alternately or differentially in different aspects). In the Austria post-war development, it clearly benefited the organised labour movement – which was certainly not the intention of capitalists or 'the capitalist state'.

5. Correspondingly, neo-corporatism is not a privileged bargain between state bureaucracies and dominant private (sectoral, professional, etc.) interests. There is no clientilistic protectionism (*corporativismo*) for agrarian, special business, professional, church, or particularistic interests at the expense of 'the

common good'. Rather, it involves global concertation and inter-class, inter-sectoral, etc. intermediation, according to solidaristic standards. At least in its Austrian, prototypical variant, corporatism is just the opposite to reactionary, particularistic, 'sectoral' or 'selective' corporatism or clientilistic protectionism.

6. In a historical perspective, new corporatism is not a universal, unilinear, irreversible and almost irresistible evolutionary pattern towards more complex, organised, collectively rational institutional arrangements; it is not a secular trend that leads to international convergence within Western societies, as did the overall trend towards catch-all parties, which radically transformed competitive party systems. New corporatism is neither a grand political vision, nor a purposeful 'project of modernity'; it is not an unintended but unavoidable evolutionary outcome. Rather, it is a temporarily stable 'historical compromise' resulting from former class conflicts, generating its own gravitational forces, proper motion, risks and self-sustaining mechanisms; it is also open to disintegration and (limited) reversal. New corporatism has many possible developments and various futures.

7. Nevertheless, it is not just a set of institutional forms, emerging and viable within a wide variety of socio-political contexts (Schmitter, 1974, pp. 86 ff). Schmitter's formalisation of corporatism did free the concept from 'corporatist' ideologies, specific national political cultures, state forms or types of regimes. But this enlarged compatibility neither implies that the range of possible frameworks is unlimited and that anything goes, nor does it mean that all socio-political contexts are equally probable and conducive to corporatist co-operation. Respecification of the purely formal concept of corporatism by looking at the Austrian paradigm case demonstrates that there is neither a fixed, determined homologue, nor a purely accidental or freely elective interdependence, between the sub-system of co-operative interest intermediation and the national polity in general. The constitutive organising principles of corporatist co-operation in the long run strongly tend to generate certain overall political formations, and the viability and stability of antagonistic co-operation depends on these highly unlikely configurations. Corporatism makes sense neither as an ex-

clusively historical category, nor as a catch-all formula.

How, then, does the Austrian, supposedly paradigmatic, variant of new corporatism work?

Pillars of the institutional infrastructure

Stable, antagonistic co-operation does not depend on specific forms of institutional infrastructure, but without certain modes in the political organisation (representation and control) of socio-economic interests, it just could not be viable. While the logic and functions of these corporatist organising principles are dealt with elsewhere (Marin, 1981c), it is necessary to outline the shape that the institutional infrastructure of neo-corporatism takes in Austria.

The chamber system

Although 'chambers' do exist in other countries, they are quite different institutions in, say, France, Italy, Great Britain or West Germany. Austrian chambers are statutory, nationwide and universal associations: no working citizen can *not* be at least a member of one and often many of the respective Chambers of Labour, Commerce, Agriculture, of the respective liberal profession, etc. With highly differentiated business interests, it is possible for one actor (a person or a firm) to hold multiple memberships in the more than one thousand regional and sectoral subdivisions of the Chamber of Commerce. This complete coverage incorporates *all* work-related interests (*Erwerbsinteressen*) and guarantees the maximum scope of functional interest intermediation.

The public law status (*öffentlich-rechtliche Körperschaften*) of Austrian chambers obliges them to represent 'common' and 'legitimate' member interests only, instead of pushing for special, particularistic interests; to take into account the 'general interest'; to intermediate internally between conflicting member interests before confronting other associations of the state; to organise internally according to democratic principles (e.g., holding elections on a one-firm, one-vote principle, the exception being the 'free' business associations). These and other obligations are undertaken in exchange for rights such as to be consulted about legislative proposals, to fulfil advisory functions in hundreds of public bodies, etc. In contrast to West Germany, the Austrian unitary chamber system leads to the primacy of the national over regional or local levels; the primacy of the Chamber of Commerce over 'free' business associations; the legally based capacity of all chambers to engage in collective bargaining – in the case of the Chamber of Labour this is voluntarily ceded to the voluntary trade union. This points to a finely tuned division of labour between compulsory union chambers and 'related' free interest associations. This leads us to a second element of the institutional infrastructure.

Parallel free associability

Despite the existence of the inclusive statutory chamber system, free associability flourishes in Austria more than in most other countries. The organisation density of the trade union confederation (ÖGB) is still more than 60 per cent. The League of Austrian Industralists (Vereinigung Österreichischer Industrieller – VÖI) mobilises more than 85 per cent of all private capital, other sectoral or special business interest associations usually reaching a similar or even higher organisational density. How is this lively free associability to be explained, given the fact that the domains of voluntary interest associations largely overlap with those of compulsory chambers? How is this associational parallelism or duplication possible?

Generally, free associations develop in order to compensate for specific 'weaknesses' of the statutory chamber system, such as the underrepresentation of special (big business, sectoral) interests, the exclusion of market and cartel functions, or sometimes too-strong internal cleavages, or to hold on to traditions such as the historical precedence of the union movement over the Chamber of Labour, which was established at union initiative. This case also illustrates some other general principles governing the delicate relationship between chambers and formally competing free associations: usually there exist multiple and subtle forms of division of labour between parallel organisations. Free associations carry higher legitimacy, spilling over to the chambers and even the overall system by the very fact of maintaining a free choice while dividing functions or sharing personnel; in the case of organised labour, additional state support (through fiscal privileges, privileged institutional access, etc.) increases union security in order to maintain the strongest Austrian mass organisation as a free counterweight to the chamber 'bureaucracy' and as a leading actor of the labour movement. With regard to business, the constellation is just the reverse – and it could not be otherwise without undermining corporatist co-operation.

A guiding directive business actor

Though unique on a global scale, the eminence of the Chamber of Commerce is widely ignored (by scholars, not by business-men, of course). A most important characteristic of the overall Austrian system lies in the simple fact that there is one, and just one, leading business representative – the statutory Chamber of Commerce which allows the transformation of the functional self-governance of capital simultaneously into a measure of indirect political control of the business class. Therefore, the guiding/directive role of the chamber on the business side is an indispensable institutional prerequisite of corporatist co-opera-tion.

Such a unified and authoritative *political* intermediation of business interests cannot be found in other capitalist market economies with decentralised *economic* decision-making. While the greater power, diversity and internal conflict potential of business interests over those of labour makes for a greater multiplicity of free associations of the business class, business pluralism is in the Austrian case limited and organised by subordinating free associations to the hegemony of the compul-sory chamber:

To function in a truly cooperative way, the system of interest intermediation must institutionally counterbalance the struc-tural asymmetry of interests between capital and labour in that it provides for more authoritative control to collectively regulate and discipline the potentially more disruptive busi-ness interests.

As it is individual businessmen/-women more than workers who have to be brought into the political arena and then in line to enable *inter*-associational interest intermediation, business representation has to be arranged through the leadership of chambers, not indispensable in the case of unions. Functional self-government of capital, contrary to that of labour, seems to need compulsory structures of *intra*-organisational interest intermediation – and hence a privilege of obligatory chambers over free associations. (Marin, 1983a, p. 208)

Organising *and* controlling business interests may be just as impossible without chambers or other statutory institutions as it cannot be accomplished by compulsory associations alone. However, whereas labour must organise freely to act as a 'responsible' interlocutor, free business associability must be regulated in order to reach an equivalent political capacity for antagonistic co-operation.

Industrial and unitary unionism

Industrial and unitary unionism are too well acknowledged as structural conditions of corporatist co-operation to need more than a short mention. In the Austrian case, the white-collar union (GPA) is the major exception to the principle of industrial unionism. However, although it has become the strongest single union since 1974, the white-collar union is – contrary to the situation in, say, Sweden or West Germany – smoothly integrated as one of fifteen affiliated unions into the trade union confederation ÖGB. Due to the extreme degree of centralisation, affiliated unions are sub-divisions of the ÖGB, with no legal personalities of their own, their activities being strongly directed by the central bodies. Centralisation and concentration of the union movement has grown steadily for over a century now.

It could be argued that unitary unionism was brought about by reconstructing the union movement as a politically independent (*überparteiliche*) unitary organisation after the Second World War. This structural change is often seen as a decisive turning point in overcoming the inter-union rivalry prevalent during the First Republic, thus probably exaggerating a valid argument. First, ideological divergences persist within the union confederation, with competing political factions as an important element of structural differentiation. Secondly, although unitary action and increased cohesion by internalised political pluralism did indeed strengthen union power and co-operative capacity in the post-war period, it lacked such a capacity much less than assumed, even in the inter-war period.

The absence of any economic policy in need of union co-operation and member control (such as 'Austro-Keynesianism') made inter-union competition a further centrifugal element but not a systemic 'disturbing' factor as it would be today.

The 'big four/two'

The Austrian system of labour relations is also highly concentrated in that it represents as many interests by as few organisations as possible. It is the 'big four' that centrally negotiate the millions of interests expressed by them or, at least, control any more decentralised bargaining of subordinated/delegated units: these are the trade union confederation ÖGB, the Chambers of Commerce and Labour, and the confederation of regional Chambers of Agriculture.

The advantages and prerequisites of expressing all demands through only a few voices for negotiation and compromise are too obvious to need much further comment. With regard to the consequences of this strategy of internalising external costs, concentrated decision-making *between* a few political actors makes for strong centralisation and the prevalence of administrative rationality *within* associational bureaucracies; and a tendency to monopolise and 'colonise' domains in their 'environments'. Finally, concentration leads to further concentration, not just inside the participating organisations but also between them: 'in the famous Parity Commission, sub-committees still involve the four most important political actors with a few representatives from each side, the informal but final decision-making within the *Präsidentenvorbesprechung* ends up as an intimate face-to-face talk exclusively between two people – the president of the Chamber of Commerce representing capital and the president of the trade union confederation representing organised labour' (Marin, 1983a, p. 209; see also, Marin, 1982a, p. 15f, p. 46f). But small numbers in strategic decision-making are not a reflection of small membership numbers or the small size of the country but of great centralised power concentration.

Centralised organisations

Any single participant association in corporatist co-operation has strongly centralised internal structures: otherwise consensus formation and member compliance with compromises obtained would be too difficult, and interest organisations could not speak to each other with one legitimate voice. While centralisation in business associations results more from the structure of state interventionism and antagonistic co-operation itself, union centralism is rooted in tradition and formal organisation and further strengthened but not produced by inter-associational co-operation. But whereas there is centralisation without co-operation, there is *no co-operation without centralisation* – a kind of iron law of intermediary interest intermediation.

Austrian union centralism may illustrate this point. There is a non-federative, unitary peak association; affiliated unions are even legally non-autonomous sub-divisions of the ÖGB; individual membership is of the ÖGB, which assigns or transfers it to specific industrial unions; central headquarters are constitutionally obliged to control 'the internal structure and activities of the individual unions' (ÖGB statutes 1971, paragraph 4, section 5); the national centre exercises control over recruitment (*Personalhoheit*) and fiscal authority (*Finanzhoheit*). Central control over organisational resources and money, when considered with the direction in which funds flow, reverses power-dependence relationships between the confederation and industrial unions. In Austria, central bodies are not dependent on subsidies of formally subordinate branch unions, as they are in all other countries. If the ÖGB is in command of 80 per cent of total membership income (not to mention additional independent sources of revenue), and not just of between 2 per cent (the TUC) and about 18 per cent (LO-Sweden), organisational authority is where the money is: at the top, where any blueprint expects union authority to be.

In everyday (administrative, political, collective bargaining) praxis, however, decentralised decision-making prevails; without informal decentralisation, such an extreme degree of formal centralisation would produce resistance and overload the top. Instead, *centralism by decentralisation* and a series of other organisational devices described elsewhere (Marin, 1983a, pp. 312 ff) allow for a combination of predominant decentralised routines and central guidance and control when required.

Modern bureaucratic interest associations

Without the development of 'modern', bureaucratic organisation, interest associations could never play their role in corporatist co-operation. Constituent associations have become so encompassing in scope that only complex and specialised 'bureaucracies' can handle internal variety and a multitude of turbulent environments. Austrian associations have gone far in their tendency towards bureaucratisation and modernisation.

One central aspect of organisational modernisation is *economising/rationalising administration*. This can easily be demonstrated in relation to the problem of acquiring sufficient resources, which is a significant issue for the institutional autonomy of any one organisation. In the case of the chambers, the supply of adequate financial resources does not even arise as a problem as membership is compulsory and all dues (*Kammerumlagen*) are automatically deducted from wage returns (after taxes) by the employer and transferred to the relevant chamber. In the case of voluntary trade unions – the financial base of which in other countries suffers from ineffective systems of dues collection – an agreement between works councils, unions, employers and union members allows for a similar arrangement of automatic deduction of union dues from wages in all public agencies and many private firms. This method of dues collection not only provides a stable and safe supply of necessary income, but also reduces administrative costs significantly by shifting the function to firms. Such rationalisation of income supply also leads to further internal power centralisation, as well as to rather rich interest associations: the 1984 preliminary budget of the Chamber of Commerce, for example, was about £204 million and the 1984 ÖGB budget was about £66 million, its funds including the central strike fund being estimated at around £800 million.

Another dimension of organisation modernisation is the *professionalisation of interest associations*, through the integration of technical competence and scientific expertise into large bureaucratic apparatuses. The Chamber of Commerce, for example, currently employs 4600 staff members and the ÖGB has a workforce of 2023 employees, many of whom are highly qualified specialists. By institutionalising a permanent co-operation between political functionaries and experts and co-opting technically competent personnel into decision-making, interest associations not only upgrade qualifications generally, but also strengthen the democratic plebiscitarian legitimation of elected/delegated leadership by underpinning it through a technocratic one.

Political linkages/interpenetration

Comparative research has explained the success of Austrian incomes policy by contrasting the failures in other Western European countries with its support from and synchronisation with the sub-system of political parties, parliament and government (Lehmbruch, 1984, p. 61). While this is clearly not a sufficient condition, corporatist co-operation could definitely not do without some co-ordination with the second institutional circuit of political life. In Austria, these links between the sub-systems of interest intermediation and that of government/party politics take the form of intensive mutual interpenetration.

Political parties are incorporated into interest associations, associations into political parties. Parties are (more or less) composed of associational segments (*Bünde* of employers, employees and agriculture) and leading positions are filled according to their strength in respective constituencies; associations are differentiated by political factions and their leadership is constituted according to their electoral strength within the chambers or the ÖGB. In this way, compulsory or unitary associations internalise political competition, parties internalise corporatist interest intermediation; and the political hegemony of socialists in workers' organisations and of conservatives in business associations allows for a political division of labour between associations and 'related' parties.

This functional differentiation between parties and associations takes many forms, with multiple functions of functionaries (*Personalunionen* and *Ämterkumulierung*) or staff-sharing among the more common ones. Accordingly, a relative majority of parliamentarians (and the most important in any *Fach-* and *Unterausschuss*) come from interest associations (Pelinka, 1981) (for example, the current president of the national assembly – *Nationalratspräsident* – is also acting president of the ÖGB), engineering parliamentary support for corporatist proposals. About 85 per cent of all legislative proposals in economic and social policy are unanimous as a result of pre-parliamentary, inter-associational consensus formation (Pelinka, 1981; Naszmacher, 1968, pp. 53ff). The same mechanism also extends to the co-ordination between associations and government, which is neither fully tripartite, nor multilateral interest-clearing, but follows a model of two-step bilateralism (Marin, 1982a, pp. 50–3). The state neither participates in balanced trilateral negotiations, nor does it serve as an arbiter between antagonists, but bases its decisions on agreements reached by associational interest intermediation. Governments cannot govern without or even against the consensus of giant interest organisations, but can only execute their common(!)will. Similarly, the division of labour and interpenetration between interest associations and parties does (as will be seen later) imply reciprocal permeation of rather unequal strength, and that involves deeply penetrating associational hegemony over political parties as well.

What history/development?

This is not the place to go into the contingencies of the (pre)history of Austrian 'social partnership'. Instead, it might be useful simply to recall a few historical turning points and evolutionary patterns in order to explain a specific and perhaps 'unique' case by general corporatist theory. A few points in this respect are less obvious and generally acknowledged than others.

Liberal corporatism did not simply follow the decay and destruction of fascist authoritarian state corporatism (1933–1945), but actually preceded it. Although the first historical attempts at institutionalising co-operative labour relations eventually failed, they nevertheless go back to the late nineteenth and early twentieth centuries. Even in the First Republic, which ended in civil war, there were serious co-operative efforts starting with the *Industriekommissionen* after 1918 to the *Wirtschaftskonferenz* and the *Wirtschaftskommission* in 1930. (Grandner and Traxler, 1984). If it makes sense to speak of an historical turning point at all, it was in 1918/19, not in 1945: practically all of the basic institutions (if not the complete institutional infrastructure) for co-operative interest politics were established during the 'Austrian Revolution'. It was the *Arbeiterkammergesetz* that universalised and extended the Austrian chamber system, initiated after the bourgeois revolution of 1848, thereby institutionalising general functional representation, bound to macroeconomic orientation and co-operative principles. It was the *Kolletivvertragsgesetz* that universalised and legally codified regular exchanges between organised capital and organised labour at the meso level of industrial branches. It was the *Betriebsrätegesetz* that created a unified and coherent system of workers' representation at plant level within the legal framework of co-operative labour relations, thereby officially recognising existing but constitutionally unfounded working class instruments like *Gehilfenversammlung, Arbeiterausschüsse* and, above all, trade union shop stewards' organisations – while at the same time getting control over a revolutionary workers' and soldiers' soviet movement (*Arbeiter- und Soldatenrätebewegung*) and preventing wildcat socialisations (*'wilde Sozialisierungen'*). Finally, an extensive social legislation established for the first time in Austrian history an interdependence between the political arena and the sub-system of interest intermediation, creating 'opportunity structures' for political exchanges between social classes and collective actors throughout the state machinery. Given all these highly important political innovations, by which the 'Austrian Revolution' set up the basic institutions for corporatist co-operation, the remaining puzzle as to why co-operative policies did not succeed until after 1945 can only be solved by reference to differences in the underlying class base, power structure and political economy of almost the same corporatist institutions.

This also explains why the co-operative arrangements emerged and were not brought about by a common plan, but rather were the unintended result of fundamentally antagonistic strategies. The logic of expansion of the associational system was that of collective actors involved in an incessant war of position in order to build up countervailing powers to their opponents, with each side expanding into empty domains, incorporating interests and later concentrating and centralising their representation and institutionalising (or legally codifying) respective gains. But it was not until the dissolution of the Austro-Hungarian Empire and the 'Austrian Revolution' that strengthened working-class organisations could successfully push for corporatist institutions, and it was not until the period after the Second World War that another shift in the balance of forces made co-operation within corporatist arrangements an unavoidable option for organised business as well.

Further basic institutions of co-operative labour relations – at bottom and top

Comprehensive corporatist co-operation cannot function without some inter-sectoral co-ordination and vertical integration of different levels of interest intermediation. In the Austrian case, the 'Parity Commission' (Marin, 1982a) serves as the very centre of a widespread network of hundreds of co-operative bodies, whereas the hierarchical integration of industrial relations at workplace and enterprise level into sectoral and national labour relations can best be demonstrated by the uses 'social partnership' makes of the works council system at plant level.

The works councillor ('Betriebsräte') system at firm level and its vertical integration

On the side of labour, effective control of national interest intermediation over industrial relations at workplace, plant and company level is achieved by integrating the statutory representational system at firm level – the works councils (*Betriebsräte, Personalvertreter*) – into the system of trade union organisation, the 'twin' Chambers of Labour and their nationwide informal co-operation with business associations. Complex interrelationships between legal provisions and organisational structures lead to a hierarchical structure of interest representation and in practice unify a formally 'dualist' works constitution. How does this vertical integration function in detail?

As industrial relations within the enterprise are regulated by legislation – the Works Constitution Act – collective labour law not only structures them explicitly according to strictly co-operative principles, but establishes a hierarchy of levels of decision and bargaining with a clear primacy of sectoral and national (macroeconomic) units of representation over firm representatives. Joint regulation at the plant is related to joint regulation at industrial and national level by a clear-cut, legally codified and hierarchically co-ordinated division of labour (Traxler 1981). It is not, as in other countries, an unpredictable outcome of an ever-changing balance of forces between shop-floor representatives and managers on the one hand, and union representatives on the other.

By extensively regulating works councils as immediate representatives of working-class interests within the firms, collective labour law specialises and establishes not only their role, but indirectly that of other actors as well. The Works Constitution Act clearly states what demands may be articulated and what means may be used by whom to put them through. By protecting *and* limiting the works councils' space of action, it simultaneously makes them rather independent from market constellations, management pressures *and* rank and file interventions or support/ mobilisation/militancy on the one hand, but quite dependent on resources of 'friendly' organisations within the labour movement on the other. Consequently, works councils can hardly perform as free floating, autonomous class fighters, but easily become 'extended arms' of trade unions and the chambers of labour.

The Works Constitution Act guarantees the very existence of representational bodies and protects them from management pressures: under the law, employers are not permitted to prevent their establishment and are obliged to provide works councillors with release from work, office and secretarial assistance and other resources. Works councillors are virtually not recallable and can pursue conflicts with management through legal channels. At the same time, they can act largely autonomously *vis-à-vis* their constituency/electorate as well: there is no imperative mandate (*freies Mandat, Weisungsungebundenheit*), there is an obligation to secrecy (*Verschwiegenheitspflicht*) on certain matters, and certain meetings are not held in public (*Betriebsratssitzungen*). These and other similar norms make them independent from direct pressures from 'below'. In regulating their control by constituents and securing freedom from interference by adversaries, both types of protection institutionalise a considerable autonomy for works councils.

Collective labour law also restricts works councils by prohibiting them legally from taking certain actions, thereby protecting the unions from interference and competition by statutory, formally union-independent representatives within the firms. Bargaining at company level (*Betriebsvereinbarungen*) is defined as a residual and ceded competence only, which cannot undermine the *bargaining monopoly* of supra-plant bodies. Works councillors are not allowed to call strikes or to initiate other forms of labour struggles (*Friedenspflicht*), making for an *effective union strike monopoly*. In general, works councils are expected to act as co-operative partners or mediators *vis-à-vis* the management and in conjunction with competent supra-plant working-class representatives. But what is even more significant within this arrangement, their own interests often become structurally congruent with those of the potentially rival unions: low collective wage agreements (in which unions´ may be interested for macroeconomic reasons) allow for additional management concessions in company-level bargaining, which in turn can be converted into comparative advantages at works council elections.

Through the Works Constitution Act unions have direct access to firms, thereby expanding the space within which they can act and making works councils susceptible to, if not dependent on, their support. Unions can initiate the very establishment of works councils; they can call for meetings and influence elections by placing union functionaries on the electoral committee (*Wahlvorstand*) or running their own candidates. Unions can advise works councils, provide indispensable expertise on legal, financial and technical matters, or assist them in negotiations with management. Works councils may object to management decisions and appeal to an arbitration board composed of sectoral union and employer association representatives or to a central state commission (*Staatliche Wirtschaftskommission*), under the influence of the large interest organisations themselves. Whatever instruction, training, courses, etc. works councils actually need and are allowed to take (during their working hours) is provided, if not paid for altogether, by the unions or the Chamber of Labour. To the extent that works councillors in large nationalised industries ('*Betriebskaiser*') are able to exert some influence on management recruitment and on management policies, their informal power is often mediated by their 'big brothers'.

Even so, one needs to take account of some additional factors to explain the *de facto* identity between works councils as statutory representatives at firm level and the union organisation at the workplace. According to union statutes, the leading committee of union workplace organisations (*Betriebsgruppe*) is composed of all works councillors belonging to the union. As almost all of them, given high union density, are already unionised, union functionaries at the lowest level are identical with elected works councillors. The same applies to the governing bodies at the local level (*Orts- und Bezirksorganisationen*), which are almost exclusively directed by works councillors. But as the central bodies at regional level consist of employed functionaries as well, and as these *Landessekretäre* are directly subordinated to the national centre, works councillors are smoothly integrated into the unions through their positions within intra-organisational hierarchies.

Many other arrangements work in the same way as an interpenetration of works councils, trade unions and chambers of labour under the 'guiding role' of the national interest associations. Statutory elections for works councils (*Betriebsratswahlen, Personalvertreterwahlen*), for instance, serve simultaneously as elections to union bodies. Under the Works Constitution Act, works councils are elected by secret ballot, with all employees eligible to vote or to stand for election, regardless of union membership. As this applies only to plants with more than five employees, some union members cannot exercise any influence on their representative bodies, while non-union members can through works council elections. The fact that all union organs from the bottom to the top rung at the national centre are proportionately composed of delegates of different political factions according to the results in works council elections, has many effects. It allows union factions to present their lists of candidates for works councillors; or to ask politically independent works councillors to declare their political affiliation or sympathy for any of the existing union factions, at least after the election. With a voter turnout of over ninety per cent, works council elections also provide a substantial plebiscitarian legitimacy for union representatives. Furthermore, the dual function of works council elections relieves union policies of general controversial issues by cutting topics down to a small scale, particularly firm-related questions.

Although the vertical integration of works councils into unions is similar to the balancing of the 'dual system' in the Federal Republic of Germany, in the Austrian case it is more encompassing and works without any frictions. Potential rivalry between statutory interest representatives and union officials is transformed into mutually advantageous co-operation – more often than not by multifunctional personnel. The existence of such perfectly smooth co-operation between statutory bodies and voluntary organisations allows for another – electoral, genuinely political – competition within this merged system. This *political* competition within an informally unified and hierarchically ordered arrangement of interest representation is not only much easier to handle than the original structural one, but it also continuously generates 'safe' plebiscitarian legitimation of the co-operative system of interest politics as a whole instead of stressing or consuming its legitimacy.

The 'Paritätische Kommission' as central body

Anyone who does not understand the working of the 'Parity Commission' in some detail cannot understand the overall system of 'Economic and Social Partnership'. While it is just one of hundreds of co-operative bodies, it preceded and initiated them and continues to play a centrally strategic and co-ordinating role. Historically, it grew out of attempts to observe and regulate prices in the period immediately after the Second World War by the *Wirtschaftskommission* (1947). After suspension of the subsequent *Wirtschaftsdirektorium der Bundesregierung* (1951) because of incompatibility with the constitution, another equivalent body without legal backing was established in 1952, leading to the *Paritätische Kommission für Preis- und Lohnfragen* in 1956–7. In 1962, the *Unterausschuss für Lohnfragen* was added, and in 1963 the *Beirat für Wirtschafts- und Sozialfragen* was institutionalised as a brains trust and centre for strategic economic planning. Its basic structure as it existed in 1985 is set out in Figure 4.1.

The distribution of functions among the various bodies constituting the Parity Commission is on the following lines. The *Preisunterausschuss* decides on claims from firms for price increases (broadly speaking, about one-third of all prices covered by the consumer price index are regulated consensually by the Parity Commission; one-third are regulated by the state; and one third are pure market prices). The *Lohnunterausschuss* decides on the timing of autonomous collective bargaining and ratifies its results, which are not valid without its consent. The *Beirat für Wirtschafts- und Sozialfragen* develops concepts and proposals for decision-making in economic policy and middle-

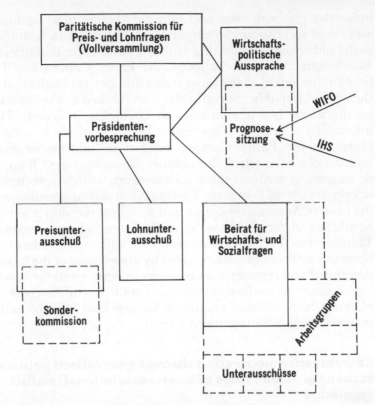

FIGURE 4.1   *Basic structure of the 'Paritätische Kommission für Preis- und Lohnfragen'*

term planning based on scientific information. The *Wirtschafts-politische Aussprache* serves as a forum for discussion of planned government measures and of actions to be taken by the Federal Reserve Bank in conjunction with other macroeconomic political actors, or as a plenum for short-term crisis management and adaptive measures (for instance, immediate exchange-rate changes). The *Vollversammlung* generally accepts decisions taken by the 'big two' in the *Präsidentenvorbesprechung*.

Since the everyday functioning and the nerves of this associational government ('*Nebenregierung*') cannot be explained in summary, three fundamental features will be mentioned here. First, the Parity Commission could not work as an isolated body but bases its internal exchanges on comprehensive co-operation in related fields and with other institutions, ranging from industrial, regional, fiscal and monetary bodies to agricultural and social security funds; labour market agencies to labour or cartel jurisdictions, operating with the participation of interest associations. Secondly, although the Parity Commission has become the kernel of the most stable and central institution of the Second Republic, not only was it established as a temporary arrangement, but it continues to be highly informal. This informality is present to an extent hardly credible to outside observers: the Parity Commission has no address or fixed meeting place, no telephone number, no independent finance, no statutes, procedural rules, membership, written agreements or even registered existence. This *institution without organisation* at the head of Austrian economic and social partnership is a most significant element of the overall system of co-operation. Thirdly, the Parity Commission, as with most other co-operative institutions, was initiated by associations of the labour movement and represents a compromise between its far-reaching attempts to institutionalise an overall system of economic planning and business resistance to any kind of substantial power-sharing with organised labour.

Antagonistic co-operation through generalised political exchanges – some rules of inter-associational conflict regulation

A barely conspicuous yet very important norm regulating inter-associational exchanges has already been referred to in relation to the informality of the Parity Commission: the *unwritten rule of not writing down rules of co-operation*, of keeping them ambiguous and revocable. This informality, voluntariness, institutional ambiguity and the existence of a 'pyramid of institutionalisation' lead to the peculiar, distinctly 'non-bureaucratic' character of inter-associational co-operation which we will call indeterminacy.

Indeterminacy

Without the concept of indeterminacy, it would not be possible to explain properly the co-operative capacity of corporatist systems such as that of Austria. It helps us to understand, for instance, how a purely informal and voluntary institution without any sanctioning powers is capable of imposing obligations on its constituent organisations and, even more, *their* membership/constituencies; how price controls can be exercised without formal sanctions, or how sanctions can be imposed without autonomous sanctioning potential (Marin, 1982a, pp. 87–120); or how interest associations conform to agreements without formal treaties, how 'social contracts' are adhered to without formal agreements.

Indeterminacy is necessary to create the *political credits* indispensable in long chains and complex networks of generalised political exchanges; formalised power could not be saved and accumulated power could not therefore produce such credits. Leaving aside all theoretical explanations of the relationship between inter-associational interest intermediation and the necessary political money created through *deconstitutionalisation/deformalisation of political power*, the outcome is very clear in a comparative perspective: conflict regulation between adversary interest associations will be more stable the more it is simultaneously *underdetermined formally but overdetermined informally*. Indeterminacy is able to create more mutual trust and binding obligations than formal coercive norms or written contracts, pacts or treaties would ever be able to generate between collective political actors.

Indeterminacy has at least four different dimensions, which will be discussed briefly:

1. *Voluntariness* of co-operation: any single participant organisation can withdraw from co-operation (or specific principles or activities) at any point in time. This option to quit is the ultimate sanction or threat of adversary associations against each other if all chances of compromise through log-rolling, etc. have disappeared. Paradoxically, so much voluntariness itself creates a necessity to co-operate, if exit is – or can be made – more costly than unwilling consensus. The longer co-operation exists, the more costly becomes any attempt at exit in terms of advantages missed – not to mention being seen as a mischief-maker by public opinion. Every participant must be able to smash doors, if necessary, to save face, knowing full well that he has to come back through another door tomorrow or the day after tomorrow. Formal freedom to co-operate or not can become a far more compelling force to continue than any formal sanction: it works by strong and morally obliging credits of trust, organisational images of reliability and faithfulness, personal-

ised transactions, by illusions of reversibility of concessions and thereby increased willingness to make them, etc. The growing stock of mutual obligations, trust and reciprocal utilities of antagonistic partners reduces the uncertainty inherent in any transaction between adversary organisations and commits them to legal co-operation to an extent legal coercion never could.

2. *Informality* of co-operation was not the original intention but, ironically, was imposed on the associations by constitutional objections against the original, legalised and formalised body (*Wirtschaftsdirektorium der Bundesregierung*). The genesis of this informality could be described as a, finally successful, search by interest associations to organise their co-operation – against the resistance of legal purists – outside constitutional competences, but in a way that was legally unassailable. Any attempt at legal formalisation (*Verrechtlichung*) has been strongly resisted as an attack on the very foundations of 'social partnership'.

3. *Institutional ambiguity* of co-operative arrangements arises from little or no formalisation and the high interdependence of structures. The cumulation of positions by functionaries, multifunctionality of roles, delegation and redefinition of competences, constant shifting of boundaries and other practices are an inexhaustible source of institutional defence-mechanisms and environmental control, not forgetting the importance of attributed public images. These ambiguities were not produced deliberately, but were skilfully used, once they had come about. They permit the drawing of boundaries and responsibilities just where they are needed at particular times: it is, for example, at the discretion of the president of the ÖGB whether a public statement should be attributed to him in this function, or as a high-ranking party official, or as president of the parliament, or whatever. With such autonomous powers of definition, problems of legitimacy scarcely arise, except with regard to this institutional ambiguity itself!

4. Indeterminacy at the top functions because it is based on a partly statutory, highly formalised institutional infrastructure at the bottom: risky transactions of associational leaders operating without explicit norms and written contracts are backed by sureties on other levels of inter-organisational exchange and intra-organisational compliance. This *pyramid of institutionalisation* prevents the disintegration of labour relations and any 'top heaviness' of co-operative arrangements by combining a solid

institutional base of formalised infrastructure with a most flexible and adaptive superstructure. Top heavy systems of industrial relations are prone to collapse: could the British tripartite National Economic Development Council, the industrial EDCs or industrial training boards function smoothly on top of a highly unpredictable and fragmented system of collective bargaining? Did not the centralised wage policy in the Netherlands eventually break down because of all too rigid over-formalisation at the top?

Double parity

Parity means simply a strictly equal composition of all economic policy decision-making bodies according to the delegation of their members by interest organisations of capital and labour. In as much as functional/class representation overlaps with the political representation of conservatives and socialists, one has double parity. Those who cannot be fitted into the interests encompassed by the traditional political code – for example, socialist entrepreneurs or farmers, conservative workers, radical consumerists or ecologists – are out of the game and the power-sharing of producer interests (Marin, 1982a, pp. 36–43). Parity is used to regulate inter-associational intermediation, as neither majority rule nor proportional arrangements would facilitate decisions about who should be allowed to take part in the game. The idea behind parity is institutionally to bind together structurally antagonistic but interdependent interests and to force them to co-operate along some common lines.

The principle of parity is contrary to any form of pluralism with which it is often confused (Marin, 1982a, pp. 43–46). Its most important effect is an equilibration of power potentials by strengthening the originally weaker side, that is institutionally compensating for structural disadvantages of organised labour in a capitalist market economy; consequently it had to be enforced on employers' associations. The most recent area of conflict over co-operation concerns the controversial domain of parity: should the principle remain restricted to the national or supra-plant level of co-determination (*überbetriebliche Mitbestimmung*), as organised capital insists, or will it be extended to the firm level (*paritätische Mitbestimmung im Betrieb*), as organised labour has to ask for in the next step towards programmatic economic democracy (*Wirtschaftsdemokratie*).

Theoretical interpolation: antagonistic co-operation and class conflict

This ongoing struggle over the terms of co-operation indicates the structural limits of co-operation in a capitalist society: although the rules of the game of antagonistic co-operation such as parity have to be agreed upon, even these rules cannot be established and developed by co-operation alone. Conflict-regulating devices like parity can channel and transform, but never remove or permanently 'freeze' the class conflicts underlying these institutional arrangements.

Antagonistic co-operation, therefore, is no counter-principle to class conflict, but transforms class struggle into a permanent war of position between associations in which they seek to gain organisational advantages over adversaries within the institutional system. Parity (or other rules of the game) between the antagonists and the very scope of their application are subject to conflict – and compromise. Under the general norm of parity, class conflict is transformed into a struggle over whose concept of the scope of the principle should previal. WSP does not simply 'institutionalise' class struggle but transforms class conflicts into conflicts over the rules of the game of antagonistic co-operation.

But conflict over co-operation that is a genuine class conflict and power struggle remains an exception, while smooth co-operation and limited distributional conflicts are the prevalent daily routine. Rules like parity provide for a certain equilibrium of class forces which makes all-out class warfare for both sides 'unwinnable' anyway. A 'realistic' appraisal of this situation consequently leads to an extension of co-operation and the minimisation of conflict over principles of co-operation, thereby generating an ever increasing propensity to compromise and self-reinforcing co-operation; a co-operation which, nevertheless, remains structurally antagonistic and conflictual in itself.

Concordance

In regulating political exchange between highly interdependent antagonists through co-operative interest intermediation, concordance is of central importance. Concordance or unanimity means mutual veto power of all participants over almost all decisions in economic and social policy-making: no decision can be taken unless it is acceptable to *all* major interest associations; any single giant organisation can block co-operative action. How is it, then, that overall stalemate and immobility do not arise?

Paradoxically, concordance facilitates co-operation by impeding it: by raising the costs of conflict *and* consensus formation, unanimity creates a strong obligation on the part of all participating associations to compromise, and strengthens any compromise once obtained. By making it easier to prevent compromises, the principle of mutual veto actually prevents participants from using it too readily. It creates strong motivations based on rational self-interest among the participants to reach consensus as long as the costs of conflict and of non-decisions are even higher than those of unwilling consensus. How this is done cannot be described in detail, but the systemic consequences of concordance are quite obvious: it ensures a minimal substantial consensus and protects the weaker side against being dominated; it makes an organisation's own decisions self-binding and *post hoc* resistance against compromises obtained morally and practically impossible; it does not allow any government to take measures against the common will of associations or to ignore their policy proposals; it spills over to other sub-systems such as parliamentarianism, making unanimous economic policy-making a rule also in areas where it is clearly not a binding rule, etc. Only to the extent that it inflicts costs on any association which by its veto inflicts external costs on all the others, will the principle of concordance be applied in such a way as to make the rationality of single organisations and collective systems rationality less divergent than they evidently are in less complex and interdependent liberal pluralist systems of 'bargaining'.

The 'philosophy' and precarious legitimacy of liberal corporatist co-operation

Economising politics

Associational co-operation is based on a latent guideline which is that of organising the (capitalist) economic system's rationality into politics. Economising politics makes (re)organising the national economy and its permanent technological upgrading a common political priority; it establishes orientations on international competitiveness, productivity and economic growth as dominant standards of social rationality and political success; it thereby institutionalises economic performance of the national economy in world markets as a primary societal/ political project and sets up its cultural hegemony over other political goals. This primacy of economic development not only makes economism/productivism a dominant integrating and latent ideological force of politics, but it also fundamentally changes the basic rules of the political game.

With macroeconomic output as the primary frame of reference, the national economy is reorganised by capital *and* organised labour according to capitalist *and* post-capitalist standards at the same time. Business profitability is used as the main yardstick for assessing success, but is occasionally subordinated to macroeconomic goals such as maintaining high levels of employment – not only in the public sector, but temporarily even in private business (Nowotny, 1979). Yet such deviations from market forces are restricted to selected interventions, limited episodes or to specific sub-sectors of the economy: political powers try in the long run not to ignore the 'silent force of economic laws' as prerequisites of prosperity. Economising politics, then, means a primacy of macroeconomic standards within politics and no predominance of political and particularistic (sectoral, regional, local, professional, status group, 'syndicalist' etc.) interests over system necessities (*'Sachzwänge'*). Austrian WSP is macroeconomic, that is to say, global and solidaristic, not selective and sectoral in orientation.

Consequently, the concerted strategy of structural adaptation works to the extent that it can neutralise the dissatisfaction of groups negatively affected, by socialising their elementary risks; and to the extent that redistributive demands can be neutralised by overall comparative economic advantages. The productivity alliance of organised labour and capital, therefore, focuses on a kind of 'supply-side politics' at national level: it favours national over particularistic or universal, productive over distributive, producer over consumer, industrial export interests over those of protected sectors, etc. Similarly, it implies a clear hierarchy of policies (with economic, fiscal, monetary, industrial, capital and labour market and social policies ranking top); a clear hierarchy of goals (with a priority of increasing growth under conditions of highest possible employment, stable prices, hard currency, constant distribution of functional incomes); and it reorganises other, 'residual' policies (health, regional, urban, educational policy, etc.) as much as possible according to standards of economic rationality and their functional contribution to modernising the national economy. Finally, the political pre-eminence of economic growth makes for a predominance of its most powerful executives that is, a functional primacy of functional interest associations over political parties, of 'economic and social partnership' over parliamentarianism and government, a guiding role for corporatist politics and its collective actors – to the extent that productivism remains a societal priority.

Ideological underdetermination

Co-operative conflict regulation presupposes adverse interests and opposing ideologies. The essence of the 'basic consensus' can be reduced to macroeconomic, pragmatic and utilitarian orientations, procedural forms, and an agreement to disagree ideologically. It has nothing to do with de-ideologisation or an 'end of ideology', nor does it allow an explicit common ideology of 'corporatist' co-operation. Antagonistic co-operation, on the contrary, needs to be compatible with incompatible, even contradictory, ideological interpretations at the same time: it has to be ideologically underdetermined. In the Austrian case, the very same praxis of co-operation is *simultaneously* interpreted as a 'counter-principle' to, and as an 'overcoming of', class struggle by business representatives, and as a 'sublimated' form of 'class struggle at the green table' by organised labour (Marin, 1982a, p. 361). 'Social partnership' allows for an ideological coexistence of interpretations as different as the Austro-Marxist conception of "functional democracy' or traditional Catholic social doctrines of the Vogelsang type or solidarism – and even wider divergences than that.

Two qualifications with regard to ideological underdetermination seem to be necessary. While continuous partisanship helps to reproduce intra-organisational cohesion and membership identification – indispensable for making compromises obtained obligatory for the respective rank and file – it has to remain somewhat restrained in order not to undermine co-operation by serious ideological warfare: inter-associational conflict regulation depends on an intermediate level of partisan ideologisation. In the Austrian case, this is sustained by a traditional split between ideological rhetoric and everyday pragmatism: 'Marx for Sundays and Keynes for working days', as the Social Democrats pointedly term this double talk on the Left.

Secondly, there are asymmetries between organised labour and capital in terms of the propensity to co-operate, which work in an opposite direction the propensity to ideologise co-operation. While it has almost always been labour organisations that have initiated and pressed for extended co-operation, they are reluctant to make an ideology of 'partnership' and see co-operation just as one more step towards *Wirtschaftsdemokratie*. The opposite holds for business: it usually resists institutionalised participation of labour in macroeconomic decision-making, but quickly insists on a normative codification of the status quo, once it is apparent that extended co-operation cannot be prevented. Organised labour benefited more than the business class from extending co-operation in terms of additional power, but it is more vulnerable to any ideologisation of co-operation, given its goal of redistributing power and resources in society. Organised business celebrates 'partnership', but resents paying the political price of power-sharing; organised labour hesitates to talk much about what it does, in ideological terms.

Overall legitimacy

'Economic and social partnership' has overwhelming support among the Austrian population: for decades, all opinion polls indicate little specific understanding but strong support for institutionalised co-operation between employers and labour organisations and government. WSP is taken to be more important and held in higher esteem than parliament; and even the overall economic system is considered to be a special case: 35 per cent of the populace (and those most satisfied) speak of a 'social partnership economy', 27 per cent of a 'socialist economy', 22 per cent of a 'market economy', 8 per cent of a 'planned economy' and only 5 per cent of a 'capitalist economy'. Although there is clearly some mental confusion and 'false consciousness', the results are quite revealing!

As far as popular support is concerned, two aspects are worth mentioning. First, there is a strong technocratic element in WSP legitimacy: 'experts' have an even higher reputation than the co-operative institution itself (Marin, 1982a, p. 283), complementing the plebiscitarian legitimation through elected leadership. Secondly, confidence in the system is generally even higher among the rank and file and works councillors than in the upper echelons, and lower social classes are even more satisfied than objectively more privileged strata. Strike patterns during the last decade confirm this trend: strikers were rarely workers, but a disproportionate number of self-employed, liberal professionals (physicians), farmers or privileged public employees (professors) etc., defending status advantages against attempts at solidaristic collective discipline. Among young Marxists of the socialist youth movement, belonging to the segments most critical of any co-operation between labour and capital, a majority of young workers or members of working-class origin considered WSP 'favourable to workers', whereas a majority of students or youngsters of bourgeois origin questioned its benefits for workers.

Criticism of WSP in general comes neither from below nor from the top but from middle levels, at the margins of the system. In terms of social structure, criticism comes from the middle class: businessmen, in particular the traditional, old middle classes, professions and farmers are more critical than the 'new', employed middle classes. In terms of ideology, criticism comes either from the traditional liberals or from Marxists or radical anti-institutionalists. In terms of politics, consequently, criticism is confined to those marginal actors who are out of the WSP-game: the national-liberal and the Communist party, corresponding right-wing conservatives and left-wing socialists and followers of the new populist movements are among the most fundamental opponents of WSP. Factions underrepresented (like Christian trade unionists) or 'outsiders' (like free-floating intellectuals, academics, journalists, etc.) are typically ambivalent. The main criticism concerns problems of democratic legitimation, and is directed against supposedly too much centralisation and overregulation. Although WSP has had very little support up to now outside the milieus mentioned above, it might well grow in the future together with the spread of diffuse but strong anti-institutionalist resentments, directed against the state and also associational (chamber) bureaucracies.

Nevertheless, the overwhelming popular support for WSP is based on a general confidence in it, the dynamics of which are difficult to understand and have been dealt with more thoroughly elsewhere (Marin, 1982a, pp. 66–70; Marin, 1981b, pp. 54ff; Marin, 1981 c, pp. 46–52; Suppanz and Robinson, 1972, pp. 46–57). The logic behind it is this: whereas comparatively superior national economic performance definitely helps to generate political legitimacy, it is not essential, as long as there is an effective capacity for symbolic control of public attribution of success, the appropriation of which is most skilfully managed by the 'economic partners'. Their superior powers of public definition allow them symbolically to appropriate whatever is experienced as a benefit or advantage of co-operation, and to externalise what people experience as shortcomings, deficiencies, burdens, strains, insecurities, conflicts, threats, disappointments, by attributing them to international factors, the government, political parties, etc. The economic partners create extensive political credits of generalised trust, loyalty and legitimacy by spreading the conviction that by and large there are no losers from corporatist co-operation, only winners.

Forgotten main prerequisites: the political economy and class base of organised mixed capitalism

Conventional corporatism is institutionalist in that it tries to explain almost everything by variations in organisational factors and institutional arrangements. The Austrian case, supposedly paradigmatic, falsifies this premise: with almost the same basic 'corporatist' institutions leading to divergent outcomes in different historical periods, non-institutional factors have to be taken into account.

Generally speaking, the viability of corporatist arrangements depends in the long run on two kinds of non-institutional prerequisites which have to 'fit' corporatist institutions:
1. Economic/social structures (such as the political economy, class base, power balance, etc.) have to fit political institutions.
2. Economic policies/programmes have to fit politics.

Both kinds of 'fit' will be briefly illustrated in relation to the Austrian case. This does not imply, of course, that this or similar forms of a political economy are preconditions for viable corporatist institutions. For example, the Scandinavian countries and Switzerland have developed functionally equivalent but different institutions to fit quite different social structures (Katzenstein, 1984). What counts is the 'fit' and not any specific social fabric, although the range of compatibilities with corporatist institutions is far from being unlimited.

Mixed capitalism and the balance of class forces

In order to understand how the institutional system outlined is possible at all, its correspondence to underlying socio-economic structures cannot be overlooked. This is most evident in contrast to an analogous 'misfit' in the First Republic, where a more unbalanced distribution of power did not allow the antagonists to co-operate within corporatist institutions.

Today, there is a *coexistence of 'family', transnational and 'state capitalism'* which can be called *'mixed capitalism'*. Each segment produces about one-third of total economic output, through rather different structures. Whereas the overwhelming majority of firms, mostly small-scale or medium-sized, are privately owned and under family control, a few large, publicly owned companies employ about one-quarter of the Austrian labour force and generate about one-third of net production and almost half of all investment. They are concentrated in strategic sectors such as banking, insurance, energy production, transport, telecommunications, large-scale industries, etc. According to La Comité Européen des Enterprises Publiques (CEEP) (Brussels, 1984), a weighted average of employment, production and investment of the public and co-operative economy is between 16 per cent and 21 per cent in Western Europe, but 25–32 per cent in Austria, higher than anywhere else (France after the 1982 nationalisations being 24–29 per cent; Italy, 20–26 per cent). Such an important share of the national economy allows for a certain political control of the central means of production (especially with regard to investment/ employment policies and management positions) and for industrial policies which steer a more flexible and adaptive private sector. But even more important with respect to the viability of corporatist co-operation is an equilibration of power potentials which could be called 'a balance of class forces'.

This 'balance of class forces' which the Austro-Marxist Otto Bauer erroneously diagnosed in 1923 as already in place in the First Republic (Bauer, 1965, pp. 228 and 257ff) is an expression of the 'historical compromise' on which current liberal cor- poratism is based. Contemporary 'organised mixed capitalism' in Austria encompasses the following features: the absence of a powerful rentier class and of a financial and strong industrial bourgeoisie, due to the nationalisation of strategic sectors after the Second World War; a limited political control of the business class through intermediary self-governance; a certain differentiation of upper classes ('the rich') and a political *and* economic 'ruling class' which consists of a new managerial class and a new class of '*technobureaucracy*' generated by corporatist institutions (Marin, 1982a, pp. 265ff). Both strata, without owning the means of production, control economic develop- ment and direct a national inter-class productivity alliance of organised capital and labour, with common perspectives, expertise and vested status interests in extending co-operation. All these equilibrating elements of a solid class base were lacking during the First Republic, where a continuous and accelerating power shift from one 'camp' to the other (as well as an excessive diffusion of power of all collective actors and an increasing incongruence between economic and political power) led to such imbalances of forces that all attempts at co-operation were destroyed despite appropriate institutions (Marin and Traxler, 1984, p. 9ff).

But corporatist institutions do not only need compatible social structures but also adequate economic programmes in order to allow for co-operation between antagonistic but interdependent interests. Economic policies are steering elements of the political economy such as the distribution of property rights and power relations are conditioning ones. A more recent and very unconventional economic policy approach in Austria, fitting WSP, is 'Austro-Keynesianism'.

'Austro-Keynesianism'

Economic policies do not just aim at realising economic goals, but also define the position of interest associations of capital and labour within the political economy and determine the con- troversiality/compatibility of antagonistic but interdependent interests. *Laissez-faire* policies (as practised in Austria during the First Republic) do not allow for any public function or participation in decision-making by unions *and* business organisations. They intensify inherent conflict potentials between market adversaries, turning all decisions into zero-sum games. The opposite is the case with 'Austro-Keynesianism', the economic policy-mix pursued by WSP, which puts interest associations in a key position instead of marginalising them; for example, 'hard currency' exchange-rate policy had to be accompanied (and is used) by an incomes policy, administered largely by trade unions and employers' associations.

'Austro-Keynesianism' is quite an unorthodox, peculiar mixture of traditional Keynesian demand management, hard currency policy, voluntary incomes policy and a wide variety of supply-side measures used to channel public expenditures into productive investment; fiscal, exchange-rate or monetary policies are chosen accordingly, e.g. to keep real interest rates lower for domestic investment. According to orthodox textbook economics, 'this policy-mix cannot work, this country simply cannot exist'; in reality, it did and does. Although it was the comparative economic success of the 'Austro-Keynesian' strategy of crisis management in the 1970s that made people reflect on what had actually been achieved, the success might well have been accidental. What counts more than comparative success is that success has been *possible* through unconventional search, experiments, trial and error, all bound together by a strong, coherent political will (to maintain full employment at any price). It is not superior goal attainment that distinguishes 'Austro-Keynesianism', but the fact that it makes any attainment of economic goals structurally dependent on associational participation, as well as on co-operation and co-ordination between all economic policy actors including the Federal Reserve Bank. This stresses the interdependence and communality of antagonistic interests and the transformation of adversarial into partially congruent interests, which is at the core of co-operative labour relations.

Outlook

This is not the place to speculate extensively about the possible future of the Austrian co-operative system of interest intermediation. There are many plausible arguments to be put forward in favour of the expectation of a viable, self-sustaining and sufficiently equilibrated system, the fundamental organising principles of which are stable and basically irreversible. But this does not imply that there are currently no inherent tensions and contradictions or even limits to co-operation under different circumstances in the future: the possibility and stability of corporatist arrangements cannot be decided *a priori* (except on purely ideological grounds) but rather it is a question open to political praxis and empirical investigation. Inherently, corporatist co-operation is neither self-maintaining nor self-negating, neither stable nor unstable; contradictions may turn out to be manageable, or lead to institutional decay if challenges are not met. Whether challenges will be met in the future, no one can say; what can be said is that it is possible to predict future challenges. Some of these hitherto latent problems are already becoming visible; here they are simply listed, not analysed.

First, there is an *essential tension between selective-protectionist,* (sectoral, regional) *and global* (concerted, solidaristic) *corporatism.* This tension arises mainly *within* the 'productivity alliance', but even more within organised labour, between workers of different branches, companies, levels of qualification, etc. These tensions increase, of course, with the length of the economic crisis and restructuring period (Marin and Wagner, 1979), but they should not short-sightedly be stylised as secular trends (towards a 'sectoralisation of interests', substituting for class differentiation). Nevertheless, particularistic interests threaten ever more concerted interest intermediation at national level, the more a growing differentiation of interests is not checked by countervailing centripetal tendencies, leading to a power shift to sectoral, regional, etc. sub-elites (Andrlik, 1984). Selective protectionism would lead to increasing social rigidities, segmentation and inequalities, and to decreasing productivity and economic effectiveness, that is, it would erode WSP.

Secondly, there is a rise of new status groups, collective identities, social movements, issues, etc. outside established institutions which can be termed *new populism* (Marin, 1980). The rather complex dialectics between new corporatism and new populism set up an increasing confrontation between the block of producer interests and these non-institutional forces (such as the ecological movement, the peace movement, consumers, mass media, marginalised segments); a shift of problems and conflict potentials from the inter-associational to other arenas; and a decreasing salience of economic growth and class cleavages and therefore a decreasing capacity of WSP to guarantee societal priorities such as prosperity, social peace, political stability, governability, etc. WSP will not be outlived by these new developments, but it will probably lose its hegemonic position. This *loss of hegemony* will unwillingly be reinforced by confrontations with the new populism, due to an ever-increasing political domain and the nature of claims made by the corporatist block, inhibiting the further growth on functional specialisation on the part of organised interests.

Thirdly, there are other tendencies towards *self-limiting evolution*, such as a loss of functions through goal attainment and goal displacement, and other well known costs of success. The current balance between adaptive/innovative and institutional sclerotic tendencies is difficult to assess. But a slow, undramatic decay and creeping decline of WSP is conceivable if it does not renew itself through self-transformation in order to meet the new challenges that are already apparent; or through linking itself to new visions and political projects such as 'economic and industrial democracy'. Both outcomes are not easily anticipated, as they would require a new system of overall co-operation.

Chapter 5

Corporatism and Local Politics

Alan Cawson

Introduction

So far the theoretical discussion of corporatism and the main body of empirical work have concentrated on the macro, or central, level of the political process. Corporatism has been identified in different ways, but whether as a new form of political economy or as a system of interest intermediation, the characteristic association of the term is with whole systems. The relevant interest organisations, whose interaction with state agencies forms the core of corporatist analysis, have most frequently been identified as the 'peak' organisations of capital and labour. Where such organisations bargain over investment and planning strategies, over incomes policies and price controls, and accept some responsibility for ensuring their membership's compliance with consensually negotiated policies, it is appropriate to speak of a 'macro-level corporatism' which takes a tripartite form involving class-based interests arising from the functional division of labour.

But as Grant has shown in Chapter 1 of this volume, this field of reference by no means exhausts the usefulness of corporatist analysis for the study of capitalist democracies. In many cases, even in countries such as Britain where macro-corporatism has developed only weakly and fitfully, there is much to be gained from analysing the interdependent bargaining process between the state and monopolistic interest organisations in specific sectors or policy fields. In examples such as milk production (Grant, 1983a) and health policy (Cawson, 1982; Mercer, 1984), a corporatist framework can clarify the interrelationships between the state and producer interests, free of the pluralist assumption that public policy is a response to the competitive play of interest-group pressures. Indeed, the merit of the corporatist approach is that it highlights the issue of the extent to which the form and nature of organised producer interests is affected by the activities of the state.

In such cases the policy agenda comprises a more limited set of sectorally defined issues than are present in macro-corporatist structures, and there is no necessity for a tripartite form involving organisations of capital and labour. What is required is an interest organisation which aggregates the interests of a defined membership, and which has achieved monopoly status and had this status recognised by the state. The National Farmers Union and the British Medical Association are both examples of such organisations: they are in this sense *structurally privileged* organisations, and differ in kind from the voluntary, competitive and private interest associations best studied within a pluralist framework. In Offe's (1981) terms, they are examples of organisations that have achieved a 'public status' which confers duties (in terms of ensuring policy implementation) as well as rights (to privileged access in policy formation).

Meso-corporatism differs from macro-corporatism in that the constituent interest organisations are not peak organisations (i.e. organisations of organisations), and the objectives of policy do not concern issues such as economic planning or incomes policy which cut across vertical (sectoral) divisions. But meso-corporatist practices involve that fusion of the processes of interest representation (input) and policy implementation (output) that is characteristic of corporatism and different from pluralism. In both types of corporatist process the distinction between 'public' and 'private' is difficult to make, to the extent that state prerogatives and powers are to some extent 'parcelled out' to nominally private bodies, and the latters' autonomy is to some extent constrained by their participation in corporatist arrangements.

In a unitary state such as Britain, the level of the state involved in both macro- and meso-corporatism is the central level; in federal systems such as Canada and West Germany provincial levels are frequently the locus of meso-corporatism. There has, understandably, been very little discussion so far about corporatism at the level of local governments, and one of the objectives of this chapter is an attempt to remedy this neglect. It does not simply extend the corporatist net, so to speak, by examining possible traces of it at the local level, but seeks to establish the local within a more general theory of interest politics and state intervention. For a number of reasons that will be explained below, corporatism is unlikely to become as significant at the local level as elsewhere, and non-corporatist modes of analysis will be necessary for looking at local political economies. But shifts in the mode of state intervention, partly in response to the economic crisis of recent years, have led to more locally based attempts to influence the behaviour of local economies which involve a search for interest organisations that might become corporatist partners in policy-making.

This chapter seeks to explore the significance of corporatist analysis at the local level in Britain, first by showing where a corporatist framework is irrelevant or misplaced, and then by examining those areas of local policy-making where explanations couched in orthodox terms seem to have little purchase. It concludes by suggesting areas where future research may be necessary to substantiate some of the hypotheses suggested by a corporatist approach.

The neglect of local corporatism

One of the reasons for the neglect of locality in the literature on corporatism in liberal democracies is the excessive attention paid to the constituent interest organisations, and the relative absence of studies of the organisation and activities of the state. By stressing the importance of class interests and role in the division of labour, corporatist theory has provided a more persuasive analysis of interest politics than was hitherto available. But since corporatism does not exist in the absence of state agencies that are willing to bargain over public policies, it is perhaps surprising that the internal politics of the state system has been so little studied (see Cawson, forthcoming, for an extended discussion of this).

In terms of interests it is true that it is the emphasis on function rather than territory that distinguishes corporatism, but if the 'state question' is firmly raised, then the issue of the distinct levels of state activity, and in particular the sub-central level, assumes importance. This is particularly the case if we recognise that interest organisations of professionals (Gilb, 1966) and of state employees (Dunleavy, 1980) are vital parts of the corporatist policy network where decisions about state spending are concerned. Associations of functional interests are hardly likely to 'peak' at the local level, but local state agencies may seek to intervene in local economies in a way that involves negotiation with local Chambers of Commerce or trade union branches. An examination of the structural characteristics of the local state, and particularly the question of local democratic institutions, will help us to evaluate the prospects for the development of local corporatism.

In one of the few contributions to the corporatist literature to date which concentrates exclusively on the local level, Hernes and Selvik (1981) adopt this approach by pointing out that the interventionist economic goals of the modern state are also relevant at this level. Writing about the Scandinavian countries, and Norway in particular, they describe the role that municipalities have increasingly adopted towards economic growth and employment maintenance which has brought them into more and more frequent contact with the representatives of economic corporate groups. The extension of public authority concerned with economic development led to a reaction among firms in which their organisational capacity to exert influence at the local level was increased (Hernes and Selvik, 1981, p. 113). Institutional responses have included the establishment of 'industrial advisory boards' and 'industrial councils' funded by parliament. Contrary to the pluralist model, interest organisation at this level *followed* rather than led to state initiatives.

In a strikingly similar development in Britain, Flynn (1983) has described the formation of 'industrial liaison groups' at the county council level in which local firms are able to discuss planning issues relevant to their corporate interests, and through which county planners seek to influence their behaviour. Such bodies are seen as advantageous both to local authorities and to local industrialists, and arise because of the lack of direct representation, particularly of large firms, in local councils dominated by professional and small business interests.

Both Flynn and Hernes and Selvik raise the question of whether a new form of 'municipal corporatism' is emerging, although they are justifiably cautious about giving an affirmative answer. Flynn considers his evidence to show 'an organisational strategy on the part of the state and a variant of interest group politics' (1983, p. 104). Hernes and Selvik describe their evidence of increased co-operation between urban governments and economic-corporate groups as having 'largely the character of *ad hoc* reactions to market conditions producing temporary coalitions for political action', but they believe that the *aggregate* of such actions is increasing and that this 'should be considered a definite corporatist trend emanating from local communities' (1981, p. 111).

Such prototypical local corporatist arrangements may indeed be part of a trend, but neither Flynn nor Hernes and Selvik have provided evidence that the real content of public policy decisions has been changed, and there may well be more elements of symbolic or 'simulated' (Bauman, 1982) politics than actual shifts in practice. Much specificity in the concept of corporatism would be lost if we were to identify *any* kind of relationship between the local state and economic groups as 'corporatist', although it may be highly significant empirically to know that the composition of actors in competitive interest group politics at the local level is changing, and that business as an organised force is becoming more involved in local politics. Future research will have to take into account the relative significance of corporatist and non-corporatist networks in policy formation: that is, it will have to concentrate on the relationships of power-dependence between actors rather than on the descriptive characteristics of the actors themselves.

We must be careful not to presuppose that all forms of local economic intervention are corporatist. In the following section I shall distinguish at a theoretical level different forms of intervention, and following that I shall show how these can be embodied in radically different kinds of economic strategies.

Representation and intervention

Elsewhere (Cawson, 1982, especially Chapter 5) I have attempted to differentiate corporatism from alternative modes of interest politics and state intervention. This is a particularly important task if we are to establish the relative significance of corporatist practices, especially in polities such as Britain and the United States where macro-corporatist institutions are largely absent, and corporatist coalitions often *ad hoc* and temporary.

First, corporatism at the local level should not be confused with managerialism and in particular with corporate management. Many local authorities in Britain in the 1970s reorganised their committee structures in an attempt to overcome the policy fragmentation that was believed to result from the traditional departmental structure. In this context 'corporate management' refers to the ideology, and to some extent the administrative practice, which sees the local authority as a single corporate body that can be more rationally integrated through a holistic and synoptic approach to policy-making. Neither the theory nor the practice of corporate management necessarily involves the incorporation of interest groups into the making or implementation of policy. Lebas (1983, p. 9) refers to Cockburn's (1977) description of the system of corporate management in Lambeth as one of 'administrative corporatism' – a highly misleading description of Cockburn's thesis which attempts to link the internal organisation of the state to the social control of subordinate classes in the interests of capital.

Likewise Byrne, drawing on Panitch (1979), argues that reformist labourism in Gateshead has led to the emergence of a 'corporatist state form' involving the 'replacement of direct instrumental control exercised through bourgeois politicians by a corporate, managerial system of administration operating in the interests of capitalism' (1982, p. 67). He argues that the labour movement, comprising the Labour Party and the trade unions, can be viewed as an organised socio-economic group and that corporate management in local government

> is essentially the imposition of co-optive mechanisms for a political leadership on to a formally democratic structure. The congruence of 'corporatism' and 'corporate management' is proper politics as well as etymology. (Byrne, 1982, p. 67, note 3)

Without wishing here to contest the empirical adequacy of these accounts of the effects of corporate management on working-class subordination, I do want to contest the alleged identity between these processes and those that have elsewhere been described as 'corporatist'. The relationship between the forms of state organisation and the processes of interest intermediation is an important theoretical question that is at the heart of the debate about corporatism, but good etymology does not necessarily make good theory! Neither Cockburn nor Byrne reports evidence of a reciprocal relationship between interest organisations and state agencies; their cases refer to forms of class domination through the instrument of bureaucracy coupled to the parliamentary form in which representative groups are co-opted, rather than play a quasi-autonomous role in policy formation and implementation.

Second, and following from this, corporatism is not co-option in the sense in which Dearlove (1975) refers to the process whereby community groups at the local level are absorbed and rendered impotent by local authorities. Indeed, the co-option of certain groups may coexist with the development of corporatist (reciprocal) relationships with others: protest groups such as squatters may be co-opted by a local authority which at the same time devolves certain housing management functions to tenants' committees on housing estates. The latter is a rare example of corporation in consumption processes at the local level; it is possible because in the case of council estate tenants, function and territory coincide within a single interest organisation.

Third, we should be careful to distinguish corporatism from examples of government by contract, which have been extensively discussed, particularly in the American context (Lowi, 1969; Hague, Mackenzie and Barker, 1975) and which at the present time in Britain can be associated with the shift to privatisation, for example in refuse disposal and hospital laundry services. Where public functions are performed by private bodies, albeit under close public regulation, we should be alert for the possibility of interest intermediation (Harrison, 1984). But the test here, as elsewhere, should be whether delegated implementation is accompanied by a real influence over the determination of policy such that the two processes are empirically inseparable.

This concept is what is identified as 'corporatism' in this chapter. There is no presumption that it involves only organisations representing the interests of capital and labour, or that it is restricted to the national level. (See Von Beyme, 1983, for the contrary view that corporatism involves *at least* three partners.) Tripartism is, of course, an important version of corporatism, and in *polities* labelled 'corporatist' there would invariably be an important element of national-level tripartism in the determination of macroeconomic policies.

Corporatism, bureaucracy and the market

Many writers on corporatism have observed that, increasingly, capitalist societies have taken on a dual character whereby pluralist politics and parliamentary forms coexist with corporatist politics and functional representation (Rokkan, 1966; Kvavik, 1976; Eliassen, 1981; Helander, 1982): in Rokkan's celebrated phrase, 'votes count but resources decide'. In recent works Peter Saunders and I have tried to specify more precisely, in ideal typical terms, the relationship of competitive democratic and concertative corporatist political processes to the levels and functions of the state (Cawson, 1978, 1982; Saunders, 1979, 1981, 1982; Cawson and Saunders, 1983). In brief, the central proposition of this 'dual state', or more properly 'dual politics', thesis is that different areas of state activity are marked by distinctively different patterns of interest politics and policy processes. The thesis bears some similarity to Lowi's (1964) argument that different policy arenas (distributive, regulative and redistributive) are associated with different political paradigms (elite non-conflictual, pluralist and conflictual elite), especially in the contention that 'policies produce politics'. But our version takes into account recent developments in the theory of the state in its distinction between state activites related to production (which produces corporatist politics) and those related to consumption (which produces pluralist politics).

We argue that it is useful to distinguish between a corporatist and a pluralist paradigm, such that there is (a) a sphere of politics and policy-making concerned with production, in which class interests dominate in the form of functional organisations of capital and labour, and negotiate agreed policies with state agencies; and (b) a sphere of consumption, in which interest organisations reflecting consumption categories not reducible to class interests compete with each other to exert

influence over state policies. Further, there exists a division of
function within the state, such that policies primarily concerned
with production are determined in arenas at central and
regional levels, whereas consumption policies are determined at
all levels, with a major element of collective social provision
organised and delivered through local governments. According
to the thesis, corporatist politics is a politics of the centre,
whereas competitive political processes are most significant at
the local level.

In addition to this link between political processes, state
activities and level of operation, is that between political
processes and modes of state intervention. Here we argue that
the state can ideal-typically act in one of three modes: it can
enforce a market mechanism for the allocation of resources; it
can intervene directly in a bureaucratic mode whereby allocation takes place according to pre-specified political priorities; or
it can formulate and implement policy through negotiation with
corporate groups in a relatively closed policy process. Often this
third mode takes place in relatively autonomous regulatory
agencies that are governed by representatives of functionally
defined interests. Corporatist intermediation thus dissolves the
institutional separation of inputs and outputs, and links directly,
albeit sometimes informally, interest representation and policy
execution, and thereby blurs the distinction between public and
private sectors.

By contrast, in the market mode and in the bureaucratic
mode, public and private domains are institutionally separated.
In the former, state intervention is limited in extent to what is
required for markets to function or develop, including the
guarantee of private property rights and the enforcement of
contacts, and, latterly, the imposed breaking up of monopolies.
It should be noted that this ideal type of market mode should be
seen as a state policy – a deliberate abstention from directive or
negotiated intervention – rather than as a *laissez-faire* situation
which presupposes the capacity of markets to function autonomously of the state. In the bureaucratic mode, state intervention operates in principle through well-defined legal-rational
procedures which are, at least in capitalist democracies, determined by a process of pluralist competition involving interest
groups and political parties. This process is, however, restricted

to rule formulation – i.e. inputs – and implementation takes place through the bureaucratic structures of the state. (For a fuller exposition, see Cawson, 1982, especially Chapter 5.)

As the functional responsibilities of the state extend into the sphere of production, because of market failures and the inadequacy of the bureaucratic mode in the determination of relevant outputs rather than procedural allocative rules (Offe, 1975), the sphere of corporatist politics may become more and more important, and corporate groups tend to become integrally involved in policies concerned with the enhancement of productivity and the maintenance of full employment. Even in a macro-political context hostile to corporatist initiatives, such as Britain under Thatcher, in certain sectors such as micro-electronics where rapid expansion is sought, or steel, where 'rationalised' production is an important policy goal, policies are still negotiated directly with producer interests rather than delegated to market mechanisms or determined by the state itself. The problems of forging macroeconomic policies through corporatist intervention have been extensively discussed else-where (Schmitter and Lehmbruch, 1979; Berger, 1981; Lehm-bruch and Schmitter, 1982), and the breakdown of corporatist arrangements in the wake of economic recession has led to the search for alternative policy instruments.

In Britain this has taken the form of the deliberate resurrec-tion of the market mode for national economic management (monetarism), a determination to return parts of the public sector to private capital (privatisation – which is not necessarily synonymous with the market mode), and a heightened concern in rhetoric with the virtues of the market, self-help and discipline (Gamble, 1981; Hall, 1983).

At the local level the response to the recession has involved a combination of corporatist and market modes of intervention with the attempt to reduce the significance of bureaucratic allocation through reduced public expenditure and the contrac-tion of state responsibilities. As I shall argue below, the market mode has proved especially troublesome to implement at the local level. Local corporatist intervention is particularly note-worthy given the association between the local level and consumption provisions discussed above in the context of the 'dual politics' thesis, which suggests that local corporatism is an unlikely combination of territorial and functional bases of political organisation. The entrenchment of welfare provision at the local level and the competitive nature of local politics should alert us to the potential difficulties of establishing local corporatist strategies, particularly in view of the absence of local arenas for interest intermediation. The examples from Norway and Britain cited above were attempts to establish just such arenas, and certainly in the case reported by Flynn it would be premature to predict how far the process of policy formation will shift to the new bodies.

In order to examine the potential and limitations of this form of policy process, I shall first examine the experience in that area of local government where concerted intervention in the economic market has been active for longest, i.e. land-use planning, and then attempt to evaluate more recent attempts at more general strategies of local economic intervention. The overwhelming evidence that corporatism to date has been primarily sectoral and central in scope and content should help us to avoid the trap of inferring the onset of summer from the presence of a few swallows.

Local corporatism and land-use planning

Land-use planning, particularly in Britain, is the one local activity that has been extensively discussed and researched within the debate on corporatism (Cawson, 1977, 1982; Jowell, 1977a; Azmon, 1980; Reade, 1980, 1982, 1984; Simmie, 1981; Flynn, 1983). Although the theoretical approaches of these works differ somewhat, there is some measure of agreement that a process of corporatist intermediation between local planning authorities and developers or industrialists has begun to emerge, both in the preparation of development plans and in the way in which development control procedures have been implemented.

In principle, the imposition of statutory controls on land development in Britain from 1947 represents an allocative process determined by formal legal-rational procedures. Land-use planning was seen in the context of the development of the welfare state as the establishment of democratic control over the land market so that community values could be embodied in planning decisions. The specific part of land-use planning primarily concerned with ensuring rationalised production – the New Towns policy – was hived off from the sphere of local government and administered through development corporations in which functional interests were directly represented.

The right to develop land was nationalised, and then planning permission was to be allocated according to criteria embodied in a statutory development plan. Changes to the legislation in 1968 introduced the concept of structure plans, which from 1974 became the responsibility of the new county councils. Structure plans were intended to be relatively flexible statements of strategic policy produced after an analysis of a range of social and economic factors affecting land use. The specific implications for land use of structure plan policies were to be the subject of one or more local plans drawn up by the new district councils. Development control decisions under the new procedures were intended to be relatively routine applications of the allocative principles embodied in the statutory plans, and in so far as there was to be consultation and participation in the planning process by individuals and organised groups, this would take place in the plan-formulation rather than the development-conrol process. In essence this conforms to the bureaucratic mode of state intervention identified in the previous section. It remains consistent with the 'dual politics' thesis because throughout the period under review, i.e. the 1950s and 1960s, economic production was not a pressing issue for land-use planners or for central governments, and the content of planning issues reflected primarily consumption and welfare concerns.

In practice, however, it has become evident that for a number of reasons planning policy-making has diverged from the formal process. The major reason for this has been the consequences of economic recession and the increased priority accorded to production issues reflected in the creation of ostensibly 'planning-free' enterprise zones, described below. But also important have been delays in formulating plans in the context of a competitive local political context (see Simmie, Chapter 7 of this volume). Even now, seventeen years after the original legislation, not all structure plans have been formally approved by central government, and a great many local plans have yet to be adopted. Thus development control is open to *ad hoc* decision-making and the exercise of political influence by developers and organised interests.

Simmie (1981), in a study of planning in Oxford from 1947 to 1977, shows clearly how the process of planning decision-making departs considerably from the theory of plan-formulation and implementation. He demonstrates how large-scale organised interests, including feudal landowners, the Oxford colleges, public bureaucracies, business and trade unions were usually effective in embodying their interests in the plan or in specific planning decisions. By contrast, the relatively unorganised interests, and especially poorer and working-class groups, were usually unable to challenge or modify planning policy which was perceived as detrimental to their interests. Simmie (1981, p. 301) describes this as a 'corporatist type of power structure in which a small number of organisations with different bases for their power exercised influence or manipulation over major planning objectives'. Now, inequalities in the distribution of power are not themselves constitutive of corporatism, and Simmie's argument seems to hinge upon the necessity of formal organisation in order to influence policy outcomes.

Simmie (p. 218) finds in the process whereby plan objectives were set 'many of the characteristics associated with a corporate state', but this is because negotiations are carried on between large formal organisations and the local state. Simmie is in large part concerned to counter the Marxist thesis that the local state acts primarily as a local instrument of capital, and in this he can justifiably claim some success in showing that the local state did maintain considerable autonomy in planning decisions, and that not all the organisations which extracted favourable policy decisions were representative of capitalist interests. However, if corporatism involves the formulation *and* implementation of public policy through negotiation between the state and organised interests, then an equally important issue is the role that organisations play in policy implementation. Simmie (p. 201) describes the process of amending the Development Plans as one in which 'the local state [was] a focus of political activity with its objectives set or altered according to the balance of power between contending interest groups', i.e. a pluralistic political process, but then shows how in major development applications public objectives were incorporated into private schemes on the basis of a closed and often secret series of negotiations. Planning at the local level is thus an interesting mixture of competitive and pluralist politics, and the giving or withholding of planning permission gives local authorities an important resource which they can use in political exchanges with developers.

Some indication of how these exchanges have been taking place can be obtained from recent discussions of bargaining in development control. Section 52 of the Town and Country Planning Act of 1971 allows local authorities to enter into agreements with developers which impose obligations on them of a kind which could *not* formally be made the subject of a condition attached to a planning permission. In the words of Heap and Ward (1980, p. 632):

> the developer is being asked to provide facilities which it is the local authority's statutory duty to provide themselves and, in addition . . . the scale of the community benefit provision which is being required of the developer is frequently assessed mainly, if not exclusively, by reference to the estimated profitability of the completed scheme.

Examples of such 'planning gains' have included open space and recreational facilities, car parking and conservation work, sometimes on sites quite unconnected with the planning application (Hawke, 1981). On one occasion bargaining concerned the nomination of households on the council house waiting list to housing in the private sector development under consideration. Sometimes local authorities have employed valuers to estimate developers' profits in a proposed development in order to bargain the appropriate level of planning gain (Jowell, 1977a). Jowell argues that these developments, which certainly can be described as 'corporatist' in terms of the strict definition adopted here, are part of a larger tendency for British planning administration to move from a judicial model to a bargaining model. In effect planning gain is a tax on land development assessed according to rules that are fashioned for each case.

Simmie (1981, pp. 231–4) shows that bargaining over planning permission is restricted to larger applications, which are more likely to come from formal organisations; smaller applications, often from individuals, are determined bureaucratically through the application of existing criteria. Unfortunately Simmie did not investigate the issue of planning gain, nor does he pursue this issue in his analysis of the major commercial development at St Ebbe's, which included a public library. But it is clear from the above that there is sufficient discrepancy between the legal-rational framework of planning, with its implicit assumption of actors as individuals, and the mode of policy determination, in practice dominated by producer interests, to warrant further empirical investigation of corporatism in land-use planning. Whether this might lead to the identification of a specifically *local* corporatism is discussed below. But first it is worth examining some evidence from a policy field with wider scope than land-use planning: recent attempts by local and central government to intervene in the local economy.

State intervention in the local economy

At the local level in Britain the first signs of an interventionist policy towards the local economy emerged as the latest phase of a series of initiatives to combat 'urban deprivation', especially in the inner city areas (McKay and Cox, 1979). From the mid-1960s onwards, a succession of urban anti-poverty programmes had focused on the sphere of consumption, emphasising service delivery and the specific characteristics of the poor themselves. But perhaps in response to the reports of the Community Development Project, which had consistently linked urban poverty to changes in the sphere of production – principally the effects of industrial decline and economic restructuring by firms – the Inner Cities White Paper of 1977 laid 'emphasis on administrative co-ordination and economic revival' (McKay and Cox, 1979, p. 253).

The range of measures since 1977 can be analysed according to the modes of state intervention outlined above. The election of the Thatcher government in 1979 introduced a more significant market element into local schemes, but at the same time bureaucratically delivered programmes were continued, and there have been some important experiments with corporatist forms in which policy determination and implementation has been a negotiative process between state agencies (at central and local levels) and producer interests. At the same time many Labour local authorities began to introduce economic strategies of their own, which embraced both corporatist and bureaucratic modes of intervention. I shall examine each of these in turn.

Bureaucratic mode

The major policy response to the Inner Cities White Paper of 1977 was the creation of seven 'inner city partnerships' in order to attempt to co-ordinate the central and local levels of the state towards a more comprehensive policy approach. Although in theory the partnerships are governed by the 'principle that all parties which have a role within the inner city, i.e. central government, counties and districts, the private and voluntary sectors, should work together for the improvement of the inner city' (Butler and Williams, 1981, p. 127), the main policy-making process seems to have been contained within the officer steering groups, which are comprised exclusively of state and public sector officials and exclude both organised interests and wider public consultation and participation (Tilley, 1979). The important feature of this programme is that it attempts to develop a unified approach to policy-making through inter-bureaucratic co-ordination – an extension of the ideas of corporate management to embrace central and local levels. In this respect it shares some features with the earlier (1974) experimental 'Comprehensive Community Programmes', which were themselves a managerialist reaction to the more radical and overtly participatory Community Development Projects. But since 1981, as mentioned by King (this volume, p.207), local authorities seeking funds under the Urban Programme, including the partnership authorities, have been obliged formally to consult local Chambers of Commerce to obtain the views of the private sector.

Corporatist mode

In analysing those initiatives where policy-making has taken the form of a collaboration between local state agencies and organised interests and groups in the private sector, it is possible to distinguish two variants, according to whether organised labour has been included or excluded. (Unlike bureaucratic/consumption policy-making it is impossible to exclude capital from either corporatist or market modes.) 'Left corporatism' may be an appropriate description for the strategies of the West Midlands County Council and the Greater London Council, both of which have set up Enterprise Boards to channel investment money to private sector firms willing to sign agreements consistent with these Labour councils' economic objectives. In the London case the Greater London Enterprise Board has adopted an overt policy of 'restructuring for labour', whereby assistance is given only to those firms willing to change their industrial relations practices to increase the level of employee and union participation (Stone, 1983). Both the WMEB and GLEB have developed their policies in discussion both with regional bodies of the Trades Union Congress and with individual local branches.

Other recent interventionist policies at the local level have had their origin in initiatives from central government, but, hardly surprisingly in view of the exclusion of trade unions from national economic policy-making by the Thatcher government, the emphasis in these programmes is on prioritising capital and seeking to reverse inner-city decay by encouraging private sector investment. Two of these 'Right corporatist' approaches will be discussed here: the Urban Development Corporations (UDCs) and Inner City Enterprises, King (this volume, p. 206) refers to a third, Business in the Community.

UDCs were established in 1980 in London's docklands area and in Liverpool in an attempt to redevelop an area that included many derelict or redundant sites owned largely by public sector bodies. The London Docklands Development Corporation is especially interesting because it was set up as an explicit rejection of the outcome of an intensive planning exercise which had involved five Labour-controlled London boroughs, local community groups, trade unions and business organisations (Newman and Mayo, 1981). The strategic plan approved in 1976 included proposals to maintain and enhance the manufacturing base of the area and build a significant amount of public sector housing, 'a real concession to working-class interests' (Newman and Mayo, 1981, p. 540), but the authorities had few powers to implement such a strategy in the face of a continued shrinkage of industrial employment. In any case, the plan called for considerable public investment (especially in housing) at a time when housing was bearing the brunt of national expenditure cuts.

In September 1979 an Urban Development Corporation was announced for the area, to be followed by the creation of an enterprise zone (see below). The UDC is closely modelled on the structure of the New Town Corporations established after 1946, and deliberately insulates control over land development from the existing local authorities and the competitive process of interest group politics at the local level which had produced the 1976 strategic plan. The UDC chairman appointed by the Secretary of the State for the Environment was also chairman of the Trafalgar House property and finance conglomerate, and board members reflect commercial and financial interests. Public money allocated to the UDC will be used for infrastructure and the attraction of private capital into joint ventures. Given the central location of the area immediately to the east of the City of London, it is likely that the development will comprise mainly offices and luxury private housing.

Inner City Enterprises was established in 1983 specifically to encourage private investment in urban areas. It was formed after discussions between the Department of the Environment and leading financial institutions, and the objective is to develop schemes jointly with local authorities and local entrepreneurs, assisted by government grants under the DoE's Urban Programme. The jointly negotiated package would then seek private sector participation using normal commercial profit criteria, although 'softened' by an element of public subsidy. (For reports of strikingly similar developments in the United States, see Kunde and Berry, 1981; Webman, 1982). The new body is likely to devise schemes like the Cantril Farm project in Liverpool, which involves a consortium of public and private bodies in the redevelopment of a run-down council estate. The local council, Barclays Bank, the Abbey National Building Society and the Barratt construction company have been involved in formulating this scheme, which with the aid of government grants and private capital will provide a mixture of new and renovated public and private housing.

These examples illustrate the integration of organised producer interests into public policy-making, and the exclusion of consumer interests. The size of the investment required, and the key role of central government grants, precludes reliance on purely local interests. In this sense they are examples of 'corporatism at the local level', rather than 'local corporatism', since the local dimension is the *target* of intervention rather than the basis for the organisation of the participating bodies. The success of such policies, apart from purely economic factors, would seem to be dependent on the efficacy of the mechanisms for co-ordinating the various interests involved. This inter-mediary organisational capacity, which involves both govern-ment officials and business organisations acting in unfamiliar roles, seems at present to be largely *ad hoc*, in keeping with the innovative and experimental nature of this form of policy-making. A good deal more research is necessary to discover how it works in practice, and who benefits. Corporatist theory, however, suggests the plausible hypothesis that it is likely to discriminate against the relatively unorganised interests of consumer groups, and the 'dual politics' thesis suggests that the representation of local communities through democratic institu-tions at the local level is unlikely to play much part in what are centralist and production-oriented processes.

Market-based intervention

In addition to corporatist modes of intervention, there has been in Britain (and in the United States – see Clarke, 1982) an attempt to restructure parts of local economies using as far as possible an unfettered market mechanism. Enterprise zones were originally conceived by Peter Hall as 'Hong Kongs in the inner cities', involving the complete removal of all government regulation and taxation, as well as all grants and subsidies (IJURR, 1982). By the time the first zones had been designated, some modifications to the original idea were evident, and although firms in the zones were exempted from local rates they would still have to comply with employment protection legisla-tion, and planning controls would be streamlined but not abolished. Some grants and subsidies that were part of regional policy would, however, be retained. A study of the two zones in Scotland shows how local authorities have used enterprise zones, not as an experiment in the free market, but as 'an adjunct to their own planning and interventionist strategies' (Keating, Midwinter and Taylor, 1984, p. 82). Given that grants remain available and that rates are waived, the zones are a means of subsidising industry rather than removing intervention. A review by the firm of economic consultants engaged by the government to monitor the performance of the zones concludes that 'the enterprise zone package is most successful when supported by other public programmes' (quoted in Keating, Midwinter and Taylor, 1984, p. 82). There are thus fewer differences than first appear between enterprise zones and more overtly interventionist urban policies, but an important one is the absence of the centre in the implementation (as opposed to the conception) of the programme. On the basis of the theoretical ideas of this chapter, one would expect that firms involved are in the market rather than the corporate sector of the economy, and that their collective interest is weakly organised. But we await more detailed studies of the zones before firm conclusions can be drawn.

Conclusion: local corporatism?

This chapter has been concerned to achieve a more precise specification of what 'local corporatism' might involve than is available in the few references in the literature. It seeks to locate the concept in the context of the levels of organisation of the state, and the relationship between state policy modes and different processes of interest intermediation.

The most striking examples of the corporatist policy mode turn out on closer inspection to be where the local defines the object of policy rather than characterises the nature of the interests involved. In this they are comparable with the activities of national quasi-bureaucratic, quasi-corporatist bodies at the local level, such as the Manpower Services Commission and the National Health Service. Both of these contain elements of functional representation: the first tripartite, involving government, business and labour; the second bipartite, where organised professional interests negotiate policy with government. They operate largely autonomously of local councils and competitive political processes. Such organisations have been excluded from the scope of this chapter because their primary concern is functional rather than territorial, and their relationship to the state is largely confined to the central level.

Taking as a starting point the local level of the state, we may begin to discuss the conditions under which a 'genuine' local corporatism might arise. First, state policy-making must have on its agenda the concern with the sphere of production, and the search for more effective policy instruments. This has certainly become evident in recent years, with a proliferation of attempts by local authorities to 'do something' about the local impact of economic decline. Part of this has been a rediscovery of the importance of small business, which means that local policy-makers have first to find out what the economic structure of their locality is like (Muller and Bruce, 1981). But although it is a precondition of effective intervention, information is not enough.

The second important factor concerns the degree of effective autonomy of local government, and its legislative and economic powers. Corporatism presupposes that state agencies are capable of making and delivering bargained policies, so that a potential local corporatism depends upon strong local state institutions. In this respect the possibilities in Britain seem more remote than in other countries, especially in federal systems where sub-central units have such powers deeply entrenched. In Britain the unitary structure of the state and the extent to which local government functions have to be centrally handed down by statute (see Sharpe, forthcoming, for a vigorous reaffirmation of the importance of this), severely constrains the possibility of a viable local corporatism. In addition, the unusually high level of concentration in the economy has diminished the significance of local markets.

The third factor concerns the degree of organisation of producer interests. We can learn from studies of the experience of corporatism at the macro and meso levels that far-reaching corporatist intervention, rather than *ad hoc* bargaining by individual firms like the planning examples discussed above, require the concertation of interests by associations and their ensuring that their members adhere to agreed policies. The relative weakness of local business associations (see King,

Chapter 8 in this volume) and local trades (union) councils represents a considerable impediment to the development of local corporatism. It also suggests that effective intervention is more likely to take place at the level of inducements and constraints on individual firms, but as Hernes and Selvik (1981) show in their example from Norway, state intervention can create the incentives for such organisation. In Britain, however, this is likely to be a response to central government, and central bodies like the Manpower Services Commission, extending their activities at the local level.

Local governments, in Britain and in many other countries, remain largely service providers, maintaining bureaucratic structures to implement social programmes according to non-market criteria, subject to both central influence and competitive pressure from local policies. But this role has been consolidated in the context of the institutional growth of the welfare state, which was able in an expansionist economic context to develop largely in isolation from the process of capital accumulation. Economic decline and mounting political pressure to alleviate its consequences, coupled with a policy of privatisation and perhaps the growth of a contract model of local service provision, may in time lead to a marked change in the role of the local state. But such a change is unlikely to be towards greater autonomy, and the kinds of corporatist interventions that may reshape the local political economy will be determined outside the reach of local political organisation.

Chapter 6

Corporatism and Urban Service Provision

Peter Saunders

This chapter reports on three case studies relating to state provision of urban services and/or state regulation of urban land-use and development. These three studies have two major features in common. First, they all document the development, in different ways and in different degrees, of corporatist strategies of urban management and policy-making. Second, all three studies were conducted using an analytical framework which has been termed a 'dual state' or 'dual politics' thesis. The aim of the chapter is both to develop insights into the role of corporatist mediation in urban politics, and to evaluate and clarify the dual politics thesis.

The dual politics thesis

Academic research in urban sociology and urban politics has progressed through three distinct phases since the Second World War. The first of these was in large part characterised by what Mills (1959) termed 'abstracted empiricism', in the sense that much research effort was devoted to qualitative or quantitative studies with little, if any, theoretical rationale. This was the period of the descriptive community study, the search for correlations in voting behaviour, the charting of the organisational structures of local governments, and so on. It was followed from the mid-1960s onwards by a second phase which represented its antithesis – what Mills described as 'grand theory'. In this phase, theoretical research was pitched at such a level of abstraction and generality that empirical work became virtually redundant. This was the period of theories of the state which paid little or no attention to variations between particular states, and of theories of urban social movements which were so preoccupied with identifying system contradictions that they entirely lost sight of the people who made these movements move.

Today we are witnessing the development of a third phase – a synthesis if you like – in which researchers are once again considering empirical and historical questions, but this time in the context of broader theoretical issues. In the work of writers such as Szelenyi (1981) and Castells (1983) we find a renewed sensitivity to the particularities of space and time and an attempt to build upon the theoretical insights of recent years through theoretically informed historical and comparative work.

If this current phase of research is to deliver on its considerable potential promise, then there is an urgent need to develop what Merton (1957) many years ago identified as 'middle range theories'. We need, that is, to develop conceptual and theoretical tools that will enable us to link the particular with the general, the concrete with the abstract, and the empirical concern with this or that phenomenon with the theoretical concern with the 'big' questions of social science such as the role of the state, the problem of class relations, and so on. As Wyn Grant notes in the Introduction to this volume, theories of corporatism are one example of middle range theory. What the dual politics thesis attempts to do is to relate work on corporatism to work on other aspects of political processes in order to develop a framework through which to link a diversity of contemporary empirical concerns with the broader theoretical issues of political science and political economy.

The core elements of the thesis are set out elsewhere (see, for example, Cawson and Saunders, 1983, and Alan Cawson's chapter in this volume). They are, first, the relation between production and consumption; second, the relation between different levels of state organisation (the local, the regional and the national); third, the relation between corporatist and competitive modes of interest mediation; and fourth, the relation between the conflicting ideologies of private property and social need. The thesis suggests that there is a tendency for political activity concerning issues of production to become focused on central state agencies, to foster relatively exclusive corporatist forms of interest mediation, and to be informed principally by values that emphasise the rights of private property and the importance of sustaining private sector profitability. Conversely, there is also a tendency for consumption questions to be relegated to peripheral or localised state agencies, where a plurality of interests become involved in political competition to realise their objectives, and where the actions of participants are often informed by values stressing the rights of citizenship and the importance of meeting different social needs.

This framework is, of course, temporally and spatially specific in that it has been constructed on the basis of empirical observation of one society (Britain) at one point in time (the early 1980s). It is not intended to be a generic framework, for the inter-relation of the different elements may be expected to vary in different countries (e.g. in the USA there is a tendency for production issues to be localised in municipal or state governments) and over different time periods (e.g. in Chapter 5, Alan Cawson suggests that local state policy-making in Britain may in future develop corporatist modes of interest mediation). Those critics (e.g. Paris, 1983; Sharpe, 1984) who argue against the dual politics thesis that, say, consumption provisions are sometimes centralised or that production questions are not always and everywhere mediated through corporatist state forms, therefore miss the point, for the question is not whether the four elements of the thesis necessarily line up in the way suggested, but rather whether the framework aids in the development of empirically testable theories and hypotheses.

The crucial hypotheses that we have developed on the basis of the dual politics thesis are, first, that Marxist-inspired class theories of politics will be more applicable the more political processes relate to questions of production, are concentrated at central level, take a corporatist rather than a democratic form, and are addressed to values of private property and profitability; and second, that pluralist-inspired interest group theories of politics will be more appropriate in explaining political processes relating to questions of consumption, to local levels of state activity, to competitive sectors of the political system and to values stressing rights of citizenship and the alleviation of social need.

One legitimate criticism that has been levelled against the dual politics thesis as set out briefly here is that it fails to provide any guidance as to the relative significance of the four elements which it identifies. Which, if any, of these elements is primary? Is the major determinant of political processes and outcomes the type of interests most affected (producers or consumers), the level at which the state intervenes (local, regional or national), the mode through which this intervention is accomplished (corporatist or competitive) or the ideology which guides it (values of property or values of citizenship)? Alternatively, is it the case that the significance of any one of these elements depends upon the way in which it is combined with the other three in any given instance? The three case studies discussed in this chapter may help to clarify this question.

The case studies and the problem of primacy

The approach adopted in this chapter is explicitly comparative in at least two senses. First, we shall be comparing political processes at different levels of state organisation (the local and the regional) and across different types of policy areas (production and consumption interventions). Second, we shall be comparing case studies conducted in two different countries (Australia and England).

The point of the cross-national comparison is partly to counter the charge of ethnocentrism which has sometimes been levelled against the dual politics thesis (e.g. by Paris, 1983, p. 224) by demonstrating its potential fruitfulness in other countries besides the UK. More importantly, however, it also enables us to consider in more detail the significance of regional levels of state organisation. In our previous work, Alan Cawson and I have tended to subsume intermediate or regional level agencies under our discussions of central level processes. We have assumed, in other words, that regional state agencies are little more than outposts of the centre and can thus be equated in the dual politics thesis with the central level. This was always a tenuous and relatively unsupported assumption to make, even on the basis of the British experience, where in recent years new and important regional bodies have been established (notably the Scottish regional councils, the regional organisation of bodies such as the Manpower Services Commission, and the regional health and water authorities established in England and Wales in 1974). In the case of a federal country such as Australia, where the regional tier (i.e. the different states) has long enjoyed its own independent identity and responsibilities, it becomes even more crucial to disentangle intermediate and central level interventions. Indeed, given that the regional level in Australia includes a strong elective element (the state legislatures), whereas the regional level in England does not, an Anglo-Australian comparison should enable us to draw some tentative conclusions concerning not only the question of levels of intervention, but also the significance of the existence or otherwise of electoral processes at any one level.

By comparing cases involving different types of policy areas, different levels of intervention and different formal modes of interest representations, we may hopefully draw some initial conclusions regarding the relative significance of the four dimensions of the dual politics thesis. Four possibilities can be assessed in the context of the case studies.

1. *The production/consumption distinction as a key factor.* If we find one form of interest mediation (corporatism) established in both England and Australia in one area of state activity (that affecting producer interests), but a different form (e.g. political competition) established in both countries in another (affecting consumer interests), then such evidence would support the hypothesis that it is the type of policy area (and hence the type of interests affected by state intervention) that is most important in determining the way in which intervention is accomplished. Furthermore, if this relationship still holds in cases where the level of intervention varies, then we may be justified in arguing that the development of a corporatist mode is a function of the type of policy area, irrespective of the level at which the state intervenes or the existence of formal electoral arrangements at regional level.

2. *The level of intervention as a key factor.* If we find one form of interest mediation (corporatism) operating at the regional level in both production and consumption-type interventions, and if in addition we find this same pattern in Australia, where there is an elected system of regional government, and in England, where there is not, then such evidence may be taken as strongly indicative of the importance of the level of intervention as a key

factor determining the character of political processes, independently of the type of interests affected by state action or the existence of formal electoral arrangements. Such a finding would, in other words, enable us to argue that it is the scale of state operation that is crucial, in that a regional level of intervention is sufficiently inaccessible to most people to allow for selective and exclusive corporatist modes to develop.

3. *The formal mode of interest representation as a key factor.* If we find that corporatist arrangements are characteristic of the regional level in England in both production and consumption-type agencies, but that these same services at the regional level in Australia are subject to more open political competition among a diversity of different interests, then such evidence may be taken as supportive of the hypothesis that it is the existence or otherwise of formal electoral arrangements that determines the character of political processes. We could then argue that a democratic-electoral system sustains competitive imperfect pluralism, irrespective of the type of policy fields in which the state is involved and of the level at which it is operating, in which case corporatism may flourish only in the interstices of the liberal-democratic state, where (as in the English regional authorities) electoral processes have not been established.

4. *Type, level and mode as non-determinate factors.* It may be that we find no consistent pattern in terms of the three possibilities outlined above. In such an event, we are left with two possibilities. One is that the implicit model of simple one-way determinacy is too crude, in which case further analysis will be required on the way these and other elements combine at particular junctures. This would involve developing a theory of causality akin to that proposed by Urry (1981) in his discussion of necessary and contingent factors. The other possibility would be that the character and outcome of state action depends crucially on the values of strategically placed actors at different points in the state system, such that, in the same objective context, state agencies operate differently under their influence and direction. Such a conclusion would provide strong support for a theory of 'urban managerialism' such as that originally proposed by Pahl (1975).

The evidence against which to assess the four hypotheses set out above will be drawn from three research projects conducted during the last few years. The first, carried out in 1981, was a study of a major land-use planning conflict in Melbourne, Victoria, in which both producer and consumer interests were directly affected and in which a dramatic shift from the local to the regional level was effected in order to resolve the resulting impasse. The second, carried out in 1982 in Canberra, the Australian capital, was a study of planning and urban service provision in a city with no elected local or regional level of government. The third, conducted in 1983–4 as part of an ESRC-funded research project which also involved Simon Duncan and Mark Goodwin, was a study of the English regional water and health authorities with particular reference to those operating in the south-east region. Fuller discussions of these studies can be found in Saunders (1984, on Melbourne; 1983a, on Canberra; and 1983b, on the English regional authorities), although much of the empirical work on the third of these studies has yet to be analysed or published.

Land-use planning in the City of Melbourne, 1981

Land-use planning is an interesting aspect of urban state intervention to consider in the context of the dual politics thesis, since it typically impinges directly on both producer and consumer interests in the locality. It is also an aspect of the state's role which in most Western countries is at least partially the responsibility of local or municipal elected governments. In the Australian state of Victoria, where local government has historically been very weak and highly fragmented, it is without doubt the most significant municipal function, for most aspects of urban service provision – housing, roads, health, public transport, education, welfare – are dealt with at the state (i.e. regional) level.

It is important to recognise that, although Victoria (along with the other Australian states) elects a state parliament, the state's responsibility for most of these services is effectively delegated to a bewildering variety of generally single-purpose statutory authorities whose membership (which is usually no more than three or four people) is appointed by the appropriate minister. These bodies enjoy considerable autonomy in making and implementing their policies, and their chairmen (for they are invariably led by men) are among the most powerful individuals in the state. Taken together, the eighty or so statutory authorities in Victoria employ over one hundred thousand people, or more than five times the number on the state government payroll. Although they are not directly our object of concern in this chapter, it is clear that these authorities are often immune to popular democratic pressures and aspirations, despite the existence of an elected state parliament, for as one observer suggests, 'Recitations about the power of voters, parliamentarians and members of the government to control public resources are highly suspect, if not obsolete, under these conditions' (Sharkansky, 1979, p. 52). Whether or not this democratic vacuum has been filled by the development of explicitly corporatist and exclusive modes of interest mediation is less certain, although Holmes has argued that the existence of these bodies has functioned 'to shield four-fifths of the state's administrative sector from the mainstream of party politics' and that this has enabled particular sectional interests to be 'brought directly into the structures of government' (1980, pp. 196 and 197; see also the special edition of the *Australian Journal of Public Administration* on statutory authorities, volume 42, number 1, 1983).

The task of land-use planning, although in part a municipal responsibility, is also subject to one of these regional-level statutory bodies, namely the Melbourne and Metropolitan Board of Works (MMBW). The MMBW is responsible for strategic planning in addition to water supply, sewerage, rivers and parks, and is largely self-financing as a result of its power to levy its own rates. At seven, its membership is somewhat larger than the norm, with four of its members representing the interests of the fifty-four different municipalities in the Melbourne metropolitan area.

Among these fifty-four municipalities is the City of Melbourne, which extends over thirty-one square kilometers and has a population of nearly seventy thousand. The City of Melbourne was, in 1981, by far the most significant of these municipalities, for not only was its annual budget three times greater than that of any of its neighbours, but its area of jurisdiction covered most of the central business district in addition to a number of residential and mainly 'gentrified' inner-city areas. The city council thus enjoyed the right to plan the use of land in an area which has traditionally been the financial centre, not simply of Victoria, but of the whole of Australia.

In 1971, the MMBW produced a strategic plan for the Melbourne metropolitan area which endorsed the then current trends towards ever-increasing suburban development and low-density population sprawl by proposing the development of radial growth corridors and new satellite towns on the periphery of the built-up area. This plan worried a number of landowners and major retailers in the city centre, who felt that it would exacerbate the flight from the centre and hence damage central land values and retail profits. Through the Melbourne Chamber of Commerce, they applied pressure on the state premier to revitalise the central area, and in this they were supported by residents in the newly gentrified fringe who were calling for a central area plan that would protect the city's older housing, smaller shops and tree-lined boulevards. The premier responded to this pressure by calling upon the Melbourne City Council, as the local planning authority, to produce a central area plan.

The City's plan was published in 1974, and it succeeded in placating both the city centre business and landowning interests and the fringe area residents by proposing that any future large-scale office development should be restricted to the existing Central Business District (CBD) area. The plan did not, however, please the MMBW, nor did it find favour with developers or owners of land in the fringe areas, and for the next six years these various competing groups battled with each other while the plan itself went into cold storage.

Throughout these years, the city council found itself squeezed between the two sets of strong and relatively evenly balanced interests, both of which enjoyed representation within the council chamber, both of which were influential with various other government agencies with which the council had to deal, and neither of which could be ignored or excluded from the policy-making process. Whatever the council tried to do, it was certain to encounter fierce and effective opposition. As a member of the MMBW put it in an interview, 'There were a lot of different groups who were applying different pressures to the situation. Given all the different pressures, you can do one of two things. You can either make the decision or alternatively you can become paralysed'. Torn by internal factionalism, hemmed in by the MMBW and the state planning department, and buffeted on all sides by commercial, landowning, developer and residential interests, the city council became paralysed.

In December 1980, the state government decided that such advanced paralysis necessitated amputation, and the premier announced in parliament that the Melbourne City Council was to be dismissed and its functions taken over by three appointed commissioners. There is strong evidence to suggest that this decision was prompted by pressure from a coalition of big business and landowning interests organised through an umbrella group formed two years earlier under the title 'Action in Melbourne' (AIM). The members of AIM, which included major retail stores, insurance companies and landowners, shared two common concerns. The first was that the climate of uncertainty created by the six-year wrangle over the city plan was damaging existing and future business prosperity: any decision, in other words, came to be seen as preferable to no decision. The second was that a loose alliance of Labor Party and residential/environmental activists seemed set to win control of the city council at the 1981 elections, thereby overturning the long tradition of business domination in the city. Faced with evidence of declining commercial profitability and the prospect of an anti-big business coalition in city hall, AIM put pressure on the state government to replace the elected council with appointed commissioners whose task would be to rejuvenate the local property market and to redraw the city boundaries in such a way as to ensure a business-dominated council when elections were finally restored. So it was that, in May 1981, the three commissioners appointed by the state government took control of Melbourne City (this being only the third time in Victoria's history that a local council had been dismissed in this way).

Within a month of taking over the city, the commissioners published a statement of aims in which they made clear their commitment to ensuring a low commercial rate (to be achieved through the sale of municipal assets and increased user charges) and a relaxation of development controls. In the first four months of their tenure of office, a record six hundred million dollars' worth of planning permits were issued, and the Chief Commissioner was able to claim with some pride in an interview that, 'We have got to the point now where the planning department is almost waiting for the next applicant to come in the door'.

The old city plan was shelved and in its place the commissioners established a planning 'task force' to draw up a new local plan. The task force, which consisted of the commissioners themselves plus representatives from the state planning department, the MMBW and the city planning department, set in motion a process of selective consultation which embraced the Chamber of Commerce, the Chamber of Manufacturers, the Building Owners and Managers Association and major retailing and development companies operating in the city. A total of thirty-one organisations were included in this planning procedure, but residential, environmental and small business interests were deliberately excluded. As the chairperson of one community group observed at the time, 'It really sounds very much like that old *déjà vu* feeling where small, select secretive bodies set down and organise a plan, release it, and the community spends the next five years trying to prevent them carrying it out'. The difference this time, however, was that 'the community' had no democratic-elected forum through which to mount its opposition to this corporatist satisfaction of privileged interests.

The only concession made by the commission to non-incorporated interests in the city was the establishment of a weekly 'access time', at which the commissioners sat in the old council chamber and listened to complaints raised by local residents. This procedure was generally recognised by all concerned as tokenistic if not ritualistic, and it is clear that the residents' right to speak carried with it no corresponding obligation on the part of the commissioners to pay attention. As the chief commissioner himself observed in an interview, 'The fact that we're a small cohesive group of three gives us surely a greater capacity to manage the situation perhaps more effectively in the short term, to manage the situation in a more coherent way, than with twenty-six people [i.e. the elected council] with all sorts of pressures being brought to bear upon them. We can absorb the pressures and come up with more positive direction more easily'.

The suspension of local democracy in Melbourne did not last for as long as business interests, the state government or the commissioners had anticipated, for in 1982 the Labor Party won control of the state and organised fresh elections in the city which resulted in victory for a Labor Party – residents coalition. What this case study shows, however, is three things. First, it provides evidence of the way in which elected local authorities may prove relatively open to a range of different and competing interests, which include producer interests concerned with questions of profitability and consumer interests concerned with questions of citizenship and use values. The six-year stalemate over the city plan demonstrates that although the latter may not prevail, nor can they be ignored. Second, the study suggests that regional-level authorities, even when they are elected, are generally less open to popular pressure and may be more amenable to producer interests. Twice – first in 1971 when they applied pressure for a local plan to counter the MMBW proposals, and again in 1980 when they succeeded in bringing about the sacking of the council – city centre land and commercial interests revealed a capacity to mobilise at state level to defend themselves against initiatives emanating from lower down the system. Furthermore, the study also makes clear that such a capacity is all the greater where the regional authorities concerned are non-elected, as in the case of the various statutory authorities in Victoria such as the MMBW, which throughout this period remained virtually immune from consumer pressure in furthering the interests of the developer lobby. Third, we see in the example of the commissioners and their task force the way in which popular demands may be side-stepped or 'absorbed', even at local level when elected agencies are replaced by appointed bodies which can develop corporatist modes of interest mediation in which the voice of the producers and values of profitability and efficiency go virtually unchallenged.

Development and urban service provision in Canberra, 1982

The most obvious contrast between Melbourne and Canberra as regards our present concerns is that, while residents in the former temporarily lost the right to elect a local council, those in the latter have never had such a right. The two hundred thousand people who live in Canberra and the surrounding area (the Australian Capital Territory or ACT) are in this respect virtually unique in Western liberal-democratic societies, for ever since the federal government established the city as the nation's capital under an act of 1908, they have been governed directly by a central department (since 1973 the Department of the Capital Territory) together with a range of statutory authorities, of which the National Capital Development Commission (NCDC), set up in 1958, is the most significant. Furthermore, when they were given the opportunity to vote for a limited degree of self-government in a referendum in 1978, nearly 64 per cent of voters rejected the proposal.

The main reason why the ACT has never been granted the right to elect its own municipal or state-level government is that, under section 122 of the constitution, the federal government administers the territory on behalf of all Australians. National institutions such as Parliament House, the National Gallery and the War Memorial were built and are administered by the federal government, and the centre has always insisted in addition that powers governing land-use in the capital must similarly be reserved to it. None of this, of course, necessarily implies that other functions which elsewhere in Australia are administered by the states or local government should also be the preserve of the centre, and for fifty years or more there have been various attempts to have these services devolved to some form of elected local assembly. These attempts came to a head with the self-government referendum of 1978, which was lost primarily because most of the city's residents believed that the proposed change would lead to a reduction in central government subsidies and hence to an increase in local property taxes. For most voters, it seems, taxation without representation was not such a bad thing if it meant low rates of taxation.

In the absence of any formal system of local democracy, Canberra and its surrounding area is administered by three sets of state agencies – federal government departments, regional-level statutory authorities, and various advisory bodies.

As noted above, the government department with primary responsibility for the ACT is the Department of the Capital Territory (DCT). The DCT is responsible for most of the functions which elsewhere are discharged by state and municipal governments, including roads, welfare, housing, water and electricity but excluding health, education and legal affairs, which remain in the hands of other federal departments. The DCT also enjoys some planning powers, for in Canberra all land is publicly owned and the Department is responsible for managing and enforcing leases, which include clauses governing land-use.

In common with the rest of the country, the ACT is also subject to the decisions made by a host of statutory authorities, although in this case the members of these authorities are appointed not by an elected state government but by federal government ministers. These authorities include the Electricity Authority, the Commercial Development Authority, the Schools Authority, the Health Commission and many others, in addition to the previously mentioned National Capital Development Commission. The NCDC occupies a particularly prominent place in Canberra, for its three commissioners are responsible for planning the layout of the city, developing public buildings and providing infrastructure, including housing, schools and services to commercial and residential developments.

In addition to the various federal departments and statutory authorities involved in running the city, there are a number of advisory bodies operating in different nooks and crannies of the system. Most of these (e.g. the National Capital Planning Committee, which advises the NCDC, and the Canberra Development Board, which advises the DCT on private enterprise developments) are appointed by ministers from among particular sections of the local population, such as academics or business people; but there is in addition one body – the ACT House of Assembly – which is elected. The House of Assembly enjoys precious little power or influence, however, for the federal government is under no obligation to seek or accept its advice, nor even to keep it informed of current policy (see Atkins, 1978), and there are many examples where the Assembly's recommendations have simply been ignored by ministers. It is, in the words of one local journalist, 'a forum lacking executive authority and which represents the window dressing of democracy' (Fitzgerald, 1981, p. 10), and it is one of the grosser ironies of urban politics in Canberra that voting in Assembly elections is compulsory when the Assembly itself is powerless.

There is, then, a democratic vacuum in the ACT. The question is whether this has been filled by the development of corporatist initiatives as a way of enabling key interests to make an input into policy-making and administration.

There is some evidence to suggest that corporatist mediation has developed to some extent among a number of statutory authorities and advisory bodies. The Canberra Development Board, for example, has provided business interests with relatively exclusive access to the DCT, and various single-purpose statutory bodies such as the Schools Authority and the Health Commission are constituted through a system of selective representation of producer and consumer interests. Such arrangements are, however, piecemeal and fragmented, and their effectiveness has often been limited by the failure of a single group to achieve any degree of meaningful liaison with the pivotal body in the entire system of ACT administration, the NCDC.

Since its inception in 1958, the NCDC has proved to be a very efficient but almost entirely non-responsive agency. Its mode of operation has been neither corporatist nor pluralist but bureaucratic, and its commissioners have maintained and defended their insularity with reference to values of professional planners' competence and expertise. As part of its submissions to a federal government review of its role and functions in 1982, the NCDC argued that, 'In practical terms a statutory authority has no legal basis for sharing its decision-making responsibilities, nor for sharing its accountability' (1982, p. 20), and the chief commissioner has on a number of occasions suggested that continued autonomy and aloofness is necessary if the city is to be planned and developed in a coherent and rational manner.

Such assertions have increasingly come under attack from various organisations in the ACT representing both producer and consumer interests. Among the former, for example, the Canberra Association for Regional Development, in its submission to the 1982 review, complained of the NCDC's 'authoritarian approach': the Building Owners and Managers Association spoke of NCDC disregard for 'suggestions and advice'; and the Chamber of Commerce pointed to the

Commission's 'patronising' manner. Similarly, among consumer organisations the Council of Social Services complained of a 'failure to consult the community', a local community council bemoaned the 'lack of meaningful consultation', and the ACT House of Assembly wrote bitterly of the NCDC's 'sweeping authority'.

But although producer and consumer interests were united in their criticisms of the Commission's insularity, they differed markedly in their proposals for change. While community groups generally argued for increased public participation in, and democratic accountability of, the NCDC, business organisations argued strongly for the development of a more selective system of participation and for more flexibility in the development and enforcement of plans. The former called for a shift from a bureaucratic to a pluralist mode, while the latter preferred instead a move from the bureaucratic form to a corporatist mode in which they would enjoy privileged access.

At the time of the study in 1982 there was little sign that the NCDC was willing to countenance any substantial move towards the development of a pluralist mode, for it recognised that increased participation would result in diverse pressures for change which have hitherto successfully been excluded from the planning system. Planning principles such as the open-plan garden city layout and the decentralised shopping areas would swiftly come under threat as residents attempted to fence off their gardens and developers sought to build high-rise blocks in the central area.

A corporatist mode, on the other hand, seemed rather less threatening, for this would allow for greater co-ordination with key sectors in the population which by 1982 were becoming uncomfortably vociferous in their criticisms, while at the same time still enabling the NCDC to retain its insularity from competing popular pressures. So it was that as the complaints of business mounted, the NCDC began to take its first faltering steps towards the development of a corporatist strategy.

The evidence for this relates to the Commission's plans, published in 1982, for the future development of the central commercial and retailing area known as 'Civic'. For some years, businesses based in Civic had been concerned about falling rates of profitability brought about by the onset of recession but exacerbated by NCDC's continued commitment to developing outlying shopping centres. In its 1982 plan, the NCDC responded to calls for more intensive development in Civic by introducing a new system under which it agreed to negotiate with private sector developers and occupiers over future developments in the area, and in this way it broke for the first time from its tradition of simply imposing plans from above.

Not surprisingly, the development of such a selective and informal method of liaison led to complaints from non-business interests that their views were being neglected. The ACT Public Land Association (whose aim is to increase public participation in the planning system) spoke for many of those interests that had been left out in the cold when it condemned the NCDC for preventing 'proper discussion' over the future of Civic as a result of its 'numerous secret discussions with development interests'. The chief commissioner's response to such complaints epitomised the NCDC's drift towards an exclusive mode of corporatist mediation. 'The user needs to be involved', he told the *Canberra Times*, 'but not every Tom, Dick and Harry'.

There are some striking parallels between the dramatic events in Melbourne in 1981 and the less dramatic but equally significant developments in Canberra the following year. In both cities, central area business interests were concerned about falling profit rates yet were unable to exert sufficient influence over the responsible planning authority to induce it to give greater priority to CBD commercial development. In both cases, this resulted in pressure to change the planning system – in Melbourne by attacking the system of local democratic control, and in Canberra by attacking the bureaucratic insularity of the NCDC. In both cases, business interests actively sought to replace the existing arrangements by a corporatist mode of mediation within which they could be assured of direct participation in the planning process while potential opponents were excluded. In Melbourne this was achieved by dismissing the elected council and removing planning functions to the regional level, while in Canberra it involved pressure to restructure the NCDC. All of this would seem to suggest that corporatism represents a mode of state organisation that is amenable to capitalist interests in a way that is not necessarily the case in democratic or bureaucratic forms.

Health and water services in south-east England, 1983-4

Before the Second World War, elected local authorities in England and Wales included among their responsibilities the administration of health services, including hospitals, and the management of water supplies and sewerage and sewage disposal. Today, local authority competence in these fields has all but disappeared, first as a result of the establishment of the National Health Service, when hospitals were nationalised and placed in the hands of Regional Hospital Boards, and then as a result of the organisational upheavals of 1974 when the reconstituted local authorities were stripped simultaneously of their remaining community health functions and of their responsibilities for water supply and sewage disposal.

This shift of health and water services out of local government has involved two significant changes. First, it has involved a change in the scale of organisation from a local to a regional basis, for both services are today organised through a small number of large regional authorities, each of which is in turn responsible for a number of divisional (in the case of water) or district (in the case of health) offices. Second, it has involved a change in the mode of organisation, for neither the Regional Water Authorities (RWAs) nor the Regional Health Authorities (RHAs) are elected. In the case of the former, this has created a unique situation in the British context of a set of authorities which are free to levy their own taxes (the water rates) while remaining immune from popular election.

Like the reorganisation of local government, which took place in the same year, the 1974 reforms of the water and health services were highly technocratic in intent. Central government's professed concern in both cases was with raising efficiency, and this was reflected in the establishment in the new regional authorities of corporate management systems designed to place effective power and responsibility in the hands of professional experts (principally the water engineers in the RWAs and doctors and health service administrators in the RHAs). Although the 1974 reforms did allow for some degree of local authority representation on the new authorities, local authority nominees were generally powerless in the face of the corporate management teams, and they were expected to perform a supportive managerial role rather than a representative one. In recent years their significance has been eroded still further, for their numbers were reduced in the health authorities after 1982, while local authority representation on the RWAs was abolished altogether under the 1983 *Water Act*.

The only other source of formal input into the planning and policy-making procedures of these authorities has been a token system of consumer committees operating at divisional or district level. Thus, each district health authority is monitored by a Community Health Council, yet these are funded entirely by the RHAs, they have no executive powers, and their members are non-elected. As Regan and Stewart observe, 'Community Health Councils do not enjoy representative legitimacy . . . In essence what has been done has been to set up one appointed body to be consulted by another appointed body . . . To such strange devices does the desire to avoid direct elected control lead' (1982, 30). Similarly, the Consumer Consultative Committees that were set up following the 1983 Act to liaise with each water authority division are generally recognised as toothless. Like the CHCs, their memberships are appointed from among various local organisations (including local authorities), and like the CHCs they have no executive powers.

As in Canberra, and Melbourne following the sacking of the City Council, there is therefore a democratic vacuum in the health and water services in England. The RWAs and RHAs are, of course, subject and responsible to central government departments, yet within the tight financial constraints imposed by central government cash limits, they can and do enjoy considerable discretion about how they spend the public's money. In the absence of any meaningful system of public participation or consultation, still less direct election, the question is again raised of how this vacuum has been filled.

The findings from the case study, which has involved interviews with officers and members of one RHA and one RWA at both regional and district/divisional levels, as well as with various representatives of groups in the population which use the health and water services most intensively, suggest that this vacuum has been filled in different ways in respect of each of the two types of authority.

In the case of the health authorities, there is little effective input from any group outside the health service itself. At both regional and district level, the health authorities closely resemble the NCDC in Canberra in their relative insularity and the emphasis they place upon professional values and technical expertise. It is true that in the health service there is a greater degree of formal representation of outside interests (through local authority and voluntary group nominations to the boards of members and the CHCs) than is the case either with the NCDC or with the water authorities in England, but, as we have seen, this representation is largely insignificant except in symbolic terms. It is also true that there is often close liaison between the health authorities and local government social services departments, but this operates almost entirely at officer level, where (as in the case of the NCDC and its advisory committee) professionally trained people who share broadly common values and career histories speak to each other with few intrusions from outsiders. By and large, therefore, the picture that emerges in the health service in England at regional and district level is one of professional and bureaucratic insularity and hegemony.

It is often suggested in the literature that this situation has provided fertile ground for the establishment of domination on the part of the doctors in general and the hospital consultants in particular (e.g. Elcock and Haywood, 1980; Navarro, 1978; Wistow, 1982), and Alan Cawson (1982), among others, has cited this as evidence for the existence of a corporatist mode in which the producers of health services liaise closely with the state in the development of these services. Yet while it is true that the medical establishment exercises considerable influence at all levels of the NHS, it is also the case that health service managers can and do pursue policies that run counter to these interests. In the case study authorities, for example, health service managers had succeded in redirecting resources away from critical hospital services and into the so-called 'Cinderella services' such as community health and geriatric care, despite the resistance of hospital consultants and others. Such policies are to be explained, not in terms of corporatist mediation, but as the product of a strong and relatively independent form of managerialism in which the values of key bureaucratic office-holders are the principal determinant of policy outcomes.

Where clearly identifiable corporatist strategies have emerged since 1974 is not in the Regional Health Authorities but in the Regional Water Authorities, and this is mainly because the latter, unlike the former, are responsible for a range of functions which have a direct bearing on private sector producer interests. As in the Melbourne and Canberra studies, it is clear from the evidence collected on the water authorities that certain business and landowning interests have succeded in developing corporatist modes of liaison in the absence of any effective form of democratic control in respect of those services that impinge directly on their own economic activity.

Most domestic water users, of course, have no effective influence over the water authorities at any level of their operation. Some consumer groups, such as angling or yachting clubs or environmentalist groups, have now achieved formal representation at divisional level on the new Consumer Consultative Committees, but as we saw earlier, these committees are, like the CHCs, virtually insignificant, and a number of organisations (including some local authorities) have simply ignored them. Where there is an outside input into water policy and planning, however, is mainly at regional level, where particular interests have developed close and informal relationships with key authority personnel. These groups fall into two categories – landowners and farmers organised through the National Farmers Union (NFU) and the Country Landowners Association (CLA); and major industrial firms which operate in relation to the RWAs on their own account or through bodies such as the regional Confederation of British Industry or trade associations such as that of the housebuilders.

Agricultural and rural landed interests enjoy a close relationship with state agencies responsible for water services at all levels of the system. This is seen most clearly in respect of land drainage services, which are organised centrally through the Ministry of Agriculture (all other water services being the responsibility of the Department of the Environment) with which the NFU and CLA have long enjoyed a special relationship (see Richardson *et al.*, 1978). Lower down the system, farmers dominate the regional and local land drainage committees which operate virtually autonomously of the RWAs and which enjoy wide executive powers, while at the lowest level they enjoy exclusive control over 273 Internal Drainage Boards, whose members are elected on a property franchise (see Parker and Penning-Rowsell, 1980). The result of all this is that farmers and landowners enjoy an extraordinary and largely unchallenged degree of exclusive influence over land drainage policies and expenditure, and the management of land drainage at all levels represents one of the purest available examples of corporatist mediation in England and Wales.

Farmers and landowners also engage in regular and informal negotiations with the RWAs on other aspects of water service provision, and here they are joined by organisations representing other industrial interests and by large companies acting on their own account. The main topic of negotiation between the RWAs and major private sector producers concerns water charges, and there is evidence from the case study that charges levied on industrial users may be varied following discussions between the interested parties. Other aspects of water policy may also be determined through such negotiations, e.g. the fixing of 'acceptable levels' of discharge of industrial effluent into rivers, or the rates of compensation payable to private landowners in respect of RWA developments such as the construction of a new pumping station, or the charges levied on private developers for the installation of new water and sewer pipes. The main point to note about all this is that the negotiation of water policy takes place informally and exclusively, and tends only to involve representatives of large-scale private sector interests. The great majority of water users (including small business and groups with a conservationist or leisure interest in water) are excluded and are left with no other option but to do what they can through the powerless Consumer Consultative Committees operating at divisional level.

Conclusions

Earlier in this chapter, four tentative hypotheses were outlined regarding the conditions under which corporatist modes of interest mediation may develop around the provision of urban services. Each of these hypotheses emphasised the significance of one element abstracted from the dual politics thesis. Thus the hypotheses variously emphasised the importance of the type of policy area and interests affected (production/consumption); the level at which intervention occurs (regional/local); the formal mode of interest representation (non-elective/elective); and the values of those responsible for managing the service in question (property/citizenship). In addition, it was also suggested that we should examine the possibility that no one of these elements on its own could be taken as causally significant.

The evidence from the three cases studies discussed above points strongly, though not conclusively, to the first of these hypotheses. In other words, it does seem that the major factor determining whether or not corporatist forms of mediation develop is the type of policy area and hence the type of interests most directly affected by state actions. In Melbourne, for example, it was precisely because the council's strategy plan had such important implications for city centre land and commercial interests that these groups eventually mobilised to have the city council dismissed and replaced by commissioners with whom they could liaise and consult more exclusively. Similarly in Canberra, the reluctant shift from a bureaucratic to a corporatist mode on the part of the NCDC directly reflected the concerns of central area business and developer interests that the commission's planning orthodoxy was harming private sector profitability. In England, too, corporatist strategies have developed within the Regional Water Authorities in respect of those aspects of water provision which impinge directly upon producer interests (e.g. agricultural land drainage, infrastructure provision for development, pollution control and charges for major users), while there was no evidence from the case study of similar arrangements having developed in the Regional Health Authorities, where it is consumer rather than producer interests that are most affected by the policies followed.

Our support for this first hypothesis must, however, be qualified in that each of the other three hypotheses can claim a limited degree of empirical validity from the case study evidence.

Hypothesis (2), which suggests that corporatism is primarily a function of the level at which urban services are organised, clearly cannot stand on its own, for the case studies have shown that corporatist strategies can evolve without any necessary shift from local to regional level. In Melbourne, the commissioners operated out of the town hall; in Canberra, the NCDC continued to operate at the same scale while evolving a different strategy; and in the English water authorities, corporatist arrangements were developed at divisional as well as regional level (although they were more significant in the latter than in the former). However, it is clearly the case (as can be seen both in the case of planning in Melbourne and that of water services in England) that a shift from local to regional level makes it easier to develop corporatist forms of mediation if only because the higher level of organisation is inherently less accessible to unorganised interests. Furthermore, it is notable in all three case studies that the state agencies concerned traced their accountability upwards rather than down (the Melbourne commissioners to the Victorian state government; the NCDC to the federal Department of the Capital Territory; and the RWAs to the central DoE and Ministry of Agriculture). This suggests that the crucial question is not so much the level at which agencies operate as the level to which they are accountable. In any event, the question of levels remains important as a secondary factor in the analysis of corporatism in urban services.

A similar point may be made in respect of the third hypothesis, which emphasises the significance of formal systems of representation for the development of a corporatist mode. It is clear from the case studies that a corporatist strategy is a lot easier to follow where electoral democracy has been sidestepped. In Melbourne, the development of corporatism followed the sacking of the city council; in Canberra it occurred in the absence of any history of local democracy; and in the case of water provision in England it took root following the 1974 reforms which removed water from local authority hands. In all three cases, furthermore, there was an attempt to seek what amounts to a spurious form of electoral legitimacy through the establishment of token popular forms of representation ('access time' in Melbourne; the ACT House of Assembly in Canberra; and the Community Health Councils and Consumer Consultative Committees in the English regional authorities) which provided the thinnest of disguises for the non-democratic arrangements that had evolved. Nevertheless, it is also clear that the creation of a democratic vacuum does not in itself foster the development of a corporatist mode of interest mediation, for as we saw in the case of the English RHAs and (until recently) the NCDC, state agencies may instead develop a strongly managerial ethos which renders the organisation immune to virtually any input from outside interests.

This brings us to the fourth hypothesis, which asserts the centrality of the values of key state personnel in influencing the development or otherwise of corporatist forms. Here the evidence suggests that the values of urban managers are important but not determinate. Strategically placed state employees can facilitate the development of corporatist strategies where (as in the case of the Melbourne Commissioners and the chairman of the water authority that was studied) their personal values lead them to emphasise the importance of maintaining private sector buoyancy and of defending the rights of private property. Equally, they can hinder the development of such strategies where (as in the NCDC in Canberra) they see the private sector as a threat to their own values and objectives. However, the fact that corporatism can develop both where it is welcome and where it is not suggests that managerial values should be treated as a secondary rather than primary factor in the analysis.

Our conclusion, therefore, is that the development of corporatist forms in urban service provision is primarily a function of the type of service in question, i.e. whether or not it has direct implications for major producer interests in society. In all three case studies, the development of corporatist forms has in one way or another reflected pressure from private sector interests such as landowners, developers and commercial and industrial firms for relatively exclusive access to state agencies that are responsible for regulating or providing resources such as development land, physical infrastructure or energy and raw material inputs, and in all three cases such access was achieved while competing consumer interests—residents, amenity groups, community organisations and so on—were kept at arm's length. However, in positing the distinction between production and consumption interventions as the major factor in explaining the growth of urban corporatist forms, it is also suggested on the strength of the empirical material discussed in this chapter that other factors – the level at which intervention is organised, the existence or otherwise of formal electoral arrangements and the values that predominate within state agencies – may have important mediating effects. In this sense, the type of policy area (and hence the type of interests most directly affected) is the 'independent variable' of our analysis, while the other three factors represent significant 'intervening variables'. Thus the most fertile ground for the emergence of corporatist forms of urban service provision relates (as suggested by the dual politics thesis) to those interventions where producer interests are most directly affected and where the resulting tendency towards corporatism is reinforced by the existence of non-local and non-elected agencies that are staffed by individuals who are sympathetic to the concerns expressed by propertied interests.

Chapter 7

Corporatism and Planning

James Simmie

Introduction

The comparatively recent revival in interest in the study of corporatism has been focused mainly on the political relationships between big capital, organised labour and national government. Much has been made of the tripartite political negotiations between those largely economically defined groups. In particular, their negotiations over such policies as those affecting prices and incomes have received considerable attention.

From the point of view of neoclassical economic analysis, however, capital and labour must be joined by land as the three major categories of factors of production. Indeed, virtually all forms of production require land on which to combine capital and labour. Conflicts over the uses of this third major factor of production and the buildings that are placed upon it are focused on both central and local government. Conflicts over the more physical aspects of the uses of land and buildings are concentrated on the town and county planning system. It is these conflicts that are the main objects of study in this chapter.

First, it is argued that disputes over land uses involve political bargaining that diverges increasingly from the pluralist democratic and accountable paradigm. Definitions of this and a corporatist paradigm are offered. The type of government planning of primary concern in this analysis is also defined.

Second, it is argued that pluralist and corporatist political bargaining depends upon the prior existence of relevant economic structures and distributions. In this analysis the major assumption is made that these structures and the relationships between them are best understood in terms of neo-Keynesian economic theory. This is shown to have some relevance for categorising the existing patterns of land-ownership and use in Britain. Their relationships to government via the formal town and country planning system are outlined.

Third, the major part of this chapter analyses the findings of the main studies conducted so far which analyse planning from the point of view of the appropriateness of the pluralist and corporatist paradigms of political bargaining. This involves summarising the development planning system as it existed between 1947 and 1973–4 (Simmie, 1981). After the legislative changes made to this system in 1968 and the start of their implementation with the reorganisation of local government in 1973–4 separate analyses need to be made of participation in structure planning (Darke, 1979) and local planning (Girling, 1980; and Doak, 1982). The day-to-day control of development can be seen at work in the development control system that has always involved informal bargaining (Simmie, 1981). Some of these deals are formalised into contractual obligations. At present this is accomplished by using section 52 of the 1971 Town and Country Planning Act (see Jowell, 1977a and b; Reade, 1982). Finally, some indication of the relative power of the different groups and organisations competing for land uses may be gained from examining the immediate physical outcomes of development planning and control (Simmie, 1981; Doak, 1982).

It is concluded from these analyses that major landowning and production organisations are involved in corporatist-type bargaining with government at the local level over land uses. Pluralist, mainly consumer-oriented groups do not generally enjoy the same type of access to government land-use decision-making. There is also a tendency to move the more significant production-related land-use decisions away from the most local levels to less local levels of government.

Definitions

'In a political system where nearly every adult may vote but where knowledge, wealth, social position, access to officials, and other resources are unequally distributed, who actually governs?' (Dahl, 1974, p. 1). With this question Dahl and his colleagues, Polsby (1963) and Wolfinger (1960), began their studies of local power in New Haven. They were to conclude that the growth and development of that town had led to a change in its local political system from one dominated by a single cohesive oligarchy to one dominated in different circumstances by different sets of leaders. This they defined as a pluralist system. Even for Dahl this was not a system in which the local community was ruled by all its people equally. Instead it was merely a political system that was dominated by more than one oligarchy and whose different oligarchies tended to dominate different key issues. This is a long way from popular conceptions of pluralist democracy in which all individuals and groups may participate equally without undue disadvantage due to various other inequalities.

In this analysis I wish to restrict the definition of pluralism to this latter 'ideal type' of political action and label it as 'perfect pluralism'. Perfect pluralism I shall define as a political system in which all individuals may participate equally in political decision-making, irrespective of the distribution of knowledge, wealth, social position, access to officials or other resources.

In contrast to pluralism, I wish to define corporatism as a political system based on participation by the ruling oligarchies of large organisations rather than individuals. These organisations are functionally differentiated from one another and for this reason they are both the singular representative of their interests and not in competition with each other. They are normally large and therefore contain an extensive and hierarchically ordered division of labour. The ruling oligarchies of these organisations have regular, often secret, contacts with the political oligarchies of government. They will be recognised by each other as speaking for their respective interests. As a result of the bargains struck between them the non-government organisations may be made responsible for implementing some of the political decisions taken in this way.

There are a number of differences between corporatist internal access to government decision-making and other types of insider connections. The first is one of degree. The ruling oligarchies of large organisations will usually have a more regular and/or higher level of direct access to key government decision-making centres than the elites of pluralist pressure groups. Second, the resources that large organisations can muster either to gain access to implement joint decisions or even to effect the national economy, mean that government will be more likely to encourage and instigate negotiations with them than with pluralist groups. The former will usually appear as a source of resources for the implementation of decisions. The latter will usually appear as a supplicant to government for resources. This puts a different complexion on internal government negotiations with them.

Both perfect pluralism and corporatism defined in these ways are 'pure ideal types' whose complete existence in practice is objectively possible but practically unlikely. Their purpose is to provide 'pure' categories or yardsticks with which observed empirical reality may be compared.

In this chapter the empirical reality to be compared against them is the political conflicts over land uses and buildings which are focused on the town and county planning system. This system is primarily concerned with the physical aspects of development which is statutorily defined as 'the carrying out of building, engineering, mining or other operations in, on, over or under land or the making of any material change of use in any building or other land' (Town and County Plannning Act, 1971).

The day-to-day political control of development is carried on by district councils in England and Wales. Strategic plannning in the form of structure plans is the responsibility of county councils. Their powers are delegated from central government through the Department of the Environment (DoE), which still retains the ultimate power of decisions over local planning authorities through the Secretary of State for the Environment.

It will be argued that political conflicts over planning decisions at these different levels of government exhibit a mixture of pluralist and corporatist elements. This mixture of pluralism and corporatism I wish to define as 'imperfect pluralism'. In general this mixture of types of political interest intermediation is characterised by interactions between the ruling oligarchies of economic and political organisations primarily concerned with production. The more contentious the land uses at stake, the higher the level of government at which oligarchical interactions take place and at which political resolutions eventually emerge. In contrast, imperfect pluralism is also characterised by interactions between individuals, voluntary organisations and government, mainly over issues of consumption. Such interactions usually involve restricted and external access to the lower echelons either between or within levels of government.

Structures

Before seeking to evaluate empirical case studies of the politics of planning, it is necessary to outline briefly the structure of political economy in general and land ownership in particular which defines the significant categories of groups and organisations with economic and political interests in planning decisions and outcomes. These categories will then be used to evaluate the significance of the pluralist and corporatist paradigms in understanding the politics of land-use planning.

Figure 7.1 illustrates a neo-Keynesian view of the structure of a political economy. It shows four main sectors and the most significant flows of expenditures and goods between them. The four main sectors are production, capital, government and consumers. The production sector includes all those organisations or individuals who produce goods or services for intermediate or final consumption. The capital sector may be defined as all those organisations or individuals who own or control the finances required by other sectors of the political economy in order to produce, govern or consume. Government includes the formal, political and administrative agencies of central and local government. Consumers are all individuals involved in the final consumption of goods and services.

For the purposes of this analysis production may be divided broadly into large public boards, private corporations and small firms. The capital sector may be divided into big (i.e. concentrated) and small capital. Government may be divided into central and local. Consumers can be broadly divided into 'middle' and 'working' class. Flows of expenditures are illustrated by broken lines, while flows of goods and services are indicated by unbroken lines. Flows of exports and imports are excluded.

From the definitions above it is to be expected that corporatist forms of political interaction are most likely to be found in the

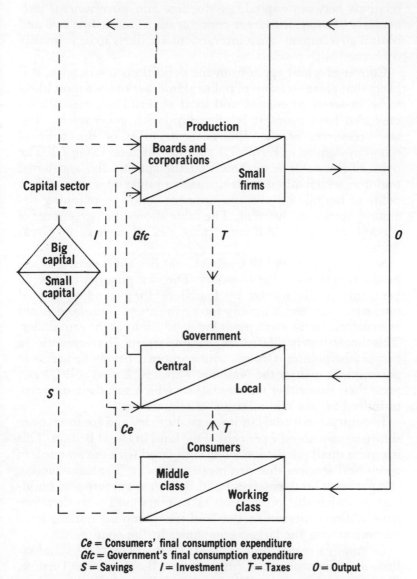

Ce = Consumers' final consumption expenditure
Gfc = Government's final consumption expenditure
S = Savings   I = Investment   T = Taxes   O = Output

Sources: Pen, J. (1965) *Modern Economics* (Harmondsworth: Penguin); Prest, A. R. and Coppock, D. J. (1978) *The U.K. Economy* (London: Weidenfeld & Nicolson).

FIGURE 7.1   *Neo-Keynesian view of the structure of a political economy*

relations between capital, production and government, particularly between the larger concentrations of the first two and central government. Such interactions are likely to be primarily concerned with production.

Conversely, and again from the definitions used above, it is likely that pluralist forms of political interactions are most likely to be between consumers and local government. Small firms may also have pluralist relationships with government. The land resources of the different categories of the political economy defined in Figure 7.1 are illustrated in Table 7.1. The point of this table is to show that the specifically land-based resources which different groups and organisations start with in political bargaining over government land-use planning decisions, are vastly different. The table shows the percentage of acreage owned by different categories of owners in Great Britain.

Some 63 per cent of all land in Great Britain is owned by the production sector of the economy. The vast majority of this (56 per cent) is still owned by feudal or long-standing landed interests. They use it mainly for agribusiness. This land is not even subject to the same planning regulations as the remainder. This immediately illustrates an important characteristic of corporatist politics. Groups with corporatist types of access to government such as the National Farmers' Union (NFU) can press their case either for regulations which suit their interests, or indeed for the minimisation of regulation.

In contrast to feudal landowners, industry and commerce are shown to own about 7 per cent of the land in Great Britain. This is a quite small proportion when compared with the amounts of goods and services that are produced on it. The construction companies, who themselves build the infrastructure and buildings in which this production takes place and who therefore have a direct interest in the land-use planning system, have become among the largest companies in the country.

Company size may be measured in terms of market capitalisation, annual turnover or employment. By the 1980s Tarmac, Blue Circle Industries, Wimpey and Barratt Developments ranked among the 100 largest companies in Great Britain on the first criterion (*Observer*, 29 January 1984, p. 26). Wimpey, Tarmac and Barratt also featured among the top ten construction companies in terms of turnover in 1980 (Grant and Streeck, 1983, p. 45). Wimpey, Laing, William Press and Taylor Woodrow also employed the largest numbers of workers in the British construction industry in 1980 (Grant and Streeck, 1983 p. 45).

Although the capital sector owns an even smaller (1 per cent) share of land than the production sector, the land it does own is often among the highest in value, with the most valuable income generating buildings upon it. For the purposes of this analysis the capital sector is defined as those financial and property companies who invest a significant proportion of their capital in land and buildings as financial assets which they do not usually occupy themselves.

In terms of market capitalisation the capital sector includes some of the largest corporations in Britain. Among them are the big four banks and the main assurance companies. Even if they only have small proportions of their total funds invested in land and buildings, these still represent very substantial amounts of capital.

Property companies with most of their funds invested in land and buildings are also among the largest companies in Great Britain. Land Securities (nineteenth, $1,336.3m) and Hammerson Properties (sixty-second, $510.0m) are two of the main examples in this category.

The capital sector is therefore much more important in the process of land-use decisions on high value sites and buildings than its proportionate ownership of the land would indicate. Because of the selective nature of its interest in planning, however, representatives of the capital sector only tend to appear in a limited number of key decisions, such as those involving Coin Street on the South Bank of the Thames in London (Girling, 1980).

Government itself is a substantial landowner. Central government owns about 9 per cent, while local government owns about 8 per cent of the land in Britain. In part this degree of government ownership (which is greater than that of industry and commerce) may give government some interests in its own right in the use of land and planning decisions. Among these interests, as with those of feudal landowners, has been an interest in avoiding the same kind of planning regulations which apply, for example, to private industry or private housebuilders.

Finally, consumers in the shape of charities and owner-occupiers may own around 20 per cent of the land in Great Britain. This figure is derived rather speculatively by deducting the other totals shown in Massey and Catalano (1978, p. 59) from a hypothetical 100 per cent. Nevertheless, as the actual amount of land owned by individuals and charities in small parcels cannot be more than one-fifth of the total, this illustrates at once the scale of the difference between landowners with potentially corporatist access to the town and county planning system and those with potentially pluralist connections with it.

Taken together, Table 7.1 and the figures showing the scale of financial resources available to the industries and the capital sector with major interests in the land uses and buildings, show the substantial differences in landownership and finance between the production and capital sectors of the economy which use land for economic purposes, and consumers who use it primarily as a place to live.

They therefore bring substantially different resources to the political bargaining that is focused on the town and country planning system. This system was established on a statutory and mandatory basis by the Town and Country Planning Act of 1947. This designated certain local authorities as local planning authorities and charged them with producing a Development Plan and then co-ordinating the mainly private applications for development according to this plan. This system was changed in the 1968 Town and Country Planning Act which split development planning into Structure (strategic) Plans and Local (detailed) Plans. In England and Wales these were made the responsibility of different types of authority. Structure plans were made the responsibility of the counties, while local plans were passed to the districts. Local, district plans had to be certified as being in accordance with the provisions of the structure (county) plans.

After the major reorganisation of local government in England and Wales in 1973–4, the division of the old-style development plan into structure and local plans also corresponded to the division between counties and districts. At that time the process of development control was also split between the two types of local authority. Districts were made responsible for

TABLE 7.1   *Landownership: per cent of acreage of land by known different owners in Great Britain*

Economic sector	Type of landowner	Total % acreage
Production	Feudal landowners	
	Crown estate	0.51
	Monarchy	0.41
	Aristocracy (great private estates	31.60
	Private individuals (gentry)	19.01
	Church	0.30
	Universities	0.56
	Trusts	3.59
	Sub-total	55.98
	Industry and commerce	
	Private companies	5.15
	Nationalised industries	1.73
	Sub-total	6.88
Capital sector	Financial companies	0.89
Government	Central government	9.18
	Local authorities	7.67
	Sub-total	16.85
Consumers	Charities	2.60
	Private individuals (owner-occupiers)	16.80?
	Sub-total	19.40?

Source: adapted from Massey, D. and Catalano, A. (1978) *Capital and Land* (London: Edward Arnold), Table 3.6, p. 59.

all routine decisions. Applications for development which had strategic implications were supposed to be passed to the counties. This division of responsibility was changed in the 1980 Local Government Planning and Land Act, which transferred virtually all responsibility for development control decisions to the districts.

Politics and planning

Having outlined the structures of the political economy and landownership in which the British land-use planning system is located, the chapter now turns to illustrative case studies of how different groups of land-owners and users relate politically to the planning system. These illustrations show the ways in which different types of feudal landowners, industry and commerce, financial interests, government, voluntary associations and individuals had their interests intermediated by local planning authorities. The case studies give a brief summary of these phenomena under the now replaced development plans, and a more lengthy exposition of them in the working of contemporary structure and local plans and development control.

Development plans

Development plans have generally been replaced by structure and local plans since the reorganisation of local government in 1973–4. They were the main statutory planning policy documents from 1947 until 1968, and in practice at least until 1973–4. They consisted of a written policy statement and a map showing, on a cartographic base, detailed land-use plans for a period of around twenty years. The politics of the production and implementation of the Oxford Development Plan have been analysed in detail by Simmie (1981). Because development plans are no longer used, the results of this study will only be summarised briefly.

The case study of the political conflicts over what should be included in Oxford's Development Plan, with respect to the central area of the city, illustrates some of the differences in the relationships between the production and corporatist sections of the local political economy, the consumption and pluralist sections, and government. Although the corporatist organisations were neither singular nor non-competitive, they were hierarchically structured, limited in number, functionally differentiated, and dominated by small oligarchies who were incorporated into various levels of government decision-making with respect to land-use planning. Apart from their significant resource advantages, their presence in the relatively secret political bargaining over the 'rules of the game' was of crucial importance in furthering their interests.

Although the corporatist groups had regular contacts with the local authority, the number of such groups was limited rather than singular. They were, however, both recognised as legitimate interest groups and subsidised in various ways by the ramifications of the planning decisions in which they themselves had been involved. Finally, their connections with planning policy were those of concertation, but there was only a very limited devolution of authority to them in the implementation of those policies. It was private contractors, for example, who demolished and rebuilt St. Ebbe's.

In contrast, the pluralist individuals were of an unspecified number, had only a voluntary organisation to further their interests, were in competition with each other for scarce housing, were not hierarchically ordered, and were not predetermined by organisation into their specification of interests. Their relationships with the local authority were generally passive, irregular and not specially recognised. Their main connections with public policy were essentially those of an ineffective external pressure group.

Structure plans

The post-war experiences of planning in Oxford were not altogether untypical. Collectively they promoted two major changes in the planning system. The first arose from a concern with the time taken to confirm development plans as statutory documents in the face of conflicts of interest. This was also linked with the realisation that by the time detailed development plans did become statutory documents they were already out of date, and the process of reviewing them could take just as long again as their original production. Accordingly a Planning Advisory Group (PAG) recommended in 1965 that development plans should be divided into general, strategic structure plans and detailed local plans. The former would become statutory plans after a general examination in public (EIP) rather than after the previous legalistic and adversarial public inquiry. Local plans, on the other hand, only had to be adopted by local planning authorities provided that they were certified as being in accordance with the relevent structure plans. These recommendations were incorporated in the 1968 Town and Country Planning Act. A further concern arose as a result of the kind of experiences suffered by the residents of St. Ebbe's. A report was produced in 1969 of the deliberations under the chairmanship of Arthur Skeffington on participation in planning. Although the production of such a report by the Ministry of Housing and Local Government indicating a widespread feeling that pluralist participation in planning had been less than adequate, the reasons deduced for this tended to blame lack of understanding by the general public of planning rather than the reverse. There was little recognition that land-use planning might be dealing with a major resource over which there were genuine and fundamental conflicts of interest within the overall political economy. Despite this, a general requirement for increased participation in town planning was also included in the 1968 Act.

An early example of public participation in the new structure plans is provided by Darke (1979) in his case study of the EIP of the South Yorkshire structure plan. This shows that public participation in the formulation of the structure plan by the Labour-controlled county council was based on the assumption that members of the public needed explanation rather than direct political involvement. The county's public participation programme at the stage of drafting the plan was therefore mainly a public relations exercise. Most of the information flows were from the county to members of the public rather than vice versa. Thus, by the time the completed plan was placed on deposit for the EIP there had been no significant difference between pluralist group participation in its formation and that characteristic of old-style development plans.

Once completed, the South Yorkshire structure plan and its EIP proved less amenable to relevant analysis than development plans and public inquiries. There were a number of reasons for this. First, there are very few organisations whose detailed territorial interests extend county-wide in scope. Government bodies are among the few whose land-use interests cover such large areas of territory. Second, the actual form of the structure plan made it difficult for individuals to comprehend its relevance for them or for their particular areas. Broad generalisations and the lack of a detailed cartographic base make structure plans obscure documents to most people. Third, in order to obtain what are regarded as relevant and expedient discussion at EIPs, the Secretary of State has been given the power to select the topics for discussion and the participants. This means that the automatic right to be heard under the old development plan public inquiry system has been dropped. Fourth, EIPs are conducted by a panel of three people who are all appointed by the Secretary of State. They operate on the principle that the discussion of detailed matters is not appropriate, and so the agenda for discussion can be managed much more easily than was the case at public inquiries. Fifth, the agenda of the South Yorkshire EIP was managed so as to give the impression that what was under discussion was highly technical. As a result, discussion was largely confined to middle-class professionals and businessmen.

Darke concludes that these procedures managed to avoid discussion of the underlying political issues. These 'were the struggle for power and legitimacy between County Councils and the Metropolitan Districts, the ideological contradictions between Labour councils and local business interests, and the social costs of continued unemployment and decline in the most depressed areas of the country' (Darke 1979).

Table 7.2 reworks some of Darke's data and shows some of the differences between corporatist and pluralist groups participating in the South Yorkshire EIP. The groups have been divided into those with potentially corporatist relationships to planning decisions and those with potentially pluralist relationships. The first category includes production, capital and government organisations. The second category includes various pressure groups and individual consumers.

Table 7.2 shows that it was virtually only corporatist organisations that were specially invited to participate in the EIP. Among these, a majority were government organisations and roughly one-third were production organisations.

The scope of government-intended participation was broadened slightly in the category of those who were asked in a general way to participate in the EIP. Although the majority of organisations that received such a request were still likely to have corporatist relationships with government, a minority, one-fifth, could be said to be pluralist consumer-oriented groups. In the case of those corporatist organisations asked to participate, roughly one-third were producers, a tiny minority represented the capital sector, and two-fifths were government organisations.

Nevertheless, in both cases where organisations were asked to

TABLE 7.2   *Participants in South Yorkshire County Council structure plan examination in public, 1978*

Interest groups	Specially invited (nos)	Asked to participate (nos)	Total making representation (nos)
Corporatist			
Production			
Agricultural interest/land owners	1	–1	1
Mineral interests	–	1	2
Motoring interests/ employers	2	2	2
Nationalised industries	1	2	2
British Rail/Inland Waterways	–	–	2
Chamber of Commerce	–	7	8
Organised labour	1	1	3
Proportion (per cent)	**35**	**38**	**32**
Capital Sector			
Home builders/property interests	–	1	·1
Proportion (per cent)	**1**	**3**	**2**
Government			
Departments and Ministries	3	2	2
Commissions	1	1	1
Advisory councils	1	1	1
Regional Economic Planning Council	1	–	–
Water Authorities	–	2	2
Local authorities	1	9	13
(Parish councils)[1]	–	–	2
Proportion (per cent)	**56**	**40**	**35**
Pluralist			
Consumers			
Pressure groups	–	–	3
Amenity groups	–	5	8
Leisure interests	–	1	2
Individuals	1	1	5
Proportion (per cent)	**7**	**20**	**29**
Total N = 100 per cent[2]	14	37	60

Notes:
1. Parish councils may be considered pluralist in so far as higher level government organisations treat them as local pressure groups rather than as integral parts of government.
2. Total numbers would normally be considered insufficient to produce percentages, but that is done here to facilitate comparisons. Numbers do not sum to 100 per cent due to consistent rounding.

Source: Adapted from Darke, R. (1979) 'Public Participation and State Power: the case of South Yorkshire', *Policy and Politics*, Vol. 7, No. 4, Table 1, p. 344.

participate in the EIP, the vast majority were likely to have corporate relationships with local planning authorities. The same is also true if the proportions of all groups making representations to the EIP, whether invited or not, are examined. This shows that out of a total of sixty organisations, 32 per cent were producers, 2 per cent represented the capital sector, 35 per cent were government organisations, and 29 per cent were pluralist pressure groups or individuals.

The proceedings of the EIP and its results generally favoured producers. They criticised the structure plan proposals to discriminate in favour of directing new production, and therefore employment, towards the declining coal-mining and industrial areas along the River Dearne.

Local district councils and local business interests joined forces to argue that instead of being dispersed to the most deprived areas, such limited new economic activity that might take place should be concentrated in existing 'prosperous' centres. In these arguments they were also supported by central government preferences for 'growth pole' regional strategies, which required the concentration of new development around existing centres. The outcome was that the Secretary of State deleted the job priority area policy and affirmed that structure plans should not include policies that would interfere with business interests in existing major centres.

Although it is not possible to generalise from the experience of one study, evidence from the South Yorkshire EIP does suggest that, under the new structure plan system, the potential for corporatist interest intermediation to dominate planning policies is even greater than it was under the old development plan system. Certainly the potential for agenda management by central government appears to be much greater in the case of structure plans than it was for development plans. This tendency to shift agenda management and strategic planning to higher levels of government does not work in favour of local pluralist interests.

Local plans

With the split between structure and local plans, a new dimension to political conflict over planning policies was introduced. This additional dimension was that each plan became a claim to power and authority by the plan-making council over other local planning authorities. Nowhere is this better illustrated than in the long-running planning saga centred on the Coin Street area of central London (Girling, 1980).

The area is located on the South Bank of the Thames between the Waterloo and Blackfriars bridges. It is adjacent to the National Theatre. The majority of it falls within the Borough of Lambeth, but a minority portion lies within the Borough of Southwark. Despite this the Greater London Council owns a substantial proportion of the site and, until 1978, it was also the local planning authority for that part of the South Bank Comprehensive Development Area which included Coin Street. There has been no clear division of responsibilities between these local authorities, and this has contributed to conflicts between them over what uses should be made of the site.

In 1976 the Greater London Development Plan (GLDP) assessed the whole of the South Bank as an area of opportunity in which offices could be encouraged where consistent with environmental enhancement and approved local plans. In the same year the Central London Planning Conference (CLPC) produced their Advisory Plan for Central London (APCL), which emphasised the importance of both working and living in the centre of London.

In 1977 the Waterloo District Plan (WDP) became the first local plan to be approved by the Secretary of State for the Environment. While it did not conflict with the broad strategies of the APCL, it did conflict with the GLDP in so far as the Coin Street sites within Lambeth were zoned for residential and recreational purposes. Such uses were in line with the interests of local, pluralist inhabitants of the area.

The new local planning system also makes provision for the adoption by local authorities of various kinds of non-statutory local plans. In 1977 the then Labour-controlled GLC adopted a planning brief for some of the Coin Street area which provided for accommodation on the site. The following year a Conservative GLC reversed that policy and made representations to the Secretary of State to have the WDP rewritten so as to zone the site for offices.

In 1978 the Labour Secretary of State confirmed the original WDP, making Lambeth the statutory planning authority for that part of the CDA which fell within its boundary. Nevertheless, the GLC remained the planning authority for the sites in Southwark because no local plan had been adopted for that area.

Although Peter Shore, the Secretary of State, supported the WDP, he also granted office development permits (ODPs) to two representatives of the capital sector, namely the Heron Corporation and Commercial Properties. Despite this Lambeth granted itself planning permission for 251 dwellings on the sites in 1978. Peter Shore called in this planning application so that a public inquiry could be held into the proposals and their consequential compulsory purchase orders.

Three further planning applications were made before the planning inquiry opened in 1979. First, an application was made by the Association of Waterloo Groups, which was an umbrella organisation for twenty-four local, plural community groups. They required 360 low-rise homes. Second, two applications were made by the same property company, Greycoat London Estates, on behalf of Phillips Petroleum. One scheme contained offices and an hotel, the other deleted the hotel. This potentially corporatist alliance was granted an ODP in the remarkably short space of twenty-four hours.

Although the evidence is sometimes circumstantial, it does appear that there was significant corporatist interest intermediation between the ruling oligarchies of the property companies and the GLC under Conservative control. For example, a Heron director was approached by the Conservative leader of the GLC, who was himself a millionaire property developer. As a result, the GLC planning committee pressed the Secretary of State to overrule the WDP and allow offices on the Coin Street sites in order to strengthen the economy of inner London. Despite the fact that the Labour Secretary of State did not appear to accept this view, he nevertheless granted ODPs to both Heron and Commercial Properties. Further evidence of corporatist interest intermediation came in 1979, when Greycoat was induced to join the fray by the head of planning at the GLC. They joined forces with Phillips Petroleum to acquire an ODP in record time. The main GLC contacts had Conservative party connections. This network facilitated corporatist interest intermediation.

The hierarchical structures and oligarchical distributions of

power within the relevant organisations contributed to corporatist types of interest intermediation focused on Coin Street.
In the GLC, for example, main policies are often initiated and
developed by the Leader's Committee. This means that the
limited number of leading councillors who sit on this committee
have a much higher degree of control over key decisions than the
rest of the ninety-two members who do not.

The significance of individuals arising from the roles they
perform within the ruling oligarchies of corporatist organisations illustrates the relevance of a neo-Weberian approach to the
understanding of power relationships. At the level of empirical
observation it may be seen that the social actions of specific
individuals and their networks of social contacts play a key
causal role in planning decisions. Admittedly the precise nature
and extent of these social interactions are very hard to trace in
detail. When they can be discovered, however, they are usually
shown to have been of crucial significance in the shaping of land-
use planning decisions.

In contrast to these important, informal and internal contacts
between key members of corporate hierarchies, pluralist groups
tend to be non-hierarchical, external to formal planning
decisions and lacking in networks of powerful contacts. The
pluralist groups representing the consumption sector of local
inhabitants of the Coin Street area were no exception.

As a result of several decades of unsatisfactory experiences
regarding participation in land-use planning decisions, pressure
groups with a particular interest in this area of government
decision-making have become better organised and more
sophisticated. Some of them have combined into coalitions such
as the Association of Waterloo Groups (AWG), mentioned
above, and the North Southwark Community Development
Group (NSCDG), which represents about twenty other voluntary groups. In addition to these umbrella organisations, the
Coin Street Action Group (CSAG) has also been fighting
proposals to commercialise the area.

From the beginning of the 1970s yet another group, the
Waterloo Community Development Group (WCDG), together
with CSAG and AWG, sought to influence local planning
policies by presenting proposals of their own. They succeeded in
establishing the local interest in housing in Lambeth's Waterloo

District Plan. CSAG and AWG also submitted a relevant planning application for much of the site in 1978. This, together with the proposals from the corporatist production sector, was called in for consideration at the requisite public inquiry in 1979.

In passing, it should also be mentioned that even pluralist pressure groups have social class hierarchies. In practice the social class composition of pressure groups and resources available to them are important determinants of their relative effectiveness. CSAG, for example, is run by middle-class interventionists. And, as Dearlove has pointed out in another London context in 1975, although middle-class activists may seek to assume a non-directive approach they soon assume a more positive and dominant role, resulting in the imposition of their own values and ideology on the rest of the group.

This often middle-class sophistication in pluralist, pressure-group politics accounts in large measure for the degree of success that CSAG, AWG and NSCG have had in the face of corporate interests in Coin Street. At the very least this has forced substantial consideration of their case at, up to now, two public inquiries.

The pluralist cause at Coin Street was assisted not only by their political skills but also by the fact that the Waterloo District Plan was the approved plan for the area, and by the ideological sympathy first of the two local boroughs and, after 1980, the GLC. These combined pressures forced the Secretary of State, Tom King, to approve both the mutually incompatible schemes from the pluralist and corporatist sectors in 1983. This unusual step provoked the GLC, Lambeth, Southwark, AWG and CSAG to challenge this decision in the High Court. Although they were unsuccessful, the continued delay and the necessity for further public inquiries eventually induced Greycoat to sell its option on the Coin Street Site to the GLC for £2.7 million in 1984.

The current (1984) situation is that the GLC is supporting the implementation of the mixed schemes proposed by the AWG. How effective this support will be in view of the fact that the GLC itself is to be abolished remains to be seen.

The Coin Street case study is particularly interesting from the point of view of the relative bargaining powers of corporatist and pluralist organisations and groups and also the difference that the ideological dispositions of different levels of government make to eventual outcomes. The study shows that, other things being equal, corporatist organisations with commercial development objectives have comparatively ready access to government decision-making, particularly at the higher and central levels. In contrast, pluralist, voluntary groups with consumption objectives do not have such ready access to any level of government.

What is so interesting about the Coin Street case study is that it shows that with sophisticated organisation, persistence and a massive investment of time and energy, pluralist groups can overcome their initial bargaining weakness and lack of access to government. It also shows that this requires essentially middle-class political skills and ideologically sympathetic government organisations. The combination of these two characteristics permits pluralist groups to become integrated, especially at lower levels, in government decisions concerning consumption issues and land-use planning.

The Coin Street study therefore shows that the outcomes of land-use conflicts between corporatist land users and pluralist land inhabitants cannot always be predicted in advance. The system does allow persistent pluralist groups to gain some successes. This is important not only in terms of significant outcomes but also for the perceived legitimacy of the system as a whole.

Nevertheless, in both the South Yorkshire and the Coin Street case studies of the new structure and local planning systems, corporatist interest representation was a key feature of land-use planning decisions. In each case the initially most influential organisations were a limited number of competing private or public oligarchies. They were hierarchically structured and functionally differentiated from other oligarchies and, indeed, from the pluralist and market sectors of the political economy. Although they were not singular organisations, they were both limited in number and had regular contacts with planning authorities. Some property companies may also be indirectly subsidised by the state in terms of not having to bear the costs of the production of the infrastructure that their buildings use, and also in having land assembled for them at less than its true market value.

The connections of corporatist organisations with planning policy are complex. They do involve concertation, some co-responsibility for policies and some internal roles in policy implementation. It is only very indirectly, however, that an organisation like Greycoat could be said to have some devolution of planning authority. The apparent success of the AWG over Greycoat may be an exception that proves the rule.

Development control

Physical planning is not a direct resource-allocating activity. Planning departments as such do not usually have budgets with which to fund development. Having established the formal 'rules of the game' in structure and local plans, public development is then funded and executed by other departments or agencies. The most important function of physical planning is then to react to proposals for development from the private, mostly production and capital, sectors of the political economy. This process is known as development control.

Until recently it was generally assumed that development control was based on rational, legal authority established in the provisions of various statutory development plans. These provisions were then supposed to be used in a judicial fashion to react to and reach unbiased planning decisions on mainly private applications for development. Leaving aside the evidence just presented on the corporatist nature of the incorporation of some interests rather than others in the provisions of development plans, evidence has also been produced to show that the judicial model of development control is being superseded by one based on bargaining, negotiations and corporatism. Almost inevitably, such plan bargaining must be between organisations drawn from the production and capital sectors of the political economy and government. This is because these organisations are the major controllers of the resources required for development.

Local authorities have had the power to enter into agreements with private owners since 1932. This power was not exercised much before the 1971 Town and Country Planning Act, whose Section 52 is the one covering most subsequent bargains. Some local authorities also have additional powers under section 126 of the 1974 Housing Act.

The nature of bargaining in development control under these powers since the reorganisation of local government has been documented by Jowell (1977a and b). He starts by making the important point that the courts have tended to strike down conditions imposed by local planning authorities in development control decisions that were not concerned with planning matters directly occasioned by the required development. Some lawyers therefore feel that planning by agreement may be seen as a device to permit the evasion of the criteria that the courts impose, and to release in development control the naked power that procedural justice attempts to restrain. Undue influence, collusion and the abuse of discretion may seem, on the surface, to be encouraged by a practice which seems close to a barter or a sale of planning permission (Jowell, 1977a, p. 415).

In 1975 Jowell conducted a survey of 28 per cent of English local authorities with development control powers. He asked which of them had acquired planning gain. This he defined as the achievement of a benefit to the community that was not part of the initial application (and was therefore negotiated) and that was not of itself normally commercially advantageous to the developer (Jowell, 1977a, p. 418).

Half of the 87 local planning authorities who responded to his questionnaire said they had acquired planning gain at some time. Among the London boroughs the proportion was much higher at two-thirds, with all but one of the inner London boroughs claiming to have acquired planning gain. Table 7.3 shows the type of bargains struck by the local planning authorities in Jowell's sample. The most significant type of bargain was the specification of an additional use to that proposed by the developer (24 per cent). This often involved seeking residential units in office developments. Other 'gains' sought involved specifying the type of use or even user in a development.

The next most typical bargain concerned the provision of public access on to land for which permission was sought (16 per cent). Land was dedicated for public use in 15 per cent of bargains and 'non-conforming' uses were extinguished in 14 per cent of bargains. The remaining types of bargains included the provision of community buildings (6 per cent), the rehabilitation of property (6 per cent), the provision of infrastructure (6 per cent), the gift of a site or buildings for residential use (6 per cent), and finally commuted payments for car parking (8 per cent).

TABLE 7.3 *Bargaining in development control*

Type of bargaining	Per cent
Specification of use	24
Public rights of way on the developer's land	16
Dedication of land to public use	15
Extinguishing existing user	14
The provision of community buildings	6
Rehabilitation of property	6
Provision of infrastructure	6
Gift of sale or buildings for residential use	6
Commuted payments for car parking	6
Total N = 100%[1]	104[2]

Notes:

1 Numbers do not sum to 100 due to consistent rounding.

2 Jowell acquired information from 87 local authorities, some of whom had struck more than one type of bargain. This figure represents the total number of bargains.

Source: Jowell, J. (1977a) 'Bargaining in Development Control', *Journal of Planning and Environmental Law*, July, pp. 414–33.

Roughly half (55) of all the bargains struck would be regarded as involving producers providing something that would be of direct benefit to consumers. This indicates the possibility that some pluralist interests may be served by local planning authority bargaining over development control. This, however, is an unpredictable outcome.

The sort of procedures employed in bargaining are generally corporatist in nature. They are normally conducted in secret. They usually only involve a few senior planning officers, possibly the chairman of the planning committee, and sometimes one other elected member. They are therefore negotiated by the top echelons of the ruling oligarchies of the potential developers and the local planning authority. They only surface before elected members of planning committees after their details have been worked out in private. The committees are under pressure to accept them because of the time and effort expended on them and by the good fortune of acquiring a 'free' community benefit.

These corporatist planning procedures may be contrasted with the 'normal' judicial model (Jowell, 1977b). In the latter conflicts of fact and value are resolved by an impartial third party according to rules and regulations that have been set down in advance by open political processes. In the case of plan bargaining, the local planning authority abandons its impartial, third party stance, and becomes involved in a two-way negotiation in which it exercises a high degree of administrative discretion.

This procedure allows developers to avoid the zero-sum possibilities of the judicial model. It also allows them a much greater degree of control over the decision-making process than they would have had in an adjudicative situation where the decision is imposed rather than agreed. In other words, the power of developers from the production and capital sectors of the political-economy is less restrained where corporatist bargaining procedures are employed rather than under the judicial model of development control.

Jowell (1977b) outlines the characteristics of the judicial model that may be contrasted with corporatist forms of decision-making. First, the adversarial process recognises the existence of conflicts and attempts to ensure that the differently perceived facts and values are at least expressed before a decision is reached. Second, decisions are made according to democratically established rules rather than at the arbitrary discretion of authorities. Third, similar cases are treated alike, thus ensuring some measure of distributive justice. Finally, the outcomes of rational-legal rules are relatively predictable.

Simmie (1981) and Doak (1982) have both shown that, at least in Oxford and Bromley, where corporatist processes are present in development control, all the requirements of the judicial model are violated to some degree. Both analyses show that, in the areas studied, the majority of applications (70 per cent and 63 per cent respectively) for development came from the production sector of the political economy. The degree of discretion exercised by the local planning authorities extended to making decisions that were quite contrary to the formal provisions of their approved planning policies. There are examples where both feudal landowners and producers were permitted large-scale developments in the green belt.

Both studies show that pluralist residents were not treated in the same way as corporatist organisations over the same area of land. The net result was often that the poorest residents lost housing while businesses gained shops and offices. This entailed some substantially unequal planning outcomes with respect to the immediate distributions of land and buildings. In such cases the power of corporatist organisations was directly reflected in development control decisions.

Finally, both studies show that actual planning outcomes could not necessarily be predicted on the basis of policies contained in the development or local plans. Thus, the informal exercise of discretion on the part of the local planning authorities usually involved a departure from rules that had been established under formal procedures.

Conclusions

Participation in the procedures of local physical planning authorities is characterised more by corporatist than by pluralist forms of interest mediation. Although both forms may still be observed, there is a tendency for the former to develop at the expense of the latter.

The reasons for this are, first, that land is a major resource owned, controlled or used by the production and capital sectors of the political economy. Together these sectors own the majority of all land and the most valuable buildings in the country. They therefore have a strong interest in land-use planning which seeks to control the uses of some of that land and those buildings. These strong interests are translated into political pressure at all the relevant levels of government.

Second, under the 1947 – 68 planning system which was based on an adversarial, judicial approach to development planning and control, the major functional interests were already incorporated, to some extent, in planning processes. Their deals could be challenged, however, by almost anyone at public inquiries. Such conflicts could be long, drawn-out and costly.

Third, the changes made to the planning system in 1968 have increased the possibilities for relatively unchallenged corporatist interest intermediation while, at the same time, making it more difficult for pluralist groups of consumers to enter into effective negotiations with local planning authorities. Structure plans are now subject to discretionary, inquisitorial examinations rather than judicial enquiries. The Secretary of State controls the agenda and most of the participants. Local plans can be adopted at the discretion of district planning authorities. The latter have also produced thousands of non-statutory, under-the-counter plans which are not necessarily the subject of any external participation at all.

Fourth, corporatist organisations are most important in the detailed implementation of these plans. The process of development control, which is supposed to decide on the merits of planning applications according to the policies laid down in plans, has always been open to corporatist types of bargaining. Since the early 1970s, however, some statutory provisions have encouraged this procedure still further.

Fifth, local councils, regardless of political complexion, are increasingly drawn to corporatist bargaining. This is either because in the few remaining areas of economic growth it is not possible for them to meet their housing requirements, or because in areas of economic decline any development is seen as beneficial.

For these reasons there has been a long-term drift towards corporatism in physical planning in Britain. Case studies have now shown that a limited number of organisations from the production and capital sectors of the political economy fill key roles in planning. Although these organisations are neither singular nor non-competitive, they are hierarchically ordered and functionally differentiated. Within them their upper echelon, controlling oligarchies are the specific individuals who deal with local planning authorities.

These dealings are with the ruling political oligarchies of top officers and committee chairmen in the authorities concerned. A limited number of external oligarchies have fairly regular meetings with their local political elites. The organisations of the former are sometimes indirectly subsidised by the state as a result of planning decisions to which they have been party. Corporatist connections with planning do involve concertation both in setting the 'rules of the game' and in manipulating those rules later on. While local councils cannot devolve their formal planning authority, developments involving bargaining do make private organisations responsible for the implementation of parts of planning policies.

While participation in planning still retains some elements of pluralist interest representation, even this favours 'middle-class' over 'working-class' pressure groups at the local level. The latter are much more reliant on organised trade union and Labour Party pressure on central government for policies leading to general local planning gains. It should be noted, however, that it is at the level of central government that their interests too can be represented in a corporatist fashion.

At the local level effective interest representation in planning is largely confined to elites drawn from functionally differentiated organisations. This is corporatism.

Chapter 8

Corporatism and the Local Economy

Roger King

Local corporatism

A particular emphasis of this book is on the importance of examining corporatism at the local level. In Chapter 1 Wyn Grant points out that corporatism is a phenomenon that can flourish in particular sectors or locations even when it is absent in a country at national level. He suggests that 'micro-corporatist' arrangements might have more of an effect on the organisation of a society than national tripartite bargaining, which, despite the high publicity it often attracts, may be only feebly implemented. A recent study of the micro-electronics industry leads to a similar conclusion. Here, as in other policy sectors in the British system, 'are to be found tripartite structures and a tendency to concentrate on smaller manageable problems rather than try for agreement on radical change' (Richardson, 1982, p. 346). Until recently, however, the relevancy of corporatist analysis for local political processes was unclear. For example, Cawson and Saunders' rejection of a unitary theory of the state in favour of an ideal-typical 'dual state' model linked corporatist forms of interest intermediation and policy implementation to national decision-making. At this level the centrality of production-related issues, the state's primary interest in securing the needs of capital accumulation, tends to lead to *ad hoc* tripartite agencies on which the interests of capital and labour are directly represented. At the local level, however, are more likely to be found non-class, consumption/reproduction struggles (over education, housing, health-care provision, etc.), and policy-making is characterised by an imperfect pluralism in which other than capitalist interests are likely to prevail (Cawson and Saunders, 1983).

Nor are these developments confined to the British case. Friedland (1982), in a study of the Federal Urban Renewal Programme in a number of United States cities, persuasively argues that the dependency of local authorities on business for production and taxes, allied to the ability of capital to move quickly in response to locational variation in profitability, allowed business to determine the outcomes of the programme. It is the local density of business's organisational resources that is important, and which does not simply shape policy, but also policy-making by affecting which local conditions affect local policy and which do not. Moreover, while local authorities may be dependent on business, the relationship is not all one-way. Firms are required to use local government to facilitate land-use changes and to provide the public infrastructure that makes their investments profitable. In effect, urban renewal put public powers – eminent domain, public subsidy and public investment – at the service of cities' office economies. Urban renewal was adopted in cities where downtown economies were not only alive, but growing, and where the downtown corporate office and retail economies were strong, not weak.

In other countries, too, closer ties can be detected between the public and private sector at local level. Johnson and Cochrane (1981, p. 132), in a comparative investigation of local authority economic policy-making in Britain and Germany, conclude that it is increasingly common for authorities in both countries to respond to problems of high unemployment and manufacturing decline by forging new 'client' relationships with local business as part of their well-established 'local welfare' orientations. Corporate systems are also developing rapidly in the Scandinavian countries. Hernes and Selvik (1981, p. 107) point to the increasing frequency and importance of contacts between business and the authorities with the interface highest and most intense at municipal level, and with more organised interaction between officials and business interests organisations (see Cawson, Chapter 5 of this volume).

The model advanced by Cawson and Saunders, however, allows for local corporatist developments, particularly if the local state becomes more involved in production issues, and they discern 'corporatist elements' in certain strategic planning functions undertaken by county councils and regional bodies. In Chapter 5 of this volume, Cawson points to corporatist developments as a consequence of increased local state intervention in the economy. In some areas production as an issue has been put back on local political agendas by deindustrialisation, which can significantly increase non-class movements based on local labour markets seeking to defend the locality by engaging in the increasingly competitive search for capital investment for their areas. Economic decline can generate corporatist alliances between local politicians, capital and labour in defence of local economies (Urry, 1983, p. 39). Jessop (1978, p. 45) detects corporatist forms of representation emerging at local and regional level as linked with the growing centralisation of local power and its insulation from popular control since local government reorganisation in 1974. In this view, corporatism steadily extends to local policy-making, despite short-term 'backtrackings', for it enables the state to support capital accumulation more effectively by insulating economic policies from popular accountability. Economic decline appears to have encouraged closer ties between government and the private sector in previously prosperous non-metropolitan areas. Flynn (1983, p. 100) has pointed to a growing interest by planners in such areas in directly involving industrialists in discussions of policy options and the presence of a 'taken-for-granted' consensus on the need to expand commercial development rather than to limit it.

If the pertinence of corporatist analysis for local politics is now more clearly recognised, how apposite is it for analysing the political practice of organised business as opposed to organised labour? A theme in this book is that corporatism is characterised by interest intermediation, and this is a significant factor in distinguishing it from pluralism. In corporatist arrangements, not only are interests represented to government, but, as a consequence of involvement in policy formulation and policy implementation, interests are mediated and controlled by associational leaders who exert discipline and control over members. However, while this may be true for trade unions, capitalist associations do not control their members in the same way. While trade unions are vital for workers in creating the bargaining power and collective will to overcome the market weakness of individual workers, business organisations tend to represent existing power – that which is defined at the level of individual capitals or member firms. Capitalist associations defend in the political arena those individual interests (taxes, tariffs, etc.) that are common to all or most member firms. Consequently, such associations have little substantial control over the actions their members choose to pursue (Offe, 1981, p. 147). We shall see, however, that the problem facing business organisations is less one of controlling demanding members than one of resurrecting any interest at all from the bulk of the membership in their representational activities.

Public and private sectors

A characteristic of liberal or societal corporatism is that the boundary between the public and private sectors becomes less clear-cut, with many 'public' functions provided by ostensibly 'private' associations or by partnerships between public and private agencies. This may result from either the state delegating functions to private bodies or from increased interventionism by the state into the realm of private activity. In Britain, however, there has long been confusion about the precise location of the boundary between the public and private sectors within the economy. Although the power of the state has expanded greatly in recent decades, as elsewhere, there has been less the growth of an all-powerful central authority than the development of shared powers between the public and private sectors. The so-called 'franchise state' (Wolfe, 1977) has had the advantage of encouraging co-operation between government and businessmen, who would have resisted having it forced on them through the state, and has often parcelled out public authority to bodies containing substantial 'private' involvement, such as the major economic interest groups (Cawson, 1982; Harris, 1972; Middlemas, 1979).

In recent years the boundary between the public and private sectors has become even more indented. The current Conservative administration is engaged in 'privatising' or 'hiving off' to the private sector what have been publicly provided services, while the number of 'public-private' organisations has also expanded. These include local enterprise agencies and bodies such as FIG (the Financial Institutions Group) that have been encouraged by the Department of the Environment (DoE) as part of its policy to induce private investment into inner-city and other neglected areas. FIG, for example, is comprised mainly of senior financial managers seconded from the private sector, working under government direction and devising schemes for facilitating local authority/private company ventures to develop industrial projects in blighted urban areas (Young, 1982, p. 1).

The development of local enterprise agencies and trusts is a further example of private-sector activity specifically related to public policies. They provide a broad-based consultancy service to start-up businesses, including financial and planning advice, and are usually sponsored by a group of large local companies. These contribute to an agency's financies and help provide its advisory services, while the director of the agency will generally be seconded from one of the sponsor firms. Chambers of Commerce are often important initiators of such ventures, and a number of enterprise agencies are located on chamber premises. Public sector support for the enterprises has come from direct local authority financial aid, usually in its role as one of the sponsors, while DoE regional staff have also specifically been asked to encourage agencies in their areas. However, even the government's facilitative role has now become partly 'privatised' in this area as the DoE has turned to a recently formed 'private' association – 'Business in the Community' – to take on the job of encouraging new agencies. Formed in 1982 with the objective of 'bringing together groups of local companies to work in partnership, together and with their local authorities' (Business in the Community, 1982, p. 1), BIC is sponsored by such major companies as IBM, Whitbread, and Marks and Spencer, while the DoE, Manpower Services Commission and the local authority associations are also represented.

An important objective in the incorporation of the private sector is the minimising of direct financial assistance by government to companies. Rather, as with urban development grants, the major aim is to reduce obstacles ('abnormals') to normal commercial activity by helping to finance land clearance and servicing in derelict areas. Similarly, the enterprise agencies provide financial advice rather than directly investing in commercial projects, which also removes one potential source of conflict between the public and private sponsors of these organisations (Young, 1982, p. 40). Joint public–private economic activity is also encouraged by the Conservative government, which sees 'private' initiatives as a useful and ideologically sound response to both economic recession and public expenditure cuts. These cuts have also forced local authorities to look more closely for private sources of finance, while public–private relationships are further reinforced by the common external front that influentials from both sectors seek to display in jointly making representation to central government and the EEC for financial assistance for 'their' local community.

Chambers of Commerce and Industry

An increasingly key organisation in the enhanced public policy involvement of the private sector at local level is the Chamber of Commerce.[1] In some areas chambers have played a major role in persuading companies to sponsor an enterprise agency and have often provided premises and staff to get one launched. Their involvement in the implementation of inner-city policy has been even more marked, for local authorities are obliged by the DoE to consult Chambers of Commerce before schemes to be included in the urban programme can go forward to central government. In 1981 ministerial guidelines issued to local authorities stated that

> Ministers see a role for the private sector not only as a source of investment but also as influencing the scope and content of inner-area programmes while they are still at draft stage. Indeed they will expect, before giving approval to programmes in future, to be satisfied that that voice of the private sector has been heard and that detailed discussion has taken place. This will normally be through members of the local chamber of commerce. (Department of the Environment, 1981, p. 2)

This statement reflected the view of the Secretary of State, Michael Heseltine, that pressure on policy-makers was one-sided and insufficiently counterbalanced by that from industry, and that the only institutions capable of forming effective pressure groups for the private sector on a countrywide basis were the Chambers of Commerce.

The Thatcher government has subsequently shown more interest in working with the Chambers of Commerce than its predecessors. In part this derives from the large proportion of small businesses in their membership, which has been a distinct advantage with recent Conservative administrations, and because chambers provide a unique combination of services and representation at local level that neither other business associations nor the local authorities can offer. However, the government has resisted claims by the Association of British Chambers of Commerce (ABCC) that chambers be granted public law status along the lines of their European counterparts. In many European nations membership of Chambers of Commerce is compulsory, and chambers undertake a range of public responsibilities, such as industrial training, or the administration of the ports, that are generally undertaken by government in Britain and which would be beyond the resources of UK chambers. The elements of compulsion and formal incorporation associated with public law status presumably sit ill with the 'anti-statist' philosophy of the Conservative government, and it has preferred to see chambers retain their voluntary character while taking on an enhanced public role.

The institutional role of UK Chambers of Commerce

Of the two systems of formal business organisation that operate in Britain, the ABCC is underfunded and relatively weak in comparison with the Confederation of British Industry (CBI), and the Chamber of Commerce movement exerts its main influence at local and regional level. The biggest chambers, with between 1500 and 6000 members, reflect the business composition of an area and include large companies and public utilities as members, although predominantly the membership is comprised of small- and medium-sized companies. Chambers offer a range of valued services and representation not available from any other single source to their members, including advice on legislation, seminars, market research, and the organisation of overseas trade missions. They are the sole, government-approved body for issuing certificates of origin for exporters and act as the Department of Trade and Industry's agents. Members receive this service at half the cost of non-members. There is thus a considerable incentive for exporters to join, and chambers receive a substantial portion of their income from this work.

Perhaps the major difference with the public law status chambers has been in the amount and quality of vocational training available through the chambers. The obligatory membership of the public law status chambers means they have greater funds than are available to their British counterparts and allows them to undertake a larger range of activities, including maintaining registers of companies, the provision of information services, administration of airports and other facilities, as well as a considerable involvement in training. In Germany, for example, around a quarter of a chamber's budget is devoted to vocational education for the young, and the chamber department dealing with it in most public law status countries is generally the largest. Although UK chambers have provided a variety of training courses, up to now they have lacked the resources to generate a commitment along the lines of those in Europe. However, the recent involvement of UK chambers in the New Training Initiative, acting as managing agents for the Manpower Services Commission's Youth Training Scheme (YTS), has moved them a little closer to the European model. It is one of the developments that indicate the increased 'public' character of locally organised business in some areas. A study of chambers and commerce in West Yorkshire, undertaken by the author since 1980, helps highlight these changes. Particular attention is paid to the Leeds Chamber of Commerce and Industry which, with over 1500 members, is around the sixth largest UK chamber, and representative of most leading chambers. Examinations of three areas – youth training, inner-city policy, and small business advisory services – reveals that Chambers of Commerce are becoming more formerly involved with public policy objectives.

Leeds Chamber of Commerce and Industry

Membership takes two different forms. The vast majority of firms pay their fees (between £50 and £345, depending upon the size of a company) to obtain the chamber's business services, primarily export documentation, and play no active role.

However, around forty to fifty 'activists' serve on the chamber's council and its committees, and are mainly managing directors or senior executives drawn from large or medium-sized firms. Formal relationships between elected and permanent officers resemble those in government. Elected officers are regarded as the equivalent of leading councillors, formulating policy through the chamber's council, which the director and his staff then carry out; it is not unusual for chamber officers to refer to their 'counterparts' in the local authorities. Although most meetings between the chamber and the local authorities consist of elected and permanent officers from both sides, the main representative link for the chamber is the director or his assistant. The director acts as the chief executive of the chamber and plays a correspondingly influential policy as well as managerial role.

Prior to local government reorganisation in 1974, relationships with Leeds local council were good, but limited. There were few meetings between 'teams' of chamber and local authority elected and permanent personnel, and chamber representation was little concerned with the local authority's general policy or strategy, but rather with members' individual complaints. Moreover, the chamber's committee structure had become moribund, diffuse and ill-attended. The result was that there were few worked-out policy documents or positions formulated in committees or working parties that could provide the basis for early strategic involvement with the local authority.

The experience of reorganisation, not least the use of increased planning powers by the larger metropolitan authorities, forced the chamber to change. The committee structure was streamlined, with the aim of producing a rolling stock of policy positions to enable quick reaction to government proposals. This provided the basis for an expanded relationship with the new local authorities, and a series of regular meetings was started with Leeds MDC (Metropolitan District Council), attended by the leading elected and official personnel from both sides. Much of the business at the first meetings was taken up with planning issues, particularly the county's structure plan and the district's central area business plan, and centred on the best way to encourage industrial and commercial development in Leeds. The chamber contributed policy papers on a number of issues and, in the words of a leading official in Leeds MDC's planning department, 'became a very valuable ally to the city council over the structure plan'. Both the chamber and the district council felt that the proposals in the structure plan would inhibit the potential for development in Leeds by restricting office and warehousing development.

A considerable amount of discussion also went on in smaller groups outside these meetings and generally involved members of the chamber's town planning sub-committee, which is composed entirely of estate agents and chartered surveyors. The chamber was particularly helpful in discussions on the central area business plan, and chaired the public forum at the invitation of the local authority. As a result, the authority asked the chamber to provide representatives from companies in the run-down inner-city areas to participate in a council-organised development study of these areas. As a chief planning officer put it, 'their knowledge of local conditions completely outclassed those of the local authority because they looked at it from the inside outwards'. These closer organisational links were increasingly reflected in closer policy positions between the public and private bodies, such as the relaxation of planning restrictions on office and warehouse development, and were buttressed by a range of informal and everyday contacts, especially at officer level, as well as attendance at the quarterly meetings of the Leeds Group on Industry and Employment. The latter is a forum instigated by the district council and is attended by employers' organisations, regional government departments, MPs, trade unions, and the local authority.

These increased contacts between the chamber and the district council can be attributed to several factors. First, there was a shared concern that even a 'prosperous' area like Leeds was experiencing rising unemployment and a declining industrial base, with particularly bad pockets in the inner-city areas and in the textile and engineering industries. The second factor was the requirements on the reorganised authorities to construct structure and local plans. The estate agents and surveyors that comprised the chamber's town planning sub-committee were especially anxious to ensure that local authority planning policies did not hamper the economic development of Leeds as a regional office centre. Third, Leeds MDC and the Leeds chamber have allied against what they have regarded as the county council's neglect of the more prosperous areas like Leeds in favour of the country's declining areas. Common 'localist' fronts such as these against county councils tend to emerge in areas that used to be county boroughs and retain a strong sense of civic pride and past strength, and resent the loss of responsibilities to the second-tier authorities. Fourth, the more 'businesslike' structure and organisation of the Leeds Chamber of Commerce, with its growing stock of well-informed policies, helped to dispel notions, especially among some Labour politicians, that the chamber consists simply of extreme right-wing 'backwoodsmen' bent on securing a ratepayers' revolt.

Since 1980 and the election of a Labour administration, relations between the chamber and Leeds MDC have become well-established. If anything, the Labour leadership has shown itself to be even more business-oriented and anxious to construct good communications with the chamber than previous administrations. The result has been that the chamber has become much more involved in the policy process than before, particularly in the areas of assistance to small firms, the urban aid programme, and the Youth Training Scheme. To a considerable extent this policy involvement follows initiatives taken by central government, particularly the Department of the Environment, and its desire to involve the private sector more in the formulation and implementation of public policy. Yet it also stems from an increased recognition in localities that economic support for an area requires increased local authority–business alliances and that chambers of commerce are often a useful and available source of expertise and legitimacy.

Leeds Business Venture

The formation of the Leeds Business Venture is an example of central government encouragement, local authority receptivity, and Chamber of Commerce initiative combining to provide an enhanced incorporation of the chamber within the public policy process. As with chambers in other areas, following encouragement from Department of Environment ministers, the Leeds chamber was instrumental in the formation of a local enterprise trust in 1980 that was set up in partnership with local large companies to offer advice to intending small entrepreneurs. Initially the Leeds Business Venture was conceived as a section of the Leeds chamber, and during its first year of operation it was supplied by the chamber with secretarial back-up, printing and general advice. However, financial support was provided mainly by twelve large sponsoring firms each donating between £250 and £450, while Marks and Spencer plc also provided a young management secondee to act as the Venture's first director.

Although the Venture is now established in its own premises and organisationally autonomous from the Chamber of Commerce, its links with the chamber are still strong. For example, at the chamber's request, it will visit firms that have submitted schemes for urban aid money and on which the Department of the Environment requires the chamber's evaluation. Moreover, the manager of the Leeds Business Venture represents the chamber on the district council's small businesses and co-operatives panel, which was set up by the authority with considerable support from the chamber to provide grants and loans from urban programme money to start-up businesses. Similarly, the director of the venture is on a panel of advisers that go through applications to the county council's small firms employment fund before these are considered by members. Where an area does not have an enterprise agency the local Chamber of Commerce provides the adviser to the panel.

In such circumstances it comes as little surprise to find that the local authority, in the view of its inner-city officer, 'regards the venture as a chamber offshoot'. The district council strongly welcomed the creation of the trust and currently contributes £18,000 per annum to its running costs. In return, as the same officer expressed it, 'it gets the views and expertise of the private business world on the viability of projects without having to go out to widespread consultation'. There is also a considerable two-way traffic between the Venture and the district council's industry and estates department. The latter refers prospective small business people to the trust for marketing and other professional advice, while the venture will refer them to the industry and estates department if they might be eligible for government grants or loans, or are seeking small unit accommodation. This division of labour is reinforced by the local authority's view that it has a special responsibility for co-operative ventures, and for community ventures that may be less profit-oriented than those seeking the assistance of the Venture. As one local authority official stated, with intended exaggeration, 'the Leeds Business Venture is more interested in whether the scheme is likely to be successful, rather than the people putting it on'.

Public–private co-operation in the provision of assistance to small firms stems from a shared recognition by the district council and the chamber that Leeds, with a highly diversified local economy and with a large number of small and medium-sized firms, is not able to attract the very large companies to the city and that effort should be concentrated on 'seed-bed' industries. The council seeks to provide small units at low rental, and along with the Venture it aims to reduce the failure rate for small firms. This strategy was discussed with the chamber and it was agreed that the provision of small business units, particularly where the costs of location were high, would not provide unfair competition for the private sector. For both the chamber and the district council the direction of activity towards small firms is a pragmatic recognition that there is little either can do to affect the location decisions of the really large firms.

While this increased public involvment by the chamber has increased its standing in the eyes of both central and local authorities, it has not been without its costs. For example, the chamber has felt obliged to breach its long-standing opposition to the provision of direct financial assistance to companies in its support of grants to start-up businesses. Although the amounts are small, and can be justified as consequently exceptional, it possibly provides a precedent for more extended direct state intervention. Moreover, a number of estate agents within the chamber have not been happy at the development of small business units by the authority, arguing that it upsets local rent levels. As a result the chamber has sought recently to resist expansion of local authority small business units, arguing for the land to be serviced by the authority but then to be sold off for private development. In this, the chamber has received the support of the district council's planning department, whose officials have tended to resist the more interventionist policy of the industry and estates department. This suggests that the chamber's quasi-governmental policy involvement rests on the acceptance that the state confines itself primarily to the provision of infrastructural support for private accumulation and that more interventionist policies are proscribed. A change in that shared public–private assumption, perhaps as a result of altered political circumstances, could lead to at least a partial withdrawal by the chamber from its more 'governmental' stance.

Urban aid programme

In discussing the Chambers of Commerce in Norwich and Birmingham, Grant (1983c, p. 16) refers to the official recognition of the chambers 'by the state, not merely as interest intermediaries, but as co-responsible "partners" in governance and social guidance'. He suggests that the 'classic case' is the formal involvement of UK chambers in briefing ministers on the deployment of Department of the Environment urban programme funds. In Leeds the chamber advises the local authority on both the balance of bids for inner-city money and individual schemes. This follows the issue of DoE guidelines in 1981 which stated that local authorities must consult the private sector on urban programme submissions and that this would normally be through the local Chamber of Commerce. Relationships between the district council and the chamber on inner-city and planning issues had already become well-established, and an added dimension in Leeds was that the DoE minister with responsibility for the urban aid programme, Lord Bellwin, was a Leeds businessman and former leader of the district council. Moreover, he is well-acquainted with chamber officers, and the local authority felt constrained to keep relationships with the chamber 'sweet', as, according to a district council official, 'the government would know very soon if there were any problems'.

Although Leeds MDC has a long-established policy of not co-opting to its committees unless statutorily required to do so, the chamber (usually the assistant director) has been granted observer status at all meetings of the inner-city sub-committee, sitting with the local authority's officers at the table, and being asked to contribute to discussions. Nonetheless, the council's inner-city officers are clear that the chamber's influence occurs before the committee meets, and that the chamber's observer status 'belies its actual role, which is very significant'. The chamber has four main tasks that it has agreed with the local authority: to express its views on the balance between social and economic projects and between revenue and capital spending; to examine the viability of the economic job-creating projects being put forward; to advance views on priorities for inner-city money; and to help some of the economic projects off the ground if management expertise is required. Consequently, the chamber receives from the local authority all the 'economic' and 'environmental-economic' applications for inner-city funds, which are then evaluated by the director and his assistant.

Prior to the inner-city sub-committee meeting, its chairman, inner-city officers, a DoE representative, and the chamber's assistant director, meet to examine applications and the views received on them. The council is conscious that if the chamber's views on a scheme are critical, then the DoE is certain to reject it. To prevent this the authority modifies or excises applications that are unacceptable to the chamber. Although the chamber denies that it has an effective veto over schemes ('we do not want to be part of the local authority and be bound by decisions we do not agree with'), it is clear that the district council believes that the chamber's support is vital for a scheme to succeed with the DoE. For its part, however, the chamber believes that it is often used as a scapegoat or as an excuse by the authority for refusing a proposal. Nonetheless, all the parties agree that conflicts of opinion are infrequent.

In effect the chamber has a much better opportunity to comment on schemes, because it receives the applications, than members of the inner-city sub-committee, who are generally provided only with brief reports on bids. Moreover, the chamber has been particularly effective in arguing (with DoE support) for a change in the balance of expenditure in the overall programme from revenue to capital, and for an increase in aid for economic and environmental-economic schemes. In the 1983–4 inner-city programme, for example, the proportion of injected schemes and new bids was comprised of 74 per cent capital and 26 per cent revenue, compared with 55 per cent and 45 per cent respectively for the 1979–83 schemes.

The chamber also plays a part in the monitoring and implementation of urban aid schemes. For example, the director

will ring Rotary Club or other contacts, often retired businessmen, to ask them to advise successful applicants, especially if the
latter are small or start-up businesses. The Rotary Club
connection has enhanced the chamber's involvement in other
directions. The local Rotary to which the chamber director
belongs, for example, initiated the idea that the club's 'social
services' activities should be focused on the inner city. The
district council was subsequently approached and asked if
Rotary could help with any of the authority's inner-city
schemes. Two schemes were suggested. One was a proposal for a
local workshop and community centre, strongly favoured by the
local community council, who mistrusted the local authority's
intentions for the scheme and suspected it lacked enthusiasm for
the idea. Rotary provided a feasibility study, thus providing the
council with expertise that was both useful and relatively
independent of the authority. The other project involved the
Rotary Club's undertaking a market survey to estimate demand
for pottery made by mentally handicapped people as part of an
inner-city project. Although these undertakings were strictly
not those of the chamber, the individuals involved, who were
closely associated with the chamber, ensured that the council's
inner-city officer's regarded it as 'really an offshoot of the
chamber connection'.

The chamber has been more specifically involved in other
projects. For example, it was instrumental in getting a secondee
to manage local workships financed from the inner-city
programme and staffed by the Leeds Council for Voluntary
Services. It was also involved in monitoring attitudes and ideas
on aid for the inner city held by local business. It interviewed
firms, developers and estate agents in a particularly derelict
district on behalf of the authority, and the resultant report was
'very well received by council members'.

Increased public involvement by the chamber carries the
attendant danger of embroiling it more clearly in political
conflict than hitherto. For example, it has become associated in
the eyes of leading figures in the authority's industry and estates
department with a concerted attack on the industry departments' inner-city submissions. Certainly the chamber has
recently cast doubt on schemes for small low-cost units,
proposals from the department for inner-city development

workers, and on schemes to extend the number of training and skills centres. Rather the chamber has preferred to see greater use of private premises in firms where training resources and facilities were under-utilised. Moreover, the industry department became disconcerted to receive reports of private discussions between the chamber's director and the authority's education department on skills training in Leeds at which the industry department was not represented. It was further alarmed at suggestons made at the inner-city discussions (see above) between the authority, the DoE and the chamber, that in future the economic schemes submitted by the industry department should be drawn up in partnership with the Chamber of Commerce. Senior figures in the department object to being subject to the views of another organisation outside of normal monitoring procedures and are disturbed by what they see as a change in attitude and assertiveness by the chamber, and by the fact that it was raising 'political' rather than technical objections to schemes. Furthermore, there was a strong suspicion that the chamber was receiving support within the authority from sections of the education department (unhappy at the industry department's criticisms that it did not provide adequate training opportunities), and from the planning department (which preferred to service land and sell it, rather than build small-business units), as well as from the DoE and Lord Bellwin who, it was thought, regarded the industry department's proposals as too interventionist. This suggests that an increased delegation of advisory and other functions to Chambers of Commerce could draw them more directly into the arena of political conflict associated with the inter-departmental rivalries of local authorities and that between central and local government.

The Youth Training Scheme

A major difference in the functions exercised by the UK chambers in comparison with the public law chambers abroad is found in the provision of training and education. The West German, Austrian and Luxembourg chambers, for example, supervise and carry out professional training which is legislated by government. The chambers register apprenticeships, supervise and advise on training in enterprises, and set examinations at the end of the apprenticeship. French chambers encourage professional training in a number of technical schools, partially financed by an apprenticeship tax introduced by law. Currently the French chambers support about 200 educational centres, with 1600 teachers and about 135,000 trainees each year.

The Youth Training Scheme (YTS) introduced by the Manpower Services Commission (MSC), which started in September 1983, has allowed Chambers of Commerce through the 'managing agency' provision to enter the field of youth training in a more systematic and comprehensive manner than hitherto. Although it does not bring them an involvement that matches the scale of that found in the public law chambers, it provides not only an enlarged public function for the UK chambers but also, just as important, the resources to sustain it.

The aim of the YTS is to generate training places for both employed and unemployed young people, and it provides one year of work experience and must include a minimum of thirteen weeks' relevant off-the-job training or further education. Under the scheme's predominant mode the employer or sponsor receives £1850 and pays an allowance of £25 per week to the trainee, leaving £550 to cover the cost of the off-the-job training programme. Additionally there is a fee of £100 per trainee paid to the employer who is acting as a 'managing agent' to cover the administrative costs and the task of organising the year-long programme. This last provision has allowed bodies such as Chambers of Commerce, local authorites and other associations to organise youth training schemes, usually to provide on-the-job experience in a number of small companies, with the off-the-job training being provided by a local college or by the managing agent making provision. The Leeds chamber, for example, because of the financial attraction of the latter option, employs a scheme organiser to hire premises and to undertake the off-the-job training.

It is not yet clear whether the fees paid by the MSC to managing agents and to those providing off-the-job training is adequate to the costs involved, or what level of recruitment is required to make the scheme financially viable for managing agencies. However, an increasing number of chambers have begun to operate, or show interest in operating, such schemes. In Leeds, by December 1983, around 200 trainees were enrolled on the chamber's scheme, and it employs three full-time training officers, each monitoring around seventy trainees, and a secretary. The chamber indicates that financially it is just about breaking even, although it has to be very careful about expenditure on administration. Although the chamber is currently still taking on trainees, each training officer is working to capacity, and the need to employ an extra officer could mean the scheme losing money. Interestingly, the company taking on most trainees is the Leeds Permanent Building Society, and each trainee is given an account with the company into which their money is paid each Friday.

This involvement by the Leeds chamber as a managing agency for the YTS has increased substantially the proportion of public money going through the chamber's account. (On a 200-trainee scheme, £370,000 is paid by the MSC, with around £130,000 going to the managing agent and off-the-job training provider.) It can be seen as part of the government's stated aim that 'In the longer term the responsibility for training must lie mainly with employers, as it does in most other major industrial countries . . . a large-scale expansion of public provision for training, parallel to the public education system, seems even more objectionable' (Department of the Environment, 1981, p. 14). For its part, having supported the disbanding of many of the industrial training boards, the chamber has expressed the desire to play a more direct role in the provision of high-quality training. Recently an influential study has recommended that Chambers of Commerce should be considered for taking over some of the work of those industrial training boards that have now been abolished, and for supporting or even replacing the MSC's area manpower boards that oversee the YTS in particular regions (Forster, 1983, p. 28). Moreover, with the local authorities also competing under the same scheme in a similar capacity as managing agents, the YTS provides a further examples of an increased indentation of the boundaries between the public and private sectors at the local level.

Other chambers

Although we have focused attention primarily on the Leeds Chamber of Commerce, there is evidence that similar tendencies can be observed elsewhere. Grant (1983c, p. 17), for example, points to the close although generally unstructured relationship between the Birmingham Chamber of Commerce and its principal local authorities, including representation on economic development committees and involvement in the Birmingham inner-city partnership. As in Leeds, the Birmingham Venture Trust is effectively a private enterprise agency that has been started by some of the city's largest companies in conjunction with the Birmingham chamber. The situation that Grant found in Norwich, a medium-sized town with a diversified economy similar to that in Leeds, involved an even closer relationship between the chamber and the local authority than that in Birmingham. The local authority and the chamber jointly launched the Norwich Enterprise Agency Trust, which operates from the chamber's premises, while the council shows all major planning applications to the chamber. When commercial sites are involved, city and chamber officials will make a joint site visit before the application goes to the relevant council committees.

Recent studies undertaken by the author of other chambers in the Yorkshire region confirm an increased relationship with government. In Bradford, for example, the chamber has a representative of the local authority on its council and is a member of the small firms panel that advises on the distribution of local authority grants and loans. A very small chamber, Barnsley (132 members), has become involved with the YTS in conjunction with a local college, and has joined with the authority in advising on the provision of enterprise workships. In Sheffield the chamber has often found itself in conflict with a radical Labour administration at district and county levels, yet areas of co-operation have emerged, particularly in representing Sheffield externally to central government.

Corporatism

We have selected three policy areas – small business advisory services, the urban programme, and the new training initiative – to indicate the increasing discharge of public functions by Chambers of Commerce, in some cases in partnership with the local authority. We could also cite chamber membership of the local Land Register 'group of three' (also including Leeds MDC and the DoE), a team set up in Leeds and other district authorities by the DoE to make recommendations, including for disposal, on underused land owned by local authorities and statutory undertakings. To what extend are these developments to be classified as corporatist? Specifically, what do government and chambers gain from the delegation of public functions to organised business?

The dimensions of corporatism

Following Offe (1981, p. 137), it is useful to regard corporatism as an 'axis' of development, rather than a situation, and to have as the criterion the extent to which public status is attributed to organised interest groups. Thus corporatism depends on the number of dimensions in which groups are affected, and increases with:

1. *Resource status*: the extent to which the resources of an interest organisation are supplied by the state, e.g. direct subsidies, tax exemptions, forced membership, etc.
2. *Representation status*: the extent to which the range of representation is defined through political decision, e.g. a public definition of the range of substantive areas in which an interest organisation may operate and/or of the political membership.
3. *Organisation status*: the extent to which internal relations between rank-and-file members of the organisation are regulated.
4. *Procedural status*: the extent to which interest organisations are licensed, recognised and invited to assume, together with a specified set of other participants, a role in legislation, the judicial system, policy planning and implementation, or even granted the right of self-administration.

The delineation of specific dimensions of corporatism allows us to recognise that positive readings on one scale could be accompanied by 'negative' showings on others. We can use these dimensions to examine the extent to which the Leeds chamber, and other chambers, display corporatist characteristics.

Resource status. Despite the absence of public law status, Chambers of Commerce derive a large and increasing proportion of their income either directly from, or under licence granted by, public authority. A recent survey of chambers estimates that members' subscription form only about one-third of the total income (Forster, 1983, p. 75). In Leeds almost one-half of the chamber's income is derived from fees for supplying exporters with certificates of origin, and this percentage has increased steadily over the last decade. Chambers are recognised as the sole agent for the Department of Trade and Industry in this respect, and for this service are in the position of state-licensed monopoly suppliers. Although this income derives from the provision of a service, and the state makes no direct grant for representational purposes, without this license many chambers would go under. Recent involvement in the YTS also provides a potentially large source of income for chambers and allows them to undertake training provision along the lines of the public law chambers. At local level the Leeds chamber receives substantial resource support from the local authorities for the local enterprise agency and for its export missions.

Representation status. Although the increased representational status of chambers has been formally and publicly encouraged by central government, especially the DoE, the extended and reciprocal links with the district council have been accomplished in an informal, almost secretive fashion. Local Labour leaders are understandably chary of being regarded by their own supporters as too close to the 'voice of local capital', while council members and officers are aware of the difficulties in justifying the special status of some groups within established conceptions of democratic authority and accountability. Moreover, it would be misleading to overlook the continuing importance of the many informal contacts between individuals from the two bodies, and the general 'unstructuredness' of chamber relations with the local authorities. Yet, more than for any other comparable local interest group, the Leeds chamber has been increasingly attributed with 'public', if not necessarily visible, status by local government in recent years.

Organisational status. There is little evidence that these developments have affected appreciably the internal relations between chamber members and its officers. Companies that do not provide membership of the chamber's council are generally disinterested in representational issues and mostly ignorant of its recently increased public activity. Most companies appear to join either for trade services or out of a vague feeling that they 'ought' to belong, and they are not discouraged in this because of the relatively low level of fees charged by the chamber. There is little sign that chamber leaders have either the capacity or necessity to exert control downwards over members. In comparatively low-rated areas such as Leeds, even annual complaints by members over rates' increases lack intensity and do little to disturb relations between the chamber and the local authorities.

Procedural status. The chamber's involvement in the urban programme provides the clearest example of corporatist development, although the other policy areas that we have examined also display similar corporatist characteristics involving the chamber. While the chamber also receives procedural recognition from the local authorities as the result of its involvement with bodies such as the Leeds Group on Industry and Employment (LGIE) or the county's Economic Advisory Board, these are little more than advisory forums and have no real powers of decision. Nor do these bodies reveal the development of forms of concerted action between capital, labour and the state. The regional trade union representatives turn up to these meetings only spasmodically, while the local trades council shows a marked hostility to the chamber. The chamber prefers and exercises most influence at bilateral and less public discussions with the local authorities. The main values of LGIE meetings to the chamber, for example, is that it allows the chamber to lobby public representatives and the opportunity to make contacts that can be followed up more discreetly later. Tripartite or 'concerted' procedural arrangements are always likely to face considerable difficulties at local, non-regional level, for trades councils are often extremely reluctant to co-operate not only with Chambers of Commerce but also with mainstream Labour councils, while there is relatively little direct trade union activity over 'place-based' or spatial issues of the kind found in more explicit 'territorial' associations such as Chambers of Commerce.

Conclusion

Increased involvement by local authorities in economic policy-making and the encouragement of central government have been instrumental in the development of corporatist tendencies at local level as these have involved Chambers of Commerce. As Grant (1983c, p. 19) notes, in so far as there has been a transfer or a sharing of power, it has been on the part of the state, which has involved the chambers in the discharge of particular functions, or has allowed them to take initiatives in particular areas (e.g. help to new enterprises) which might otherwise have been a state responsibility. The chambers have been asked to forfeit little, if any, autonomy in return. Despite its increased involvement with public policy implementation, there is little sign of increased control exerted downwards on members by chamber officers. Most member companies are unconcerned with the chamber's representational activity. Investment and other key economic decisions are the prerogatives of individual companies, and the chamber does not negotiate with labour over wages and working conditions, but confines itself in advancing interests common to all its membership. Consequently it is not required to 'deliver' its membership to government in the way expected of trade unions.

The corporatist tendencies observable in government–chamber relationships are less an instance of state-induced restraint on the chambers than a recognition by the state of its relative powerlessness to influence the accumulation of capital. It expresses the institutional self-interest of the state in capitalist societies 'which is conditioned by the fact that the state is denied the power to control the flow of resources which are indispensable for the use of state power' (Offe and Ronge, 1982, p. 251). Although the local state may be less directly reliant for its funding than the central state on the process of accumulation within its jurisdiction (because of central grants to it), economic recession and rising unemployment have accelerated local government's direct interest in promoting conditions conducive to capital accumulation in its own area. Local councils have also felt forced into a competitive struggle between localities to attract capital investment. As it is beyond their power to organise or control the process of accumulation, local authorities turn to the organised 'voice of local business' for help in encouraging business to perform.

In Leeds the return of a Labour council, most of whose members were well-acquainted with the public sector but only dimly aware of the private sector, yet committed to promoting industrial expansion, resulted in a strengthening of links between the authority and the chamber. Leading councillors know little of the chamber, or how representative it is of local business, but they are aware that it is available and possesses the status and increasing competence to provide both legitimacy and expertise to the council's economic policy-making. In supporting chamber activities the local authority was able to draw upon the skills of the private sector in support of its policies in a way that would have been denied the council if it had directly undertaken such a task itself. These public-private initiatives may provide a more flexible form of interventionism, and are more finely tuned to the needs of local small capital, than would be provided by more directly statist or bureaucratic prescriptions.

We should be clear, however, that corporatist developments involving the chamber at local level are, in part, dependent on the local authority's limiting the type and extent of its intervention. While the chamber recognises an increased need for councils to support local capital, it is resistant to the 'socialisation' of the accumulation process. For example, it seeks a limited and specific form of local state interventionism which guarantees government assistance in capital accumulation without exacerbating demands that state policies should be oriented away from private needs and more to public use values. Proposals to offer direct financial assistance by government to companies are generally anathema to the chamber. Because of the costs involved, such incentives are necessarily selective, to particular companies or sectors. They are therefore regarded as both unfair – taking ratepayers' money from successful companies and giving it to less successful companies or to competitors from outside – and dangerous, the probable start of a slippery slope in which financial assistance is given in return for government control of the company. Furthermore, a general representative business body like the chamber, unlike an employers' or trade association representing a particular industry, has its own organisational reasons for opposing incentives or subsidies, as these would pose difficulties in retaining the confidence of local capital generally for its policies. Therefore the chamber seeks public money to be used in the provision of infrastructure, such as road or house-building, the clearing and servicing of land, or the provision of company accommodation. This facilitates capital generally, can be seen as support for the community as a whole rather than special business interests, and minimises the risk of government controls in exchange for assistance. However, it is doubtful whether local authorities possess the necessary information from private capitalists to enable them to intervene directly in the accumulation process in a major fashion, while they also lack the resources and the ability to get them to do this. To raise rates, for example, on the scale required to generate such resources would be counter-productive, for it would invite the economic and political hostility of local capitalists ('rates revolts') and scare off potential investors, thus threatening the local accumulation process. Moreover, extensive productive functions may be beyond the capacities of bureaucracies.

Thus, in Leeds, the chamber and the local authorities adopt a strategy of 'administrative recommodification' in which the effort is directed to expanding public infrastructural investment designed to help broad categories of commodity owners (including labour) to engage in exchange relationships (Offe and Ronge, 1982, p. 253). As part of this infrastructural provision is provided by the central state, the local authorities and the chamber join forces on behalf of 'the locality' to advance their claims to central government. In such instances the chamber allies with the local authority as a 'policy-taker' *vis-à-vis* the central state (Offe, 1981, p. 138).

In the manner and type of services it provides for business, the boundaries between the chamber and the local state seem hazy. For example, both sets of officials are involved in offering advice to potential investors, in collecting trade data, and in furnishing advice on current legislation to local businessmen. They meet regularly and are found in the same public and social gatherings. The interface between the two organisations is increasingly indented and is likely to become more so as the chambers take over public functions, while some local authorities have shown interest in themselves directly providing some services presently offered by chambers (for example, export missions, legislative and loans advice).

We can discern a convergence of public and private officialdoms in style, aims and habitat. Lindblom (1977) has argued that distinctions between administered and market systems are blurred in that in all industrial systems production is directly organised not by the market but by bureaucratic authority. Certainly, the managing directors and chief executives that are active in the Leeds chamber are used to 'authoritatively' directing large organisations, and their work-a-day activities are not dissimilar to those of public officials, supervising and directing other individuals. The permanent chamber officials, of course, are even more accustomed to the workings of administrative life spaces and bureaucratic structures. Consequently, the Leeds Chamber of Commerce has come to resemble the commercial counterpart of a local government department and has adjusted comfortably to its enhanced interaction with other public authorities.

Chapter 9

Corporatism and the European Community

Jane A. Sargent

The exploration of corporatism at the European Community level has been strangely neglected, despite the fact that the Commission of the European Economic Community (EEC) has encouraged the development of interest organisations at European level and attempted to foster a 'social partnership' with representatives of labour and capital. This chapter attempts to fill this gap in the literature. Its principal objective is to establish whether or not there is any evidence of corporatist structures and/or corporatist functions in the Community and to examine the direction of trends towards, or away from, corporatism in the Community.[1]

The term corporatism is used to refer to societal or neo-corporatism rather than to state corporatism (Schmitter, 1977, p. 12), and the terms 'corporatist structures' and 'corporatist functions' should be taken to mean the particular style of interest intermediation and mode of policy formation defined by Philippe Schmitter (Schmitter, 1977, p. 9 and 1981a, p. 295).

Attention is not restricted to the Community level in this chapter as the Community's legislative processes involve two sets of decision-making bodies: EEC bodies and the legislative bodies of the member states. As a result, consideration is given to evidence of corporatism at Community level, as well as to any impact the Community has had on the development or erosion of corporatist structures and/or functions in the member states. In connection with the latter, attention is focused on Britain, a late entrant to the EEC (and thus not one of the member states upon which the Community's political system was modelled), and one of the member states that is generally regarded as exhibiting few corporatist features. Of particular interest is the question of whether EEC membership has stimulated corporatist developments in Britain and, if not, whether it is likely to do so in the future.

As this is a study of corporatism, the main theme of this chapter is the nature of the relations that have developed between interest organisations which represent labour, capital, and both EEC and the member states' legislative bodies (which together can be said to form 'the state' in an EEC context) in connection with EEC policy formation and implementation. Special attention is given to the relationship between evidence of corporatist structures and functions and evidence of a pluralist style of interest intermediation and/or a parliamentary form of policy-making. This is because during the past decade numerous advisory committees, or 'Euroquangos' as British observers tend to refer to them, have been set up at Community level. During the same period, the European Parliament has developed from an appointed body with little or no legislative powers to a directly elected body with greater budgetary powers and, according to some observers, the potential (by virtue of being directly elected) to assume greater *de facto* if not *de jure* powers during EEC policy formation than it has exercised hitherto. (See, for instance, Coombes, 1977; Fitzmaurice and Jackson, 1979; Jackson, 1979, and Herman and Lodge, 1978.) Both corporatist and parliamentary structures appear to have coexisted and developed in parallel at Community level during the past ten years, and so an examination of corporatism in the EEC seems particularly useful in the light of the difference of opinion that exists about the relationship between such developments. Lehmbruch (1977, p. 94), for instance, argues that corporatist and parliamentary structures may coexist, while Cawson (1982, p. 42) maintains that the corporate sector of representation will grow at the expense of the pluralist one.

Definitions of corporatism are not restricted to the nature of relations between representatives of labour and capital and the state. Cawson (1982, p. 66) claims that a state which assumes an interventionist role in the economy, as opposed to a facilitative or directive one, in association with a social democratic/reformist ideology, displays important defining characteristics of corporatism. In the light of this argument an examination of corporatism in the EEC seems to be particularly useful for a number of reasons. First because, as its name suggests, the European Economic Community is primarily concerned with economic issues. Second, because the EEC has the authority to intervene directly in the economies of the member states by virtue of the fact that it can make its decisions legally binding in the member states. Third, because some EEC bodies have adopted what may loosely be termed a social democratic/ reformist approach to the Community's activities during the past decade, for example the Commission and the directly elected European Parliament, while others, namely the Council of Ministers and the European Council, have moved away from such an approach towards a more conservative one as the political complexion of most of the member states' governments changed from socialist or social democratic in the early 1970s to conservative in the early 1980s.

Britain also constitutes an interesting case in the light of Cawson's argument because the policy pursued for most of the 1970s of incorporating representatives of labour and capital into the policy-making process was replaced by the stance of the 1979 Thatcher Government, which did not perceive a need for clearing policy with such interests.

Most writers on corporatism assume that it implies a particular relationship between corporate groups (representatives of labour and capital) and their representative members in which the groups are able to discipline and control their members. This argument forms another of the themes pursued in this chapter, namely the ability of European and British representatives of labour and capital to act as pillars of corporatism.

To return to the relationship between corporate groups and legislative bodies that are involved in EEC policy-making, attention is given to any differences between the relations that have developed between such bodies and, on the one hand, representatives of labour and, on the other, representatives of capital. This is because many writers maintain that corporatism implies parity in such relations. This chapter does not seek to test such claims. They simply form the main issues addressed by the chapter in its three sections; the first of these is on the style of interest intermediation that has developed at Community level, the second is on the mode of policy formation practised by the Community, and the third deals with the impact of EEC membership on Britain.[2]

Interest intermediation at European level

In his ideal-typical distinction between pluralism and corporatism as styles of interest intermediation, Schmitter (1977, p. 9) defines pluralism as characterised by multiple, voluntary units, not licensed, supported or controlled by the state, and not exercising a monopoly within their category of interest. Corporatism is characterised by a limited number of units, recognised or licensed by the state, and granted a representational monopoly within their category of interest. Schmitter's scheme leads to a focus in this section on the number and organisation of European representatives of capital, the impact the EEC as a whole and/or individual EEC bodies have had on the organisation of interests, and upon the relations of European-level organised interests with EEC bodies and the styles of operation of such interest.

The number and organisation of European representatives of capital differ from the number and organisation of European representatives of labour. The former are more numerous than the latter and their organistion is more complex, more fragmented and possibly more competitive. Over 400 European interest organisations have emerged to represent the interests of capital. Together they represent industry, commerce and various crafts. Manufacturing industry has the most European spokesmen, however – nearly 300 compared with just over 150 representatives of commercial interests. There is very little hierarchical ordering of the European representatives of capital. Some of these organisations developed following the creation of the EEC, others emerged as the scope of the Community's activities, especially its competition policy, expanded. (For details see Haas, 1958, and Economic and Social Committee, 1980.) The representative organisations of capital range from those which organise sector unspecific national peak associations, such as the Union of Industries of the EEC (UNICE), to which the Confederation of British Industry belongs, through European Federations for Branches of Industry (FEBIs), which organise

sector-specific associations, down to the European representatives of product- or craft-specific associations, such as the
Association of European Tomato Processing Industries.

Numerous different elements of capital within the EEC have
a separate voice at European level. This arrangement reflects
the multiplicity of national representatives of capital in the
member states, which, in its turn, reflects the essentially
individualistic nature of European capital. This individualistic
nature has also resulted in a low level of co-ordination between
European representatives of capital. Few organisations of this
type are affiliated to others, and there is little evidence of
collaboration between European representatives of capital,
including those which speak for the same sectors of the economy.
Some collaboration has developed, however, and some of this
has been inspired by UNICE: for example, the formation of an
Employers' Liaison Committee (ELC) to facilitate co-ordination of employers' views, primarily on EEC-related social
questions. However, membership of the ELC does not require
any European interest organisation to surrender its autonomy,
as any collaboration fostered under the auspices of the committee is purely voluntary.

Neither the Commission nor any other EEC body appears to
have encouraged simplification of the organisation of European
representatives of capital. There has been no encouragement of
mergers between the organisations which represent similar
interests, nor support for greater hierarchical ordering of
European representatives of capital. As an alternative, elements
within the Commission have set up committees to which they
have invited the appropriate European representatives of
capital to send delegates. The aim of these committees is to
reduce the problems the Commission faces when seeking to
consult with industrial and/or commercial interests that are
represented at European level by numerous interest organisations. The 'Davignon Committee' and its successor, the Committee for Commerce and Distribution, are examples of this type
of arrangement. These committees were set up in 1978 and 1981
respectively by Commission officials, the former on an informal
basis, the latter on a formal footing (by decision of the Council of
Ministers) in response to the demise of the European group for
retailing and distribution (COCCEE). Similarly, the Commit-

tee of Credit Associations was set up in 1979 to ease the practical difficulties the Commission faced when trying to consult the various European representatives of the financial services sector.

It should also be noted that the Commission has repeatedly expressed a preference for national interest organisations which represent similar interests in each member state to present their views collectively through a European interest organisation rather than individually. This has encouraged many national representatives of capital to join and even to form the appropriate European interest organisation. Very occasionally, the Commission expresses this preference by encouraging the formation of specific interest organisations. Commissioner Mansholt's part in the creation of European farming organisations has been well documented (Lindberg and Scheingold, 1970, p. 173). Less well publicised is the support officials within the Commission directorates III and XV have expressed since 1981 for the establishment of a Community-based association of financial organisations specialising in the funding of innovation as a means to promote the Community's industrial policy. The Commission hopes that such an association will act 'as a centre for exchange of experience and information in this specialised field, for the development of risk-assessment and financing used and also for the establishment of standards of conduct' (EEC Commission, 1982, p. 12). Moreover, the Economic and Social Committee played some part in establishing a liaison committee as a replacement for COCCEE after its disappearance.

The evidence of direct intervention by individual EEC bodies in the number and organisation of European representatives of capital reflects the Community's need for intermediaries through which to consult with organised business interests. It also reflects the need of EEC bodies for assistance when seeking to make policy decisions that will be acceptable to member states. They turn to interest organisations for both legitimacy and support for their own activities because none of the EEC bodies in question has the authority to impose its decisions on the member state governments which make up the membership of the EEC's main decision-making body, the Council of Ministers. Any of the member states' governments has the right to veto any proposal they are required to approve if they believe that the proposal affects the national interest of their country.

The evidence of intervention by individual EEC bodies in the number and organisation of European representatives of capital does not suggest the development of a corporatist style of interest intermediation at European level. Indeed, capital itself would seem to prefer a pluralist style of intermediation, if the number and organisation of the European-level representatives it has produced can be taken as a reliable indicator. Such a pattern of representation is not surprising when one considers that the interests of fragments of capital might best be safeguarded at the Community level by conducting discussions on a highly technical level through sector- or product-specific groups, thus preserving a low profile and preventing the wider politicisation of the issues being discussed, which might in its turn bring into the decision-making process other groups less well disposed to capital's interests.

The organisation of labour at the Community level

The existing organisation of labour at the Community level reflects the organisation of labour in European states in that it consists of two types of interest organisation. These are the umbrella organisation, the ETUC, which organises national peak associations for trade unions, and the fourteen European Industry Committees, which are composed of the national trade union or trade union bodies that organise workers in individual industries such as agriculture, chemicals, metal-working and transport. By the summer of 1984, the ETUC had 'recognised'[3] ten of these European Industry Committees and maintained working relations with the others, the 'recognised' unions being able to participate in a variety of ways in the work of the ETUC. It is not uncommon for the ETUC and the appropriate European Industry Committee to make a joint statement on EEC-related matters of interest to both, but the ETUC has no authority over European Industry Committees. Any collaboration between them is purely voluntary.

The creation of a single peak association for European labour in 1973 represented European labour's response to the creation and growth of multinational groups of companies and reflected the essentially collectivisit philosophy of European labour. Thus, creation of the ETUC was inspired largely by non-EEC-related matters. This does not mean to say that EEC-related matters did not act as additional incentives for the creation of the ETUC. Kirchner (1977, p. 28) has argued that formation of the ETUC also reflected the strength of European representatives of employers and aspects of Community policy, in particular the Common Agricultural Policy and the Community's policy on the free movement of labour.

The Community's failure to produce a common economic policy and a common policy on industrial relations, however, has contributed to a situation in which the number of European representatives of labour is less than the number of European representatives of capital. Moreover, the scope of labour's EEC-related activities is narrower than that of capital, as a comparison between the range of policy areas covered by European Industry Committees and FEBIs shows (see, for example, Editions Delta, 1984).

It would seem, then, that the number and organisation of European representatives of labour and capital suggest that the style of interest intermediation that has emerged at European level is essentially a pluralist one which has developed a few, immature corporatist features as a result of initiatives by European labour and certain EEC bodies. However, the number and organisation of European representatives of capital and labour do not constitute sufficient indicators of the style of interest intermediation that has developed at European level. Consideration should also be given to relations between these interest organisations and EEC bodies. Are the interest organisations recognised or licensed by EEC bodies, have they been granted a representational monopoly by EEC bodies, and do EEC bodies have a say in such matters as their styles of operation and internal affairs?

The multiplicity of European representatives of capital in particular, and the considerable size of the Commission's workload, together with the nature and scope of the Community's activities, have prompted the Commission to be selective in its consultations with European interest organisations. The Commission has instituted a policy of 'recognising' certain European interest organisations to which it gives preferential treatment during EEC policy formation and/or implementation. A European interest organisation is said to be 'recognised' by the Commission if its name appears on the Commission's list of such organisations (the 'green book'), if it is invited to nominate members to EEC advisory committees, and/or if it is regularly consulted by the appropriate divisions or services within the Commission.

Few European interest organisations are granted a monopoly of representation of a particular interest by virtue of being recognised by the Commission, because the Commission maintains a policy of consulting widely. Hence the names of four European interest organisations appeared on the list of representatives of small and medium-sized enterprises drawn up in November 1981 (EEC Commission, 1981). This list also included the names of national and international interest organisations. This is not exceptional. Apart from cases where there is no European-level organisation for a particular interest, the Commission also consults national interest organisations when the appropriate European organisation is unable to produce general agreement among its members, when a European interest organisation's policy does not reflect agreement between its members about the details of a Commission's proposal, and/or when a European interest organisation produces a majority view that is not acceptable to one or more of its leading members. This practice of consulting national interest organisations has become more widespread as a means whereby the Commission seeks to increase the legitimacy of, and support for, its proposals in order to increase their chances of being adopted by the Council of Ministers, and as a means to increase the chances of these proposals being implemented without difficulty once adopted.

Although the Commission does not grant representational monopolies to individual interest organisations, it does give preferential treatment to those that are affected by certain aspects of EEC policy. In 1968, for instance, national and European representatives of agricultural interests were co-opted into the Community policy-making processes on agricultural questions 'so as to give them a maximum sense of participation in the great European enterprise' (Lindberg and Scheingold, 1970, p. 173). This incorporation of the representatives of agricultural interests took place through advisory committees and went beyond the consultation procedures then usually practised by the Commission.

Since the early 1970s, the incorporation of certain interest organisations into EEC policy formation and/or implementation has been extended to the European and national interest organisations the Commission recognises as representatives of the two sides of industry: labour and management, or the 'social partners'. This initiative followed the December 1972 Paris Summit Agreement, which stated that it was essential to ensure the increasing involvement of representatives of labour and capital in the Community's activities on social and employment questions in order to facilitate adoption (by the Council of Ministers) and implementation in the member states of EEC policy on such questions.

On general social and employment questions the Commission recognises the ETUC, of which the TUC is a member, as the social partner for labour, but does not grant the ETUC a representational monopoly on such issues. The Commission also consults the French Communist trade unions, which are not members of the ETUC. The counterpart social partners for management are recognised as the members of the Employers' Liaison Committee. In connection with sector-specific social and employment matters, the appropriate European Industry Committee (for labour) or the appropriate FEBI (for management), or the appropriate national employers' organisation and trade union, are recognised as the social partners.

Various mechanisms have been established by the Commission to facilitate consultation with the social partners. These include the Social Partners Office, which was set up within the Secretariat-General of the Commission following the Paris Summit Agreement. In addition, the social partners have been granted access to the cabinets of various directorates-general, especially D-G V (Employment and Social Affairs) and have been invited to consult with the Commission under the auspices of various joint labour–management committees (Economic and Social Committee, 1980b). Two EEC advisory committees provide for consultation between the social partners and both representatives of the Commission and the member states' employment and/or social affairs ministers. These are the Tripartite Social and Economic Conference and the Standing Committee on Employment, which were reconvened in 1974 in response to the Paris Summit Agreement. The tripartite conference was last convened in December 1978, when disagreement arose between the labour and management representatives over work-sharing.

Relations between the Commission and the social partners consist of regular meetings between Commission personnel and the social partners during which the latter are consulted over reports and proposals before they are adopted by the Commission, either bilaterally or under the auspices of various EEC advisory committees. Although the social partners are granted preferential treatment in connection with the Commission's activities on social and employment questions at the expense of other European representatives of capital, this does not necessarily mean that the Commission has granted parity to those representatives of labour and capital which it recognises as the social partners.

Grant (1978, p. 92) has suggested that the employer's grouping, UNICE, is a 'house insider' at the Berlaymont (Commission buildings) and attributes this to the fact that Commission officials share the values and objectives held by UNICE's members and, as a result, are prepared to give UNICE's views a sympathetic hearing. This may be the case. It is important to note, however, that as the Commission has become less and less confident that its proposals will be accepted by the Council of Ministers and/or implemented without difficulty in the member states, Commission personnel have become increasingly more anxious to consult those representatives of interests which do not share their values, especially if, as in the case of trade unions, these interest organisations have political significance in the member states. The Commission's anxiety stems from the fact that ever since the Luxembourg Compromise decision of 1965–6, the balance of policy-making powers in the EEC has favoured the member states' governments at the Council of Ministers. Hence, representatives of trade unions now have greater access to the Commission than was the case in the 1960s, and the Commission has taken steps to help the standard of trade union participation in the Community's legislative processes to match that of the representatives of management. For example, EEC financial assistance has been provided for the European Trade Union Institute, a research and information centre.

According to Schmitter's ideal-typical conception of corporatism as a style of interest intermediation, the extent of state intervention in the internal activities of corporate groups is an important indicator of the evidence of corporate structures. The evidence just cited indicates that the Commission has been prepared to take positive action in order to facilitate participation by certain corporate groups in EEC policy formation and/or implementation. The Commission and the Economic and Social Committee also reimburse the expenses incurred by representatives of corporate (and other) groups which participate in the work of EEC advisory committees. It would seem, then, that certain EEC bodies have attempted to assist national and European interest organisations to act as intermediaries by providing them with financial resources. Whether or not their objective has been to increase the potential of particular interest organisations to act as pillars of a corporatist mode of policy-making is discussed in the next section. The existence of mechanisms to facilitate participation by organised interests in EEC policy formation and implementation has influenced the style of operation that such interests have adopted, adding weight to the view that the style of interest intermediation at European level has developed certain corporatist features in reponse to the development of EEC policy, especially the agricultural and social policies.

Policy formation and implementation at Community level

A corporatist style of interest intermediation and a corporatist mode of policy formation may be related, but they are not synonymous according to Schmitter (1981a, p. 296). He defines the latter as 'a mode of policy formation in which formally designated interest associations are incorporated within the process of authoritative decision-making and implementation. As such they are officially recognised by the state not merely as interest intermediaries but as co-responsible "partners" in governance and social guidance' (Schmitter, 1981a, p. 295).

We have seen that the Commission has recognised certain (national and European) interest organisations as interest intermediaries, has granted preferential treatment to such organisations when seeking to consult the interests they represent, and has attempted to assist some of these organisations to act as interest intermediaries. Does the preferential treatment extend to incorporating all or some of these organisations, especially the social partners, into EEC policy formation and implementation processes? In other words, to what extent does the social partnership the Commission has attempted to develop with corporate groups amount to a corporatist mode of policy-making? In order to answer this question, it is necessary to examine the powers conferred upon such groups through the EEC advisory committees upon which they are represented, and as a result of their bilateral relations with EEC bodies.

The establishment of numerous consultative and advisory bodies in the EEC, or 'Euroquangos' as they are familiarly known to British observers, is regarded by some observers as synonymous with the development of corporatism in the Community (Fallon, 1983). Two arguments are generally advanced in justification of this observation. First, the composition of the Euroquangos and, secondly, the powers they have acquired.

There are over 200 EEC advisory and consultative bodies, but not all of these include representatives of economic interest organisations among their members. Several categories of Euroquango do so, however. These include the following:

1. Committees that are designed to assist the Commission with the implementation of EEC policies. These include the agricultural advisory committees and several general committees such as the Advisory Committee on the European Social Fund.
2. Committees set up under the Community's structural policies, such as the Advisory Committee on Questions of Agricultural Structural Policy.
3. Advisory Committees on the approximation of laws, such as the Advisory Committee on Foodstuffs.
4. Committees that are designed to assist with the formation of EEC policy, such as the Advisory Committee on Vocational Training.
5. Joint Labour-Management committees for particular industries, such as construction and textiles.
6. Miscellaneous bodies such as the Committee for Commerce and Distribution. (Economic and Social Committee, 1980a)

Although all the Euroquangos included in these six categories have representatives of labour and capital among their members, this does not make them corporatist in the sense that the term is used in the Introduction to this book.

The composition and powers of the Euroquangos vary considerably. Some draw their members from European interest organisations, while others include national representatives among their members; few include both. Most Euroquangos do not restrict their membership to the social partners; indeed, many do not include this particular category of representatives of labour and capital. Although some Euroquangos restrict their membership to the representatives of labour and capital, others include consumer, environmentalist and other 'various interests'.

The majority of the Euroquangos are purely advisory, both officially and in practice. This is indicated by the fact that they do not, and are not required to, produce consensus opinions. Their role is limited to recording the views of their members. This is because, first, few European interest organisations and far from all national ones have the authority to make their decisions binding upon their members, and few can guarantee that their members will comply voluntarily with any agreement that might be made with EEC bodies. Second, although the Commission seeks to redress the imbalance of policy-making powers that has developed between itself and the Council of Ministers by means of consulting interest organisations on the Community's legislative activities, the Commission is reluctant to delegate any of its remaining powers to, or share them with, European or national interest organisations. Third, ever since the creation of the EEC, one or more of the member states' governments has objected to EEC advisory bodies assuming policy-making powers whether, as in 1957, because of a fear of the development of state corporatism at the Community level or because of a reluctance to surrender EEC policy-making powers to EEC advisory bodies, as is the case for most of the member states' governments today. As a result, few Euroquangos reflect the development of a partnership between EEC institutions and either European or national representatives of labour and capital.

There are two Euroquangos that invest *de jure* policy-making powers in national representatives of labour and capital – the European Centre for the Development of Vocational Training and the European Foundation for the Improvement of Living and Working Conditions in the EEC. However, although there is a sharing of power on the management boards of these bodies between representatives of the Commission, member states and national representatives of trade unions and employers' organisations, they do not deal with very significant aspects of the Community's activities. There are a few cases of Euroquangos investing *de facto* policy-making powers into corporate groups. For example, the Advisory Committee on the European Social Fund is officially restricted to advising the Commission on applications for assistance from the Fund, but in practice the Committee is generally considered to have acquired extensive influence over allocation of the fund. As a consequence, there has been some extension of the Commission's authority over these allocations to the national representatives of employers and trade unions who sit on the Committee.

It would seem, then, that although the Commission is willing officially to recognise particular organisations as interest intermediaries, it is not willing to accord them the status of partners in the formation of EEC policy. The Commission does, however, seem to be more willing to implement certain aspects of EEC policy through representatives of labour and capital. This is due largely to the size of the Commission's workload, which requires it to delegate certain tasks simply in order to remain effective, and to the Commission's desire to facilitate the implementation of EEC policy in the member states by recruiting the assistance of the national representatives of those whom these policies affect.

The Commission attempts to implement EEC policies with the assistance of national and European representatives of labour and capital, both under the auspices of advisory committees such as that on the Social Fund, and through agreements with individual interest organisations. The latter are negotiated on a bilateral basis. For example, in 1981 part of the Community's budget was allocated to increasing awareness of the opportunities the Community makes available to small and medium-sized enterprises. In the process of implementing this measure, the Commission made separate agreements with the Union of Industries of the EEC, the European Association of Crafts and Small and Medium-Sized Enterprises, and *La Confédération Euopéenne de Commerce du Detail*, whereby these organisations were required to hold awareness-building conferences for those members representing small and medium-sized enterprises. Also in 1981, the Permanent Conference of Chambers of Commerce and Industry in the EEC signed a contract with the Commission to undertake a pre-development study for data processing and information exchange in the European Chambers of Commerce. The Commission hopes that, ultimately, Chambers of Commerce will establish a network of computerised data banks containing information about companies, their products, markets and trade regulations.

These and similar arrangements have in common the fact that they do not require the European or national interest organisation concerned to be able to make its decisions binding upon its membership. Voluntary compliance on the part of members is sufficient, or the agreement does not require the members' approval. The evidence does not point to the development of a corporatist mode of policy-making in the EEC, but arrangements with interest organisations do provide the Commission with a means of reducing its workload and of facilitating the effective implementation of EEC policies.

The inadequacies of some European interest organisations have led the Commission to implement some aspects of policy through individual national interest organisations. Occasionally, the Commission has developed corporatist arrangements with individual companies. The most important of these co-operation schemes has been ESPRIT (the European Strategic Programme for Research in Information Technologies). It is intended to enable Europe to catch up with its foreign competitors over the next decade. Running from 1984, the Community provided the scheme with an initial budget of £855 million over five years. ESPRIT represents an agreement between the Community and industry, laboratories and universities under which innovation is stimulated by a pooling of research efforts and results.

Most of the cases of co-operation between the Commission and interest organisations related to the development of relationships with representatives of capital rather than labour. Indeed, it seems that arrangements with interest organisations during EEC policy formation apply more often to aspects of the Community's commercial and industrial policies than to the Community's employment and social policies. The latter category of policy is more likely to suggest a need for corporatist arrangements that involve organised labour.

Any delegation or sharing of policy-making powers with representatives of labour and/or capital that has occurred has taken place in relation to the Commission rather than in relation to the Council of Ministers or the European Council. This may be due to the fact that these two bodies have no role during EEC policy implementation – the legislative stage at which the Commission appears to find corporatist arrangements most attractive. More significant, however, is the fact that the member states' governments do not perceive a need to delegate their collective EEC decision-making powers to, or share them with, European or national representatives of labour and/or capital. The political complexion of the member states' governments has changed over the past decade, so that fewer of these governments favour the development of corporatist arrangements than was the case a decade ago.

In the early 1970s, the majority of the member states' governments were socialist or social democratic. Today, conservatism is the prevailing ideology. This trend from socialism or a social democratic ideology to a conservative one is reflected by the fact that although the heads of state and governments of the EEC agreed to greater involvement of representatives of labour and capital in EEC policy-making on social and employment issues in December 1972, by 1976 the heads of state and governments had turned their attention to development of the European Parliament. Members of the Parliament have subsequently become directly elected, and many observers expect the Parliament to increase its authority in relation to the Commission and the Council of Ministers in EEC policy formation.

It seems, then, that policy-making and implementation at Community level reflects a tension between the attitudes of the two arms of the Community's executive towards the incorporation of interest organisations into these processes. Most members of the Council of Ministers and the European Council now favour the development of a parliamentary mode of policy-making, but not at their own expense. The Commission, however, is attracted by corporatist arrangements, especially during policy implementation. In this it has the support of European trade unions, which would like to see the Commission and the Council of Ministers take more notice of the recommendations of various Euroquangos. European capital, by contrast, is opposed to the development of a corporatist mode of policy-making at Community level.

The Commission's attitude also reflects another underlying tension. The Commission does not wish to delegate, or share, any more of its remaining policy-making powers than necessary to interest organisations. At the same time, in its search for legitimacy and support for its proposals, it has had to seek collaboration with interest organisations. Development of the European Parliament may offer the Commission an alternative and, ultimately, more reliable source of legitimacy and support given the inherent weaknesses of most European interest organisations in relation to their members. As yet, however, the European Parliament is little more than a Parliament in name. Its legislative, control and budgetary powers are not comparable to those of the Westminster Parliament, for instance (Herman and Lodge, 1978).

Weak Euroquangos and a weak Parliament appear to have coexisted and developed in parallel – up to a point – at Community level over the past decade. The development of a corporatist mode of policy-making at Community level has been constrained by, among other things, the inability of most interest organisations to act as pillars of corporatism, the attitude of European capital and EEC member states' governments towards the development of corporatism at Community level, and the development of a parliamentary mode of policy-making at that level, albeit in a weak form. In the light of these observations, it seems unlikely that EEC membership has stimulated the development of corporatism in Britain.

The impact of EEC membership on Britain

In order to assess the impact of EEC membership on the development of corporatist arrangements in Britain it is necessary to examine the following areas to see whether changes have taken place which could be attributed wholly, or in part, to British membership: the organisation of British representatives of labour and capital; the ability of such interest organisations to act as pillars of a corporatist mode of policy-making; and relations between British economic interest organisations and the British government.

The organisation of capital and labour

A number of changes have been made in the last decade which have sought to promote a more coherent organisation of labour and capital for representational purposes, and some of these changes have been linked to British membership of the EEC. Among the examples are the rejuvenation and subsequent development of the British Bankers' Association; the creation of the Food and Drink Industries Council, and subsequently the Food and Drink Federation; the formation of the Council of Mechanical and Metal Trades (COMMET); and the extension of the role of certain TUC industry committees such as the Textile and Clothing Industries Committee. Closer links have also developed between the CBI and the Association of British Chambers of Commerce to co-ordinate their lobbying on EEC matters.

The influence of Community developments on British interest organisations is well illustrated by one of the examples listed, that of the British Bankers' Association. The rejuvenation of this organisation was encouraged by the policy adopted by the relevant European-level organisation, the European Banking Federation (BFEC), to admit to membership only one organisation per member state and by the fact that the traditional, principal representative of the British banking community, the Bank of England, was not eligible to join BFEC. In addition, the EEC made a series of proposals that affected the vital interests of British bankers. It should also be said, however, that development of the British Bankers' Association was further influenced by non-EEC-related factors such as the secondary banking crisis (Sargent, 1982).

On the other hand, some factors associated with EEC membership seem to have undermined any incentive to change the organisation of certain groups of British representatives of labour and capital. The multiplicity of European representatives of financial interests, for example, would seem to have offset any incentive for the multiplicity of British representatives of the financial services industry to develop the Confederation of British Financial Institutions recommended by the Inter-Bank Research Organisation (IBRO) in 1973.

As far as labour is concerned, some TUC industry committees have been required to co-ordinate the views of the unions in the particular industry on EEC questions. This development was not inspired by the composition of European industry committees, however, because these interest organisations do not restrict their membership to one organisation per member state. As a result, some European industry committees include more than ten British unions among their members. The main incentive for co-ordinating British trade union input into the appropriate European Industry Committee has been the introduction of EEC policy proposals which threatened to damage the British component of the industries concerned. Not all industries are equally affected by EEC policies, and thus not all TUC industry committees are put to this use. In the case of the Textile and Clothing Industries Committee, for example, the incentive for extending the committee's role was the introduction of Commission guidelines on the textile and clothing industries in 1979 and the Community's Multifibre Arrangement.

One can cite a number of examples of alterations to the structure of British interest organisations representing labour and capital which can in some way be associated with EEC membership. However, such changes are isolated; they relate to particular groups of economic interest organisations, and they vary in nature from greater hierarchical ordering of interest organisations, through the establishment of new or the development of existing co-ordinating machinery, to *ad hoc*, informal liaison between the staff of interest organisations. It would seem that the organisation and composition of European representatives of capital have influenced some, and constrained other, alterations to the organisation of British representatives of capital. Moreover, it appears that the existence of EEC legislative proposals that affect the vital interests of a group of economic interest organisations, especially negatively, can encourage such organisations to forget their traditional competitiveness and to co-ordinate their responses to these policy proposals. However, such co-ordination is purely voluntary. It does not require any of the interest organisations concerned to surrender any of their autonomy against their will. It seems, then, that EEC membership cannot be said to have made the style of interest intermediation in Britain significantly more corporatist.

British interest organisations and corporatist policy-making

EEC membership has neither increased nor decreased the ability of British representatives of capital and labour to act as pillars of corporatist forms of policy-making. Rather, the number and organisation of European representatives of labour and capital would seem to have contributed towards the maintenance of the status quo. British peak associations have been unable to increase their influence over their member associations as a result of developing greater expertise on EEC-related matters, as their members are often not interested in this expertise. Similarly, a British peak association's expertise on EEC-related matters cannot influence that organisations's influence over its membership if, as is often the case, that membership or components of it have access to an alternative source of this expertise in the form of a European interest organisation of their own. (This would seem to differ from the experience of other countries. See, for example, Neunreither 1968.)

EEC legislation has neither required British peak associations to increase their authority over their members, nor motivated the members of British organisations representing labour and capital to surrender decision-making autonomy to such organisations. However, the nature, and even the absence, of certain pieces of EEC legislation have affected relations between British economic interest organisations and the British government. The absence of EEC legislation to harmonise the member states' laws on Chambers of Commerce, for example, has contributed to the fact that British Chambers of Commerce have not been granted public law status and, as a result, their relations with government in Britain have not altered significantly over the past decade.

The EEC and existing corporatist arrangements

Some EEC legislation has had the effect of undermining corporatist relationships that have developed between government and economic interest organisations in Britain. The British Agrochemicals Supply Industry Scheme (BASIS) rested on an agreement with the British Agrochemicals Association that any BASIS member de-registered for selling products that were not cleared by the government-operated Pesticides Safety Precautions Scheme (PSPS) would not be supplied with agrochemicals by the BAA's members. The EEC Commission maintained that this scheme contravened the Community's free trade laws, and in February 1983 agrochemical manufacturers were told by the Commission that their support for BASIS contravened Community regulations. As a consequence, responsibility for policing agrochemical trading was left to the Health and Safety Executive. In this case the Community's competition laws have served to dismantle a corporatist arrangement in Britain.

This is not always the case, however. Although the Thatcher government advocates a policy of liberalisation, it sometimes finds itself supporting and even initiating corporatist arrangements as an alternative to statutory provisions. For example, the government has acted in this way since 1981 in connection with a proposed EEC draft directive on quick frozen foods. Various early versions of this proposal provided for mandatory standards to be applied to freezer cabinets at retail level, which, if adopted, would have required wide-scale re-equipping of freezer cabinets in Britain. In response, the government encouraged representatives of the retail trade, with the agreement of consumer organisations, the enforcement authorities and frozen food producers' organisations, to draw up guidelines for the handling of quick frozen foods at retail level which would remove any need for the proposed EEC legislation in Britain. The Government has acted in a similar way since 1982 in response to proposed EEC draft directives on the energy labelling of domestic electrical appliances such as washing machines and freezers. In these cases, too, the Government has encouraged the relevant manufacturers' and retailers' organisations to agree to voluntary arrangements in order to render the proposed EEC legislation unnecessary.

Although the Commission's preference for harmonising member states' laws by means of common, statutory rules rather than voluntary arrangements suggests that EEC membership is likely to have prevented the development of corporatist arrangements in Britain, the reverse has sometimes been the case under the Thatcher government.

In addition, the British Government has sometimes developed corporatist arrangements with representatives of capital when implementing EEC codes of conduct. In 1978, for example, a new Council for the Securities Industries was set up to supervise the operations of the securities market in accordance with the then newly published EEC Code of Conduct for dealings in the capital markets, the method of implementation of which was left to each member state to decide.

It would seem, then, that contrary to Cawson's expectation, corporatist arrangements are sometimes promoted and defended by conservative governments which advocate a policy of minimal state intervention in the economy, but are not supported by social democratic/reformist EEC bodies which adopt a more interventionist stance. In some cases, however, corporatist arrangements in Britain have come under a dual threat from the EEC and Thatcherism, most importantly in the dairy industry. Corporatist arrangements in the dairy industry rest on an intricate piece of political design with a complex set of internal balances, which include the delegation of public authority to a state-sponsored co-operative (the Milk Marketing Board) and a Joint Committee of the Milk Marketing Board and the Dairy Trade Federation which represents processors (Grant, 1983a, 1983b). The government's commitment to free enterprise economics led it to decontrol retail milk prices (at first in Scotland, to be followed by England and Wales in 1985), thus introducing a new element of instability into arrangements that had operated for fifty years. At a community level, Irish milk marketing interests have taken legal action aimed at the two-tier system of pricing in Britain which involves a lower price for milk for manufacturing—action which, if successful either legally or politically, could lead dairy processors to re-think their attitude towards the existing corporatist arrangements. More importantly, the imposition of milk quotas by the EEC in 1984 undermined the confidence of some farmers, particularly smaller producers, in the Milk Marketing Board and led them to demand changes in the system (such as the abolition of the 'cow vote') which could unbalance it.

Conclusions

It appears that EEC membership has not had a consistent impact on Britain, nor the impact which various contributors to the debate on corporatism might have expected. EEC membership has undermined some, and promoted other, corporatist arrangements in Britain, although it should be noted that each of the examples cited concerns relations between the British government and representatives of British capital. EEC membership has not produced parity in the relations it has fostered between the state and representatives of labour and capital in Britain. Also important is the finding that the corporatist arrangements identified all relate to EEC policy implementation and not to EEC policy formation. The evidence also suggests that EEC membership is likely to continue to foster corporatist arrangements between the British government and representatives of British capital as a means of implementing EEC decisions that are binding in the member states, and which seek to harmonise the member states' policies, laws and/or practices, at least for the foreseeable future.

At the Community level, there is relatively little evidence of the development of corporatist structures and functions. Nevertheless, the style of interest intermediation and the mode of policy formation that have developed at Community level do exhibit some, albeit not very significant, corporatist features. At the same time, the EEC is tending to develop a more parliamentary form of policy-making than it has produced hitherto. In summary, the Community exhibits a combination of weak corporatist structures and functions which tend to favour representatives of capital, and weak pluralist and parliamentary arrangements. Moreover, both are prevented from further development by various tensions which effectively cancel each out. One example is the tension between the approaches towards policy-making that have been adopted by the two arms of the Community's executive, the Commission and the Council of Ministers, whereby the former favours the development of certain corporatist arrangements, and the latter has increasingly favoured a parliamentary mode of policy-making over the past decade. In addition, the Commission's attitude towards its relations with interest organisations reflects an underlying tension between different aspects of the Community's policy. Aspects of the social and agricultural policies, for example, would seem to favour corporatist arrangements, especially during policy implementation, whereas other aspects of Community policy, such as its competition policy, have not produced corporatist arrangements. A tension also exists between the attitudes of European capital and labour towards corporatism at the EEC, with capital opposing corporatist modes of policy-making, and labour being more favourable towards them.

Corporatist structures and functions have emerged at Community level only in relatively insignificant contexts and in an immature form. Yet the Community's social and employment policies remain relatively undeveloped, and its industrial policy is only in its infancy. Further development of the European Parliament would not seem to be sufficient to secure the further development of these policy areas, and thus of the Community as a whole. It could be argued that the effective incorporation of interest organisations into policy-making and implementation in the social, employment and industrial fields is essential for the future development of Community policies in these important areas. In order for this to happen, however, there will need to be at least a partial reconciliation of the tensions outlined above, and it is difficult to be optimistic about the likelihood of such a development.

Notes

Chapter 2   Neo-corporatism and the state

1. As is the case with much of what I have been writing on this and related subjects recently, I am indebted to Wolfgang Streeck of the International Institute of Management, Berlin, for his helpful comments, criticisms and encouragements. Alan Cawson, Wyn Grant, Andreas Kunz and Jelle Visser also gave the manuscript a close reading at an earlier stage and I have incorporated several of their suggestions. The European University Institute in Florence has provided research funds specifically for this project, as well as a generally congenial atmosphere in which to work on it. For what has resulted from all this support, I alone am responsible.

Chapter 3   Corporatism in industrial relations: a formal model

1. Game theory in the strict sense cannot be applied to actual cases of industrial relations, since they contain too much scope for informal communicative bargaining outside the 'rules'. I therefore use the terms 'zero-' and 'positive-sum' loosely. However, given the difficulties that the parties in industrial relations have in trusting each other, it is likely that they often rely on revealed behaviour rather than on 'nods and winks'. A genuine pure games theory may therefore have more to contribute to this subject than is generally recognised. However, in a paper of this length we should not be able to reach anything as complex as bargained corporatism by treading that austere path.

2. If strict game theory were being applied, this could be analysed as a 'co-ordination game'. Here, two actors, X and Y, are faced with a choice between two strategies, i and j. If they both choose j they both maximise their outcomes. However, if X chooses j, but Y chooses i, does worse than if he too chooses i, and *vice versa*. The problem is to discover under what circumstances they will both be able to choose j. (For further applications of these and similar concepts to social science problems, see Schotter, 1981).

Chapter 8   Corporatism and the local economy

1. Much of the material used in this chapter was collected as part of an Economic and Social Research Council funded project on 'The Organisational Structures and Political Practice of Selected Chambers', E/00/23/0028/1.

Chapter 9   Corporatism and the European Community

1. Most of the data on which this chapter is based were collected between 1979 and 1983 in connection with research for a PhD at the London School of Economics. This research included approximately seventy-five interviews with members and officials of EEC bodies and representatives of both British and European interest organisations which speak for various aspects of capital and labour.

2. The terms 'European level' and 'Community level' are not used interchangeably in this chapter, as many European interest organisations do not restrict their membership to the appropriate representatives from the EEC member states and many do not restrict their interests to the Community's activities.

3. The ETUC 'recognises' those European industry committees which have two standing bodies and their own operating budget; which cover at least the EEC countries; which group at least the appropriate trade federations of the confederations affiliated to the ETUC; and which have arranged for the mutual exchange of regular information and mutual attendance at meetings with the ETUC.

References

ALMOND, G. (1983) 'Corporatism, Pluralism and Professional Memory', *World Politics*, 35, pp. 245–60.

ANDERSON, C. (1977) 'Political Design and the Representation of Interests', in P. Schmitter and G. Lehmbruch (eds) *Trends Towards Corporatist Intermediation* (London: Sage), pp. 271–97.

ANDRLIK, E. (1984) 'Die Sozialpartnerschaft in der Wirtschaftskrise: Der Fall VEW (1975–1984)', *Journal für Sozialforschung*, 24, pp. 395–421.

ARMINGEON, K. (1982) 'Neo-Korporatistische Einkommenspolitik', dissertation, Sozialwissenschaftliche Fakultät, Universität Konstanz.

ARMINGEON, K. (1983) *Neo-Korporatistische Einkommenspolitik* (Frankfurt am Main: Haag und Herchen Verlag).

ARMINGEON, K., LEHMBRUCH, G. *et al.* (1983) 'Neokorporatistische Politik in Westeuropa', Universität Konstanz, Diskussionbeitrag No. 1.

ATKINS, R. (1978) *The Government of the Australian Capital Territory* (St. Lucia: Queensland University Press).

ATKINSON, M. and COLEMAN, W. (1983) 'Corporatism and Industrial Policy', paper presented to the European Group for Organisation Studies, Florence.

AZMON, Y. (1980) 'Bargaining in Physical Planning in Israel: a Comparison with the British Experience', *Policy and Politics*, 8, pp. 443–56.

BAGLIONI, G. and SANTI, E. (eds) (1982) *L'Europe Sindicale del 1981* (Bologna: Il Mulino).

BAUER, O. (1965) *Die österreichische Revolution* (Vienna).

BAUMAN, Z. (1982) *Memories of Class: The Pre-History and After-Life of Class* (London: Routledge & Kegan Paul).

BERGER, S. (1981a) 'Introduction', in S. Berger (ed.) *Organising Interests in Western Europe* (London: Cambridge University Press), pp. 1–23.

BIRNBAUM, P. (1982a) 'The State Versus Corporatism', *Politics and Society*, 11, pp. 477–501.

BIRNBAUM, P. (1982b) *La Logique de l'Etat* (Paris: Fayard).

BLANK, S. (1977) 'Britain: the Politics of Foreign Economic Policy, the Domestic Economy and the Problem of Pluralist Stagnation', *International Organisation*, 31, pp. 673–722.

BLOCK, F. (1977) 'The Ruling Class Does Not Rule: Notes on the Marxist Theory of the State', *Socialist Review*, 33, May–June.

BOTZ, G. (1979) 'Politische Gewalt und industrielle Arbeitskämpfe in Wirtschaftskrisen. Versuch einer Extrapolation aus der Geschichte der Ersten und Zweiten Republik', in B. Marin (ed.) *Wachstumkrisen in Österreich?*, Volume 2, *Szenarios*, Vienna.

BUSINESS IN THE COMMUNITY (1982) 'Objectives, Activities', London, pp. 1–8.

BUTLER, P. and WILLIAMS, R.H. (1981) 'Inner City Partnerships and Established Policies: the Newcastle/Gateshead Experience', *Policy and Politics*, 9, pp. 125–36.

BUXBAUM, J.M. (1981) *The Corporate Politea: A Conceptual Approach to Business, Government and Society* (Washington: University Press of America).

BYRNE, D. (1982) 'Class and Local State', *International Journal of Urban and Regional Research*, 6, pp. 61–82.

CAMERON, D. (1978) 'The Expansion of the Public Economy: a Comparative Analysis', *American Political Science Review*, 72, pp. 1243–61.

CAMERON, D. (1983) 'Social Democracy, Corporatism and Labour Quiescence in Advanced Capitalist Society', paper presented at the SSRC Conference on Order and Conflict in Western Capitalism, Buchenbach bei Freiburg, May 1983.

CARPENTER, L.P. (1976) 'Corporatism in Britain 1930–45', *Journal of Contemporary History*, 11, pp. 3–25.

CARRIER, M. and DONOLO, C. (1983) 'Oltre l'orrizzonte neo-corporatistsa. Alcuni scenari sul futuro politico del sindacto', *Stato e Mecarto*, 9, pp. 475–503.

CASTELLS, M. (1983) *The City and the Grassroots* (London: Edward Arnold).

CAWSON, A. (1977) 'Environmental Planning and the Politics of Capitalism', Working Papers in Urban and Regional Studies, University of Sussex, No. 7.

CAWSON, A. (1978) 'Pluralism, Corporatism and the Role of the State', *Government and Opposition*, 13, pp. 178–98.

CAWSON, A. (1982) *Corporatism and Welfare: State Intervention and Social Policy in Britain* (London: Heinemann).

CAWSON, A. (forthcoming) 'Is There a Corporatist Theory of the State?', in G. Duncan and R. Alford (eds), *Democracy and the Capitalist State* (Cambridge: Cambridge University Press).

CAWSON, A. and SAUNDERS, P. (1983) 'Corporatism, Competitive Politics and Class Struggle', in R. King (ed.) *Capital and Politics* (London: Routledge & Kegan Paul), pp. 8–27.

CERI, P. (1980–1) 'Le condizioni dello scambio politico', *Quaderni di Sociologia*, XXIX, pp. 640–41.

CHUBB, J. (1983) *Interest Groups and the Bureaucracy: The Politics of Energy* (Stanford: Stanford University Press).

CLARKE, S.E. (1982) 'Enterprise Zones: Seeking the Neighbourhood Nexus', *Urban Affairs Quarterly*, 18, pp. 53–71.

CLEGG, H. (1975) 'Pluralism in Industrial Relations', *British Journal of Industrial Relations*, XIII, pp. 309–16.

COCKBURN, C. (1977) *The Local State: Management of Cities and People* (London: Pluto Press).

COLEMAN, W. (1984) 'State Corporatism as a Sectoral Phenomenon: The Case of the Quebec Construction Industry', prepared for A. Cawson and I.

Scholten (eds) *Meso-Corporatism: the State and Organized Interests in Policy Formation*, Sage, forthcoming.

COLEMAN, W. and GRANT, W. (1984) 'Business Associations in Public Policy: A Comparison of Organisational Development in Britain and Canada', *Journal of Public Policy*, 4, pp. 209–35.

COLEMAN, W. and JACEK, H. (1982) 'The Role of Business Interest Associations in the Canadian Food Processing Industry', paper presented at the Organisation of Business Interests project conference on the food processing industry, Wroxton St Mary, September 1982.

COOMBES, D. (1977) *The Future of the European Parliament* (London: Policy Studies Institute).

COOMBES, D. (1982) *Representative Government and Economic Power* (London: Heinemann Educational).

COSER, L. (1956) *The Functions of Social Conflict* (London: Routledge).

COX, A. and HAYWARD, J. (1983) 'The Inapplicability of the Corporatist Model in Britain and France: the Case of Labor', *International Political Science Review*, 4, pp. 217–40.

CROUCH, C. (1977) *Class Conflict and the Industrial Relations Crisis* (London: Heinemann).

CROUCH, C. (1978) *The Politics of Industrial Relations* (London: Fontana).

CROUCH, C. (1979) 'The State, Capital and Liberal Democracy', in C. Crouch (ed.) *State and Economy in Contemporary Capitalism* (London: Croom Helm), pp. 13–54.

CROUCH, C. (1980) 'Varieties of Trade Union Weakness: Organised Labour and Capital Formation in Britain, Federal Germany and Sweden', *West European Politics*, 3, pp. 87–106.

CROUCH, C. (1981) 'State, Market and Organisation: a Classification of the Contribution of Neo-Corporatist Theory', mimeo. Italian version published as 'Stato, Mercato e Organizzazione: la Teoria Neo-corporative', *State e Mercato*, No. 2 (1981), pp. 333–58.

CROUCH, C. (1982a) *The Politics of Industrial Relations*, 2nd edition (London: Fontana).

CROUCH, C. (1982b) *Trade Unions: The Logic of Collective Action* (London: Fontana).

CROUCH, C. (1983a) 'Corporative Industrial Relations and the Welfare State', in R.J. Barry-Jones (ed.) *Perspectives on Political Economy* (London: Frances Pinter), pp. 139–66.

CROUCH, C. (1983b) 'Pluralism and the New Corporatism: a Rejoinder', *Political Studies*, 31, pp. 452–60.

DAHL, R.A. (1961) *Who Governs?* (New Haven: Yale University Press).

DAHL, R.A. (1974) *Who Governs?* (London: Yale University Press).

DAHRENDORF, R. (1959) *Class and Class Conflict in an Industrial Society* (London: Routledge).

DARKE, R. (1979) 'Public Participation and State Power: The Case of South Yorkshire', *Policy and Politics*, 7, pp. 337–55.

DEARLOVE, J. (1975) 'The Control of Change and the Regulation of Community Action', in D. Jones and M. Mayo (eds), *Community Work One* (London: Routledge & Kegan Paul).

DEPARTMENT OF THE ENVIRONMENT (1981) 'A New Training Initiative: A Programme for Action', pp. 1–14.

DEPARTMENT OF THE ENVIRONMENT (1982) 'Ministerial Guidelines on Inner City Programmes'.

DEVLIN COMMISSION (1972) *Report of the Commission of Inquiry into Industrial and Commercial Representation in Britain* (London: ABCC/CBI).

DICKENS, P. and GOODWIN, M. (1981) 'Consciousness, Corporatism and the Local State', Working Papers in Urban and Regional Studies, No. 26, University of Sussex.

DOAK, J. (1982) 'Corporatism, Pluralism and Planning: the Case of Local Planning in Bromley', unpublished M.Phil thesis, University College London.

DORE, R.P. (1973) *British Factory-Japanese Factory* (London: Allen & Unwin).

DUNLEAVY, P. (1980) *Urban Political Analysis* (London: Macmillan).

ECONOMIC AND SOCIAL COMMITTEE (1980a) *European Interest Groups and Their Relationships with the Economic and Social Committee* (Farnborough: Saxon House).

ECONOMIC AND SOCIAL COMMITTEE (1980b) *Community Advisory Committees for the Representation of Socio-Economic Interests* (Farnborough: Gower).

ECONOMIC AND SOCIAL COMMITTEE (1981) *The Right of Initiative of the Economic and Social Committee of the European Communities* (Brussels: Editions Delta).

EDITIONS DELTA (1984) *Directory of the Professional Associations Set Up at Community Level* (Brussels: Editions Delta).

EEC COMMISSION (1981) *Repertoire des Organisations Internationales et Nationales des Petites et Moyennes Enterprises Industrielles et de l'Artisanat* (Brussels: EEC Commission).

EEC COMMISSION (1982) 'Communication of the Commission to the Council and Draft Council Decision Concerning: A Plan for the Transnational Development of the Supporting Infrastructure for Innovation and Technology Transfer', Brussels, 5 May 1982.

ELCOCK, H. and HAYWOOD, S. (1980). 'The Buck Stops Where? Accountability and Control in the National Health Service', University of Hull Institute for Health Service Studies.

ELIASSEN, K. (1981) 'Organizations and Pressure Groups', in E. Allardt *et al.* (eds), *Nordic Democracy* (Copenhagen: Det Danske Selskab).

ELLIOTT, J. (1978) *Conflict or Cooperation? The Growth of Industrial Democracy* (London: Kogan Page).

ESSER, J. (1982) *Gewerkschaften in der Krise* (Frankfurt: Suhrkamp Verlag).

ESSER, J. and FACH, W. (1981) 'Korporatistische Krisenregulierung in "Modell Deutschland"' in U. von Alemann (ed.), *Neokorporatismus* (Frankfurt: Campus Verlag), pp. 158–79.

FALLON, M. (1983) *Euroquangos* (London: Adam Smith Institute).

FARAGO, P., RUF, H. and WIEDER, F. (1984) 'Wirtschaftsverbände in der Schweizer Nahrungsmittelindustries', Bericht No. 1, Forschungsprojekt: Die Organisation von Wirstchaftsinteressen in der Schweiz, Sociologisches Institut, Universität Zürich.

FITZGERALD, A. (1981) 'Introduction', in Committee for Self-Government (ed.), *Self-Government for the ACT* (Canberra: Committee for Self-Government).

FITZMAURICE, J. and JACKSON, R. (1979) *The European Parliament: a Guide for the European Elections* (Harmondsworth: Pengiun).

FLYNN, R. (1983) 'Co-optation and Strategic Planning in the Local State', in R. King (Ed.) *Capital and Politics* (London: Routledge & Kegan Paul), pp. 85–106.

FORSTER, N. (1983) *Chambers of Commerce* (London: Industrial Aids Limited).

FOTHERGILL, S. and GUDGIN, G. (1982) *Unequal Growth: Urban and Regional Employment Change in the UK* (London: Heinemann).

FREMANTLE, A. (1956) *The Papal Encyclicals in Their Historical Context* (New York: Mentor-Omega).

FREY, B. and SCHNEIDER, F. (1981) 'A Politico-Economic Model of the UK: New Estimates and Predictions', *Economic Journal*, 91, pp. 737–40.

FRIEDLAND, R. (1982) *Power and Crisis in the City* (London: Macmillan).

FROEBEL, F., HEINRICHS, J. and KREYE, O. (1979) *The Changing International Division of Labour* (New York: Cambridge University Press).

GAMBLE, A. (1979) 'The Free Economy and the Strong State', in R. Miliband and J. Saville (eds) *The Socialist Register 1979* (London: Merlin Press).

GAMBLE, A. (1981) *Britain in Decline* (London: Macmillan).

GAMBLE, A. (1984) 'Conclusion: Part B' in A. Gamble and S. Walkland (eds), *The British Party System and Economic Policy 1945–83* (Oxford: Oxford University Press), pp. 170–87.

GIRLING, D. (1980) 'The State and Urban Development: Corporatist and Pluralist Elements', unpublished M.Phil thesis, University College London.

GILB, C.L. (1966) *Hidden Hierarchies: the Professions and Government* (New York: Harper & Row).

GOETSCHY, J. (1983) 'Néo-corporatisme et Relations Professionelles dans Divers Pays Européens', *Revue Française des Affaires Sociales*, 3, pp. 65–79.

GOLDTHROPE, J. (1984) 'Introduction', in J. Goldthrope (ed.) *Order and Conflict in Contemporary Capitalism: Studies in the Political Economy of West European Nations* (Oxford: Oxford University Press), pp. 1–13.

GRANDNER, M. and TRAXLER, F. (1984) 'Sozialpartnerschaft als Option der Zwischenkriegszeit? Liberalkorporatistisches Krisenmanagement am Beispiel der Wirtschafftskonferenz von 1930' in Dr Karl Rennerinstitut (ed.), *Der 12 Februar 1934: Ursachen, Faktem, Folgen*, Vienna.

GRANT, W. (1978) 'Industrialists and Farmers, etc.', *West European Politics*, 1, 1 (February).

GRANT, W. (1981) 'The Development of the Government Relations Function in UK Firms', labour market policy discussion paper (Berlin: International Institute of Management).

GRANT, W. (1983a) 'Gotta Lotta Bottle: Corporatism, the Public and the Private, and the Milk Marketing System in Britain', Sussex Working Papers in Corporatism No. 3.

GRANT, W. (1983b) 'Private Organisations as Agents of Public Policy: the Case of Milk Marketing in Britain', paper presented at the sixth EGOS colloquium, Florence, November 1983.

GRANT, W. (1983c) 'Chambers of Commerce in the UK System of Business Interest Representation', University of Warwick, Department of Politics, Working Paper No. 32.

GRANT, W. (1984) 'Is Corporatism Necessarily Interventionist? A Discussion of the Thatcher Government in Britain' (Salzburg: Ludwig Boltzmann-Institut).

GRANT, W. and STREECK, W. (1983) 'Large Firms and the Representation of Business Interests in the British and West German Construction Industry', labour market policy discussion paper (Berlin: International Institute of Management).

GRANT, W. and NATH, S. (1984) *The Politics of Economic Policymaking* (Oxford: Blackwell).

HAAS, E.B. (1958) *The Uniting of Europe: Political, Social and Economic Forces 1950–67* (London: Stevens & Sons).

HAGUE, D.C., MACKENZIE, W.J.M. and BARKER, A. (eds) (1975) *Public Policy and Private Interests: the Institutions of Compromise* (London: Macmillan).

HALL, P. (1982) 'Economic Planning and the State: the Evolution of Economic Challenge and Political Response in France', *Political Power and Social Theory*, 3, pp. 175–213.

HALL, S. (1983) 'The Great Moving Right Show', in S. Hall and M. Jacques (eds) *The Politics of Thatcherism* (London: Lawrence & Wishart).

HARBISON, F.H. (1954) 'Collective Bargaining and American Capitalism', in A. Kornhauser, R. Dubin and A. M. Ross (eds) *Industrial Conflict* (New York: McGraw Hill).

HARRIS, N. (1972) *Competition and the Corporate Society* (London: Methuen).

HARRISON, M.L. (1984) 'Corporatism, Incorporation and the Welfare State', in M.L. Harrison (ed.) *Corporatism and the Welfare State* (Aldershot: Gower), pp. 17–40.

HAWKE, J.N. (1981) 'Planning Agreements in Practice', *Journal of Planning and Environment Law*, 1981, pp. 5–14 and 86–97.

HEAP, D. and WARD, A.J. (1980) 'Planning Bargaining – the Pros and the Cons – Or, How Much Can The System Stand?', *Journal of Planning and Environment Law*, 1981, pp. 631–7.

HELANDER, V. (1982) 'A Liberal-Corporatist Sub-System in Action: the Incomes Policy System in Finland', in G. Lehmbruch and P. Schmitter (eds), *Patterns of Corporatist Policy-Making* (London: Sage), pp. 163–87.

HERMAN, V. and LODGE, J. (1978) *The European Parliament and the European Community* (London: Macmillan).

HERNES, G. and SELVIK, A. (1981) 'Local Corporatism', in S. Berger (ed.), *Organising Interests in Western Europe* (London: Cambridge University Press), pp. 103–22.

HOLMES, J. (1980) 'The Hamer Government and Urban Planning in Victoria', in R. Scott (ed.) Interest Groups and Public Policy (Melbourne: Macmillan).

HU, Y-S. (1975) *National Attitudes and the Financing of Industry* (London: Political and Economic Planning).

IJURR (1982) 'Urban Enterprise Zones: A Debate', *International Journal of Urban and Regional Research*, 6, pp. 415–45.

INGHAM, G.K. (1982) 'Divisions within the Dominant Class and British "Exceptionalism"', in A. Giddens and G. Mackenzie (eds), *Social Class and the Division of Labour* (Cambridge: Cambridge University Press).

INTER-BANK RESEARCH ORGANISATION (1973) *The Future of London as an*

International Financial Centre (London: HMSO).

JACKSON, R. (1979) *The Powers of the European Parliament* (Reading: Eastern Press).

JESSOP, B. (1978) 'Capitalism and Democracy: The Best Possible Political Shell?', in G. Littlejohn *et al.* (eds) *Power and the State* (London: Croom Helm).

JESSOP, B. (1980) 'The Transformation of the State in Post-War Britain', in R. Scase (ed.), *The State in Western Europe* (London: Croom Helm), pp. 230–93.

JESSOP, B. (1982) *The Capitalist State* (New York: New York University Press).

JOHNSON, N. and COCHRANE, A. (1981) *Economic Policy-Making by Local Authorities in Britain and West Germany* (London: Allen & Unwin).

JORDAN, A.G. (1983) 'Corporatism: the Unity and Utility of the Concept', University of Strathclyde Papers on Government and Politics, No. 13.

JOWELL, J. (1977a) 'Bargaining in Development Control', *Journal of Planning and Environment Law*, July 1977, pp. 414–33.

JOWELL, J. (1977b) 'The Limits of Law in Urban Planning', *Current Legal Problems*, 30, pp. 63–83.

KATZENSTEIN, P. (1984) *Corporatism and Change. Austria, Switzerland and the Politics of Industry* (Ithaca: Cornell U.P.).

KEATING, M., MIDWINTER, A. and TAYLOR, P. (1984) 'Enterprise Zones: Implementing the Unworkable', *Political Quarterly*, 55, pp. 78–84.

KEYNES, J.M. (1963) *Essays in Persuasion* (New York: Norton), first published in 1926.

KING, R. (1983) 'Corporatism, Capital and Local Politics', paper presented to the annual conference of the Political Studies Association, University of Newcastle, April 1983.

KIRCHNER, E. (1977) *Trade Unions as a Pressure Group in the European Community* (Farnborough: Saxon House).

KLOSE, A. (1970) *Ein Weg zur Sozialpartnerschaft. Der österreichische Modell* (Vienna).

KORPI, W. and SHALEV, M. (1979) 'Strikes, Industrial Relations and Class Conflict in Capitalist Societies', *British Journal of Sociology*, pp. 164–87.

KUNDE, J.E. and BERRY, D.E. (1981) 'Restructuring Local Economies Through Negotiated Investment Strategies', *Policy Studies Journal*, 10, pp. 365–79.

KVAVIK, R.B. (1976) *Interest Groups in Norwegian Politics* (Oslo: Universitetsforlaget).

LACLAU, E. (1975) 'The Specificity of the Political: The Poulantzas–Miliband Debate', *Economy and Society*, 4, pp. 87–110.

LAKOFF, S. and RICH, D. (eds) (1973) *Private Government* (Glenview, Ill. Scott, Foresman).

LANGE, P., ROSS, G. and VANNICELLI, M. (1982) *Unions, Change and Crisis: French and Italian Union Strategy and the Political Economy, 1945–1980* (London: Allen & Unwin).

LEBAS, E. (1983) 'The State in British and French Urban Research or The Crisis of the Urban Question', in V. Pons and R. Francies (eds) *Urban Social Research: Problems and Prospects* (London: Routledge & Kegan Paul).

LEHMBRUCH, G. (1967) *Proporzdemokratie. Politisches System und politisches Kultur in der Schweiz und in Österreich* (Tübingen).

LEHMBRUCH, G. (1977) 'Liberal Corporatism and Party Government', *Comparative Political Studies*, 10, pp. 91–126.

LEHMBRUCH, G. (1979) 'Consociational Democracy, Class Conflict and the New Corporatism', in P. Schmitter and G. Lehmbruch (eds) *Trends Towards Corporatist Intermediation* (London: Sage), pp. 53–61.

LEHMBRUCH, G. (1982) 'Neo-Corporatism in Comparative Perspective', in G. Lehmbruch and P. Schmitter (eds) *Patterns of Corporatist Policy-Making* (London: Sage), pp. 1–28.

LEHMBRUCH, G. (1983) 'Interest Intermediation in Capitalist and Socialist Systems: Some Structural and Functional Perspectives in Comparative Research', *International Political Science Review* 4, pp. 153–72.

LEHMBRUCH, G. (1984) 'Österreichs sozialpartnerschaftliches System in internationalen Vergleich', in Beirat für Wirtschafts- und Sozialfragen (ed.) *Methoden der Politikberatung im wirtschaftspolitischen Bereich*, Vienna, pp. 41–62.

LEHMBRUCH, G. *et al.* (1983) 'Neokorporastische Politikentwicklung in Westeuropa', special issue of *Journal für Sozialforschung*, 23, 4.

LEHMBRUCH, G. and HALLE, A. (1983) 'Verflechtungen zwischen Parteien und organisierte Interessen im Neokorporatismus', paper presented at the Deutsche Vereinigung für Politische Wissenschaft, Mannheim, October 11–12.

LEHMBRUCH, G. and SCHMITTER, P. (eds) (1982) *Patterns of Corporatist Policy-Making* (London: Sage).

LIJPHART, A. (1968/69) 'Typologies of Democratic Systems', *Comparative Political Studies*, 1, pp. 3–44.

LIJPHART, A. (1969) 'Consociational Democracy', *World Politics*, 21, pp. 207–25.

LIJPHART, A. (1977) *Democracy in Plural Societies: A Comparative Exploration* (New Haven: Yale University Press).

LINDBLOM, C. (1977) *Politics and Markets* (New York: Basic Books).

LINDBERG, L. and SCHEINGOLD, S. (1970) *Europe's Would-Be Polity: Patterns of Change in the European Community* (Englewood Cliffs, NJ: Prentice-Hall).

LOWI, T. (1964) 'American Business, Public Policy, Case Studies and Political Theory', *World Politics*, 16, pp. 677–715.

LOWI, T. (1969) *The End of Liberalism* (New York: Norton).

LOWI, T. (1979) *The End of Liberalism*, 2nd edition (New York: Norton).

LUSTIG, R. (1982) *Corporate Liberalism: The Origins of Modern American Political Theory 1880–1920* (Berkeley: University of California Press).

McBRIDE, S. (1983) 'Public Policy as a Determinant of Interest Group Behaviour: "The Canadian Labour Congress" Corporatist Initiative 1976–1978', *Canadian Journal of Political Science*, XVI, pp. 501–17.

McCONNELL, G. (1966) *Private Power and American Democracy* (New York: Knopf).

McKAY, D.H. and COX, A.W. (1979) *The Politics of Urban Change*, (London: Croom Helm).

MAKLER, H. *et al.* (eds) (1982) *The New International Economy* (Beverly Hills: Sage).

MALLOY, J. (ed.) (1977) *Authoritarianism and Corporatism in Latin America* (Pittsburgh: University of Pittsburgh Press, 1977).

MARAFFI, M. (1983) 'The Neo-Corporatist Model and the Theory of the State', paper presented at the IPSA 12th World Congress, Rio de Janeiro 1983.

MARIN, B. (1980) 'Neuer Populismus und "Wirtschaftspartnerschaft". "Neo-korporatistische" Konfliktregelung und ausserinstitutionelle Konfliktpotentiale in Österreich', *Österreichische Zeitschrift für Politikwissenschaft*, 9, pp. 157–76.

MARIN, B. (1981a) ' "Freiwillige Disziplin". Preiskontrolle ohne autonome Sanktionspotenzen – Österreichs Paritätische Kommission', labour market policy discussion paper (Berlin: International Institute of Management).

MARIN, B. (1981b) 'What is Half Knowledge: Sufficient For – and When? Theoretical Comment on Policymakers' Uses of Social Science', in *Knowledge: Creation, Diffusion, Utilisation*, 3, pp. 43–60.

MARIN, B. (1981c) 'Cooperative Interest Politics. Organising Principles of Technocorporatism', unpublished MS, Vienna.

MARIN, B. (1982a) *Die Paritätische Kommission: Aufgeklärter Technokorporatismus in Österreich* (Vienna: Internationale Publikationen).

MARIN, B. (1982b) 'Wie ist die "Wirtschafts- und Sozialpartnerschaft" möglich? Einige Funktionsbedingungen des Vierteljahrhundertprovisoriums Paritätische Kommission', *Österreichische Zeitschrift für Politikwissenschaft*, 11, pp. 325–38.

MARIN, B. (1983a) 'Organising Interests by Interest Organisation. Associational Prerequisites of Cooperation in Austria', *International Political Science Review*, 4, pp. 197–216.

MARIN, B. (1983b) 'Associationalism – Bureaucracies Beyond Bureaucracy?', paper presented at the 6th Egos Colloquium, Florence.

MARIN, B. and TRAXLER, F. (1984) 'Corporatism between Ständestaats-Dictate and Arbeitsgemeinschaft der Klassen', paper presented at the Arbeitstagung 'Korporatismus in historischer und internationaler Perspektive', Ludwig Boltzmann-Institut für Historische Sozialwissenschaft, Salzburg.

MARIN, B. and WAGNER, M. (1979) *Wachstumkrisen in Österreich*, Volume 1, *Grundlagen* (Vienna).

MARTIN, A. (1979) 'The Dynamics of Change in Keynesian Political Economy: the Swedish Case and its Implications', in C. Crouch (ed.), *State and Economy in Contemporary Capitalism* (London: Croom Helm), p. 88–121.

MARTIN, R. (1983a) 'Pluralism and the New Corporatism', *Political Studies*, 21, pp. 86–102.

MARTIN, R. (1983b) 'Pluralism and the New Corporatism: a Reply', *Political Studies*, 21, pp. 461–2.

MASSEY, D. and CATALONO, A. (1978) *Capital and Land* (London: Edward Arnold).

MEIDNER, R. (1978) *Employee Investment Funds* (London: Allen & Unwin).

MERCER, G. (1984) 'Corporatist Ways in the NHS?' in M.L. Harrison (ed.), *Corporatism and the Welfare State* (Aldershot: Gower).

MERTON, R. (1957) *Social Theory and Social Structure* (Glencoe, Ill.: Free Press).

MIDDLEMAS, K. (1979) *The Politics of Industrial Society* (London: Deutsch).

MILLS, C.W. (1959) *The Sociological Imagination* (Oxford: Oxford University Press).

MILWARD, H.B. and FRANCISCO, R.A. (1983) 'Subsystem Politics and Corporatism in the United States', *Policy and Politics*, 11, pp. 273–93.

MINISTRY OF HOUSING AND LOCAL GOVERNMENT (1965) *The Future of Development Plans* (PAG Report) (London: HMSO).

MINISTRY OF HOUSING AND LOCAL GOVERNMENT (1969) *People and Planning* (Skeffington Report) (London: HMSO).

MOLITOR, M. (1978) 'Social Conflict in Belgium', in C. Crouch and A. Pizzorno (eds) *The Resurgence of Class Conflict in Western Europe*, Volume 1, *National Studies* (London: Macmillan), pp. 21–52.

MULLER, R. and BRUCE, A. (1981) 'Local Government in Pursuit of an Industrial Strategy', *Local Government Studies*, 7, pp. 3–18.

MUTTI, A. (1983) *Stato e Scambio Politico* (Rome: Edizione Lavoro).

MYRDAL, H-G. (1980) 'The Swedish Model – Will It Survive?', *British Journal of Industrial Relations*, XVIII, pp. 57–69.

NAJEMY, J.M. (1982) *Corporatism and Consensus in Florentine Electoral Politics 1280–1400* (Chapel Hill, NC: University of North Carolina Press).

NASZMACHER, K.-H. (1968) *Das österreichische Regierungssystem, Grosse Koalition oder alternierende Regierung?* (Köln).

NATIONAL CAPITAL DEVELOPMENT COMMISSION (1982) 'To Plan, Develop and Construct: the Functions of NCDC', in Committee of Review of NCDC Submissions, *Review of Appropriate Responsibilities and Scale of Activity of the NCDC* (Canberra: Department of Capital Territory).

NAVARRO, V. (1978) *Class Struggle, the State and Medicine* (Oxford: Martin Robertson).

NEDELMANN, B. and MEIER, K. (1979) 'Theories of Contemporary Corporatism: Static or Dynamic?', in P. Schmitter and G. Lehmbruch (eds) *Trends Towards Corporatist Intermediation* (London: Sage), pp. 95–118.

NEUNREITHER, K. (1968) 'Wirtschaftsverbände im Prozess der Europäischen Integration', in C. J. Friedrich (ed.) *Politische Dimensionen der Europäischen Gemeinschaftsbildung* (Köln).

NEWMAN, I. and MAYO, M. (1981) 'Docklands', *International Journal of Urban and Regional Research*, 5, pp. 529–45.

NEWMAN, O. (1981) *The Challenge of Corporatism* (London: Macmillan).

NEWMAN, R. (1980) *The Road and Christ Church Meadow* (Oxford: Oxford Polytechnic).

NORDLINGER, E.A. (1981) *On the Autonomy of the Democratic State* (Cambridge, Mass.: Harvard University Press).

NOWOTNY, E. (1979) 'Verstaatliche Unternehmen als Instrument der Beschäftigungspolitik in Österreich', in *Zeitschrift für öffentliche und gemeinwirtschaftliche Unternehmen*, Vol. 2.

OFFE, C. (1975) *Berufsbildungsreform: Eine Fallstudie über Reformpolitik* (Frankfurt: Suhrkamp).

OFFE, C. (1981) 'The Attribution of Public Status to Interest Groups', in S. Berger (ed.) *Organising Interests in Western Europe* (Cambridge: Cambridge University Press), pp. 123–58.

OFFE, C. (1983) 'Korporatismus als System Nichtstaatlicher Makrosteurung?', mimeo, Universität Bielefeld, October 1983.

OFFE, C. and RONGE, V. (1982) 'Theses on the Theory of the State', in A. Giddens and D. Held (eds) *Classes, Power and Conflict* (London: Macmillan), pp. 249–56.

OFFE, C. and WIESENTHAL, H. (1980) 'Two Logics of Collective Action:

Theoretical Notes on Social Class and Organisational Form', *Political Power and Social Theory*, 1, pp. 67–115.

ÖHMAN, B. (1982) *Fonder i en Marknadsekonomi* (Stockholm: Studieförbundet Näringslivoch Samhälle).

ÖHMAN, B. (1983) 'The Debate on Wage-Earner Funds in Scandinavia', in C. Crouch and F. Heller (eds) *International Yearbook of Organisational Democracy, Volume 1* (Chichester: Wiley).

OLSEN, J.P. (1983) *Organized Democracy, Political Institutions in a Welfare State – the Case of Norway* (Bergen, Oslo and Tromso: Univcrsitctsforlaget).

OLSON, M. (1982) *The Rise and Decline of Nations* (New Haven: Yale University Press).

PAHL, R. (1975) *Whose City?*, 2nd edition (Harmondsworth: Penguin).

PAHL, R. and WINKLER, J. (1975) 'The Coming Corporatism', *Challenge*, March/April 1975, pp. 28–35.

PANITCH, L. (1979) 'The Development of Corporatism in Liberal Democracies', in P. Schmitter and G. Lehmbruch (eds) *Trends Towards Corporatist Intermediation* (London: Sage), pp. 119–46.

PANITCH, L. (1980) 'Recent Theorisations of Corporatism: Reflections on a Growth Industry', *British Journal of Sociology*, 31, pp. 161–87.

PANITCH, L. (1981) 'Trade Unions and the Capitalist State', *New Left Review*, 125.

PARIS, C. (1983) 'Whatever Happened To Urban Sociology?', *Society and Space*, 1, pp. 217–25.

PARKER, D. and PENNING-ROSWELL, E. (1980) *Water Planning in Britain* (London: Allen & Unwin).

PELINKA, A. (1981) *Modelfall Österreich? Möglichkeiten und Grenzen der Sozialpartnerschaft*, (Vienna).

PEMPEL, T.J. and TSUNEKAWA, K. (1979) 'Corporatism Without Labour? The Japanese Anomaly', in P. Schmitter and G. Lehmbruch (eds) *Trends Towards Corporatist Intermediation* (London: Sage), pp. 231–70.

PIZZORNO, A. (1978) 'Political Exchange and Collective Identity', in C. Crouch and A. Pizzorno (eds) *The Resurgence of Class Conflict in Western Europe since 1968, Volume 2* (London: Macmillan), pp. 277–98.

POLSBY, N.W. (1963) *Community Power and Political Theory* (New Haven: Yale University Press).

PONTUSSON, J. (1983) 'Comparative Political Economy of Advanced Capitalist States: Sweden and France', *Kapitalstate*, 10/11, pp. 43–74.

POULANTZAS, N. (1972) *Political Power and Social Class* (London: New Left Books).

POULANTZAS, N. (1975) *Classes and Contemporary Capitalism* (London: New Left Books).

RAINBIRD, H. and GRANT, W. (1984) *Employers' Associations and Training Policy* (University of Warwick: Institute for Employment Research).

READE, E. (1980) 'Town Planning and the Corporatism Thesis', Association of Sociologists in Polytechnics, Working Paper No. 10.

READE, E. (1982) 'Section 52 and Corporatism in Planning', *Journal of Planning and Environmental Law*, January 1982, pp. 8–16.

READE, E. (1984) 'Town and Country Planning' in M. Harrison (ed.) *Corporatism and the Welfare State* (Aldershot: Gower).

REGAN, D. and STEWART, J. (1982) 'An Essay in the Government of Health: the Case for Local Authority Control', *Social Policy and Administration*, XVI, pp. 19–42.

REGINI, M. (1983) 'Le condizioni dello scambio politico. Nascita e declino della concertazione in Italia e Gran Bretagna', *Stato e Mercato*, 9, pp. 353–84.

RICHARDSON, J. (1982) 'Tripartism and the New Technology', *Policy and Politics*, 10, pp. 343–61.

RICHARDSON, J., JORDAN A. and KIMBER R. (1978) 'Lobbying, Administrative Reform and Policy Styles: The Case of Land Drainage', *Political Studies*, 26, pp. 147–64.

ROKKAN, S. (1966) 'Norway: Numerical Democracy and Corporate Pluralism', in R. Dahl (ed.) *Political Opposition in Western Democracies* (New Haven: Yale University Press).

RUSCONI, G.E. (1981) 'Scambio Politico', *Laboratorio Politico*, 1, 1981, pp. 65–87.

RUSCONI, G.E. (1983) 'Scambio, patto, autorita', *Il Progetto*, 3, pp. 17–21.

SARGENT, J. (1982) 'Pressure Group Development in the EC: The Role of the British Bankers' Association', *Journal of Common Market Studies*, 20, pp. 269–85.

SARGENT, J. (1983) 'The Politics of the Pharmaceutical Price Regulation Scheme', labour market policy discussion paper (Berlin: International Institute of Management).

SAUNDERS, P. (1979) *Urban Politics: A Sociological Interpretation* (London: Heinemann).

SAUNDERS, P. (1981) *Social Theory and the Urban Question* (London: Hutchinson).

SAUNDERS, P. (1982) 'Why Study Central-Local Relations?', *Local Government Studies*, 8, pp. 55–66.

SAUNDERS, P. (1983a) 'The Canberra Tea-Party: Bureaucracy, Pluralism and Corporatism in the Administration of the Australian Capital Territory', Sussex Working Papers in Corporatism No. 2.

SAUNDERS, P. (1983b) 'The Regional State: A Review of the Literature and Agenda for Research', University of Sussex Urban and Regional Studies Working Papers No. 35.

SAUNDERS, P. (1984) 'The Crisis of Local Government in Melbourne', in J. Halligan and C. Paris (eds) *Australian Urban Politics* (Sydney: Longman Cheshire).

SCHAIN, M. (1980) 'Corporatism and Industrial Relations in France', in P. Cerny and M. Schain (eds) *French Politics and Public Policy* (New York: St Martin's Press), pp. 243–66.

SCHMIDT, M. (1982) 'Does Corporatism Matter? Economic Crisis, Politics and Rates of Unemployment in Capitalist Democracies in the 1970s', in G. Lehmbruch and P. C. Schmitter (eds) *Patterns of Corporatist Policy-Making* (London: Sage), pp. 237–58.

SCHMIDT, M. (1983) 'Stato ed ecomia in tempo di crisi. Ventitre democrazie industralia a confronto', *Rivista Italiana di Scienza Politica*, 1, pp. 103–38.

SCHMITTER, P.C. (1974) 'Still the Century of Corporatism?', *Review of Politics*, 36, pp. 85–131.

SCHMITTER, P.C. (1977) 'Modes of Interest Intermediation and Models of

Societal Change in Western Europe', *Comparative Political Studies*, 10, pp. 7–38.

SCHMITTER, P.C. (1979) 'Still the Century of Corporatism?', in P. Schmitter and G. Lehmbruch (eds) *Trends Towards Corporatist Intermediation* (London: Sage), pp. 7–52.

SCHMITTER, P.C. (1981a) 'Interest Intermediation and Regime Governability in Contemporary Western Europe and North America', in S. Berger (ed) *Organising Interests in Western Europe* (Cambridge: Cambridge University Press), pp. 285–327.

SCHMITTER, P.C. (1981b) 'Needs, Interests, Concerns, Actions, Associations and Modes of Intermediation: Toward a Theory of Interest Politics in Contemporary Society', unpublished MS, Wissenschaftszentrum, Berlin, March 1981.

SCHMITTER, P.C. (1982) 'Reflections on Where the Theory of Neo-Corporatism Has Gone and Where the Praxis of Neo-Corporatism May be Going', in G. Lehmbruch and P. Schmitter (eds) *Patterns of Corporatist Policy-Making* (London: Sage), pp. 259–79.

SCHMITTER, P.C. (1983a) 'Democratic Theory and Neo-Corporatist Practice', European University Institute Working Paper No. 74. Also in *Social Research*, 50, pp. 885–928.

SCHMITTER, P. (1983b) 'Organizzazione delgi interessi e rendimento politico', in G-F Pasquino (ed.) *Le Societa Complesse* (Bologna: Il Mulino), pp. 9–86.

SCHMITTER, P. and LEHMBRUCH, G. (eds) (1979) *Trends Towards Corporatist Intermediation* (London: Sage).

SCHMITTER, P. and STREECK, W. (1981) 'The Organization of Business Interests', labour market policy discussion paper (Berlin: International Institute of Management).

SCHOTTER, A. (1981) *The Economic Theory of Social Institutions* (Cambridge: Cambridge University Press).

SHARANSKY, I. (1979) *Whither the State?* (New York: Chatham House).

SHARPE, J.E. (forthcoming) 'Central Coordination and the Policy Network'.

SHARPE, L.J. (1984) 'Functional Allocation in the Welfare State', *Local Government Studies*, 10, pp. 27–45.

SHONFIELD, A. (1984) *In Defence of the Mixed Economy* (Oxford: Oxford University Press).

SHORTER, E. and TILLY, C. (1974) *Strikes in France: 1830–1968* (Cambridge: Cambridge University Press).

SIMMIE, J.M. (1981) *Power, Property and Corporatism* (London: Macmillan).

SIMMIE, J.M. (1984) 'The Planning Profession in 1984', *The Planner*, 7, pp. 7–9.

SKOCPOL, T. (1982) 'Bringing the State Back In', *Items*, 36, pp. 1–8.

SPANN, O. (1931) *Der wahre Staat* (Jena: 3 Aufl.).

STONE, D. (1983) 'The Local State and Economic Restructuring: a Study of the Greater London Enterprise Board', MA thesis, University of Sussex.

STRANGE, S. (1971) *Sterling and British Policy* (London: Oxford University Press).

STREECK, W. (1983) 'Die Reform der beruflichen Bildung in der westdeutschen Bauwirtschaft 1969–1982', labour market policy discussion paper (Berlin: International Institute of Management).

STREECK, W. (1984) *Industrial Relations in West Germany* (London: Heinemann Educational).

STREECK, W. and SCHMITTER, P. (1984) 'Community, Market, State – and Associations? The Prospective Contribution of Interest Governance to Social Order', European University Institute Working Paper No. 94.

STRINATI, D. (1979) 'Capitalism, The State and Industrial Relations', in C. Crouch (ed.) *State and Economy in Contemporary Capitalism* (London: Croom Helm).

STRINATI, D. (1982) *Capitalism, the State and Industrial Relations* (London: Croom Helm).

SUPPANZ, H. and ROBINSON, D. (1972) *Prices and Incomes Policy: the Austrian Experience* (Paris: OECD).

SZELENYI, I. (1981) 'Structural Changes of and Alternatives to Capitalist Development in the Contemporary Urban and Regional System', *International Journal of Urban and Regional Research*, 5, pp. 1–14.

THOMPSON, D.L. (1983) 'Public-Private Policy: an Introduction', *Policy Studies Journal*, 11, pp. 239–85.

TILLEY, J. (1979) 'The Inner City Partnerships: a Critical Assessment', in M. Loney and M. Allen (eds) *The Crisis of the Inner City* (London: Macmillan).

TRAXLER, F. (1981) 'Organisationsform des ÖGB und "Wirtschaftspartnerschaft"' in *Wirtschaft und Gesellschaft*, 7, pp. 29–52.

TRAXLER, F. (1983) 'Prerequisites, Problem-Solving Capacity and Restrictions of Self Regulation: A Case Study of Social Autonomy in the Austrian Milk Industry', paper presented at the sixty EGOS Colloquium, Florence.

TRUMAN, D. (1951) *The Governmental Process* (New York: Knopf).

URRY, J. (1981) 'Localities, Regions and Social Class', *International Journal of Urban and Regional Research*, 5, pp. 455–74.

URRY, J. (1983) 'Deindustrialisation, Classes and Politics', in R. King (ed.), *Capital and Politics* (London: Routledge & Kegan Paul), 22–48.

VON BEYME, K. (1983) 'Neo-Corporatism: A New Nut in an Old Shell?', *International Political Science Review*, 4, pp. 173–96.

van WAARDEN, F. (1983) 'Bureaucracy Beyond the State. Varieties of Collective Self-Regulation in the Dutch Dairy Industry', paper presented at the sixth EGOS Colloquium, Florence.

WASSENBERG, A. (1982) 'Neo-Corporatism and the Quest for Control: the Cuckoo Game', in G. Lehmbruch and P. Schmitter (eds) *Patterns of Corporatist Policy-Making* (London: Sage), pp. 83–108.

WEBMAN, J.A. (1982) 'UDAG – Targeting Urban Economic Development', in R.C. Rist (ed.) *Policy Studies Review Annual*, 6, pp. 305–23.

WILLIAMSON, P.J. (1982) 'Corporatism in Theory and Practice in Contemporary British Politics', unpublished PhD thesis, University of Aberdeen.

WILSON, F.L. (1983) 'Interest Groups and Politics in Western Europe: the Neo-Corporatist Approach', *Comparative Politics*, 16, pp. 105–23.

WILSON, G. (1982) 'Why Is There No Corporatism in the United States?', in G. Lehmbruch and P. Schmitter (eds) *Patterns of Corporatist Policy-Making* (London: Sage), pp. 218–36.

WINKLER, J. (1976) 'Corporatism', *European Journal of Sociology*, 17, pp. 100–36.

WINKLER, J. (1977) 'The Coming Corporatism', in R. Skidelsky (ed.) *The End of the Keynesian Era* (London: Macmillan), pp. 78–87.

WISTOW, G. (1982) 'Collaboration Between Health and Local Authorities', *Social Policy and Administration*, XVI, pp. 44–62.

WOLFE, A. (1977) *The Limits of Legitimacy* (New York: Free Press).

WOLFINGER, R.E. (1960) 'Reputation and Reality in the Study of Community Power', *American Sociological Review*, 25, pp. 636–44.

YOUNG, S. (1982) 'The Changing Boundary Between the Public and Private Sectors', paper presented to the annual PAC conference, University of York.

ZYSMAN, J. (1983) *Governments, Markets and Growth* (Oxford: Martin Robertson).

Index